Ireland: a social, cultural and literary history, 1791–1891

Ireland: a social, cultural and literary history, 1791–1891

James H. Murphy

FOUR COURTS PRESS

Published by
FOUR COURTS PRESS LTD
7 Malpas Street, Dublin 8, Ireland
email: info@four-courts-press.ie
http://www.four-courts-press.ie
and in North America by
FOUR COURTS PRESS
c/o ISBS, 5824 N.E. Hassalo Street, Portland, OR 97213.

ISBN 1-85182-727-7 hbk
1-85182-728-5 pbk

A catalogue record for this title
is available from the British Library.

Printed in Ireland
by Betaprint Ltd., Dublin

For Mark Butler, Stewart Roche,
Jürgen Auer and Uwe Wartha,
and John and Yvonne Cuddigan

Contents

Introduction

The century between 1791 and 1891 was one of enormous political change in Ireland, beginning with the foundation of the United Irishmen and ending with the death of Parnell. It saw the 1798 rebellion; the union of Britain and Ireland in 1801; the campaign for Catholic emancipation and then for repeal of the union, both led by Daniel O'Connell; the Young Ireland movement; the Fenians; the Irish Parliamentary Party; and the home rule crisis of the 1880s.

Political movements are also movements involving large numbers of people. The social causes, compositions and consequences of such movements are a concern of this book. Social history, however, is usually tied to economic history. Irish economic history in the nineteenth century was about food and land. Clearly the most important event of century as far as people's lives were concerned was the cataclysm of the famine in the 1840s. The famine was also part of a radical restructuring of the system of land-holding which reached its climax in the land war of the 1880s.

This book is especially focused on the links between social, cultural and literary history. Because of Ireland's contested status – country, region, nation or colony – in the nineteenth century its popular culture was continuously scrutinized by the literature produced by its high culture as part of an argument about whether Irish people were to be seen as normal or eccentric, as civilized or savage. Further, the lack of local political institutions meant that culture found itself called on to play a unifying role, though in this it did not always succeed.[1]

The social, cultural and literary history of Ireland in the period begins properly with a glance backwards towards the late seventeenth and eighteenth century settlement, which survived the radical assault of the 1790s only to be more gradually dismantled. This study ends designedly in 1891 because for far too long later nineteenth-century Ireland has been seen, at least in terms of culture and literature, as a mere trough. From it, the brilliance of those various movements (they may be called the Irish revival for convenience) was seen to spring and flourish over the three decades following 1891.

This book has its own particular aims. One is to see the literature of the times in its political context and to support new trends in its reading. But it also attempts to report on current thinking and research on nineteenth-century Ireland from a variety of disciplines including political and social history, liter-

1 Eagleton, *Heathcliff*, p. 228.

ary and cultural studies, economics and famine and Diaspora studies, geography and the study of religion, education, gender, music and the visual arts. It seeks to indicate the broad areas of agreement and to highlight areas of disagreement and debate. Overall, the purpose of the book is to offer an accessible picture of life in Ireland based on a synthesis of current scholarship. In doing so it does not claim to be anything other than eclectic when it comes to underlying assumptions. For example, it reflects the influence of theories of nationalism – in particular the notion of frustrated economic and social expectations leading to alienation and the embrace of nationalism.[2]

Perhaps this is an auspicious moment to produce a work of this kind. The debate between nationalist, revisionist and post-revisionist paradigms remains ongoing though its ferocity has somewhat abated. What came to be called 'revisionism' began as a movement in Irish history writing in the 1930s that was suspicious of a nationalist teleology and strove, as it now seems perhaps naively, for objectivity. By the 1980s it was coming under scrutiny within its own discipline on the grounds that it had detached itself from any sense of the trauma of Irish history. Meanwhile, literary studies had embraced a more theoretical approach to the past and, in particular, had begun to see Irish experience in terms defined by post-colonial studies. Suddenly Irish history could be read as issuing not in a restricting nationalism but in a struggle for liberation from a colonial status which was debilitating in cultural as well as in economic and political terms. Post-colonial studies, however, far from merely recuperating a nationalist history as has been alleged, have tended to problematize the notion of the nation, in its bourgeois formulation at least, and even more to descry the independent nation state as a scarring legacy of, rather than as a liberation from, imperialism. The post-colonial fervour has now itself somewhat abated in face of those who say that it delineates the past in over-sharp contours.

A final aim of this book is to further foster the growing climate of multi- and inter-disciplinary research in nineteenth-century Irish studies. The founding in 1992 of the Society for the Study of Nineteenth-Century Ireland was a significant moment in this process. At its inaugural conference, the keynote addresses were given by an historian and a literary scholar, each on the familiar territory of his discipline. At its tenth anniversary conference, an historian and literary scholar also gave the principal lectures but each spoke confidently in appropriately inter-disciplinary terms. The founding of the Society in 1992 came at a time of renewed interest in nineteenth-century Irish culture from scholars such as Terry Eagleton and David Lloyd. The social history of the century has long been well-established through the work of James S. Donnelly Jr and many others. The newer literary studies of the period are beginning to yield

2 Boyce, *Nationalism in Ireland*, pp 375–90.

remarkable results, now that much of the past canonical thinking about the literature or the century has been cleared away.

I am grateful to Margaret Kelleher, Colin Graham, Clíona Ó Gallchoir and Larry Geary who read this book in draft form and made most helpful suggestions. The notes give short titles of sources; fuller titles can be found in the extensive bibliography of secondary literature that has been provided. As the book is intended as a resource for further exploration of the period, works are divided under headings that reflect important themes from the text. Entries for chapters from books which themselves feature in the bibliographies use the short versions of the titles of the books in question.

CHAPTER 1

Radical climax, 1791–1800

The 1790s were climactic years in Ireland, a time when the social and religious settlement that had existed since the end of the seventeenth century came close to unravelling completely.

The seventeenth century had seen the defeat of the Ireland of the Gaels and Old English, the imposition of a new class of English Anglican landowners throughout the country and the emergence of a sizeable community of Scots Presbyterians in Ulster. Eighteenth-century estates varied greatly in size, but there were 2,000 large estates of between 2,000 and 4,000 acres and by the end of the century several dozen estates as large as 50,000 acres.[1] Relations between landowners and those who rented land from them, though not idyllic, were often better than might be expected. A 'moral economy' of respect and cordiality existed which was based on easy-going farming practices such as long leases, low rents and a tolerance of arrears, and landlords often sponsored popular entertainment and sports such as hurling. Long-standing notions of a very impoverished and resentful 'hidden Ireland' of the Gaelic Catholic majority coexisting but not interacting with the ruling order are true in part but tend to overstate the reality.[2] The collapse of the moral economy, however, with the new commercial spirit of the late eighteenth century and the adoption of metropolitan manners by the landed class did create a greater space for popular discontent and an opportunity for political radicalization.[3]

In politics, support for the Catholic Jacobite cause (the return of the dispossessed Stuart monarchy to the British and Irish thrones, now occupied by the Hanoverians) sustained a 'nascent national ideal' in politically-disenfranchised, Gaelic Ireland.[4] It was reinforced by the aisling tradition of Gaelic poetry, in which Ireland in the form of a young woman laments her condition and longs for the Stuarts. However, it was to be the Patriots, a movement within the politically-enfranchised, English-descended, Protestant community, who came to see themselves as the Irish nation at odds with Britain over the economic constraints that it had placed on Irish economic development. Taking the opportunity afforded by the American war of independence, the Patriot-led Volunteers succeeded in obtaining legislative independence for the parliament of the king-

1 Dickson, *New foundations*. p. 117. **2** Cullen, *Hidden Ireland*. **3** Bartlett, 'An end to moral economy,' in Philpin (ed.), *Nationalism and popular protest*, pp 191–218; Whelan, 'The United Irishmen,' in Dickson, Keogh and Whelan (eds), *The United Irishmen*, pp 269–96. **4** Leerssen, *Mere Irish*, p. 239. **5** Ibid., p. 324. **6** Connolly, 'Eighteeenth-century Ireland' in Boyce and O'Day (eds), *Revisionist controversy*, pp 15–33; Leighton, *Irish ancien régime*.

dom of Ireland, though the London executive continued to control affairs in Ireland.

The colonial nationalism of the Patriots was of a civic kind, but they also came to see themselves as the inheritors of Gaelic antiquity.[5] This was deeply ironic, because most Patriots opposed the inclusion of the Catholic descendants of the Gaels in the nation and supported the continuance of those laws, the 'penal laws', which excluded them from public or political life and curtailed their right to own land.

The centrality of religion to the constitution of eighteenth-century Ireland is one reason why it is proper to see it not only as a colony but also as an *ancien régime*, with much in common with other societies in pre-revolutionary Europe.[6] Adherence to the Protestant Established Church was necessary for full participation in civic life. Not only Catholics but also dissenting Protestants, such as the Presbyterians, were penalized for their failure to conform. The measures against Catholics were particularly strong, however, as 'popery' was seen as a political threat to personal liberty and the very existence of the Hanoverian state, though in practice the laws provided most difficulties for Catholic landowners rather than for Catholic tenants or merchants.

By the middle of the eighteenth century, however, the official anti-Catholic mood was changing, and in 1760 a Catholic Committee was founded to press for relief acts from the penal laws by seeking to convince the state that Catholics could be loyal subjects. A series of such acts did follow in 1778, 1782, 1792 and 1793, though often at the behest of the London government rather than on the initiative of the Protestant Irish parliament. However, they fell short of full 'Catholic emancipation', which came to be symbolized in the demand for Catholics to be able to become Members of Parliament.

Catholics were well represented in the merchant community, though they were probably not as dominant as was once claimed. In 1775 around one third of wholesale merchants were Catholics in Dublin and one quarter in Cork.[7] Nor was the situation concerning land ownership, where Catholics were hindered from inheriting or buying land by the penal laws, quite as desperate as it might have seemed, though it was still very restricting.

One fifth of the land remained in Catholic hands if one takes into account those individuals and families who converted to the Established Church in order to retain property, for they formed a group which was by no means seen as lost to the Catholic interest.[8] In addition, Catholics were eligible to become middlemen. These were technically tenants who rented large tracts of land from landlords and then sublet them to farmers.[9] Many were Protestant, but

7 Dickson, *New foundations*, p. 134. **8** Power, 'Converts,' in Power and Whelan (eds), *Endurance and emergence*, pp 101–27; Whelan, *Tree of liberty*, p. 6. **9** Cullen, *Emergence of mod-*

members of the former Catholic gentry were often able to become middlemen and to maintain a lifestyle consonant with their former status. The Scullys of Tipperary were thus enjoying a profit rent of £6,700 by 1803.[10]

The middleman system lasted into the first third of the nineteenth century. As time went on and a more mercantile tone developed, the Catholic ex-gentry were joined as middlemen in increasing numbers by Catholic farmers who had risen from the ranks of the tenantry. Noted for their frugality, they were the basis for the Catholic big-farmer class that was of such importance in the nineteenth century. Just at the time when landed and ex-gentry Catholics were abandoning their claim to 'aboriginal ownership' and seeking to convince the state of their loyalty, this rising class of big farmers embraced the claim. Over the next century, the sense that the Protestant landlord class lacked legitimacy was one which would percolate through the Catholic community and bolster the struggle against landlordism.[11]

As highlighted by Kevin Whelan, the 'Catholic core' area, where Catholic ex-gentry, middlemen and big farmers were strongest, was in south Leinster and east Munster, on an axis between Limerick and Wexford. It was also the area with the highest rate of attendance at mass, and it was a base from which the confident Catholicism of the nineteenth century was to emerge.[12]

The Munster and south Leinster area was also noted for outbreaks of agrarian protest, which consisted in attacks or threats of attack on persons and property. The Whiteboy movement flourished in 1761–5 and again in 1769–75 and the Rightboys in 1785–8. On each occasion there were outbreaks of unrest in counties Tipperary and Kilkenny, while Limerick, Waterford and Cork were each affected during two of the periods. The reasons for the protests varied but generally included opposition to tithes (taxes paid to ministers of the Established Church) and for this very reason the protests were sometimes tacitly encouraged by the gentry, who were in competition with clergymen for income from the peasantry.

Of more long-term importance, though, was rural disorder in Ulster, where the three principal denominations were represented at the lower levels of society and where agrarian protest was thus overlaid by sectarian tensions. The Oakboy disturbances of 1763 in counties Armagh, Tyrone and Monaghan involved Catholics, Presbyterians and members of the Established Church in a protest against tithes and other taxes. The Steelboys of the early 1770s were exclusively Protestant, however. Co. Armagh was one of the few areas with a large, lower-class population that adhered to the Established or Anglican Church. The Peep of Day Boys arose in the mid 1780s among the weavers of

ern Ireland, p. 99. **10** Whelan, *Tree of liberty*, p. 26. **11** Ibid., p. 38. **12** Whelan, 'Regional impact of Irish Catholicism,' in Smyth and Whelan (eds), *Common ground*, pp 253–77; Whelan, 'Catholic mobilization, 1750–1850.' *Culture et pratiques politiques*, pp 239–58.

north Armagh who were increasingly independent of landlord control and who resented the rising position of Catholics in the linen industry and on the land. In response, the Catholic Defenders were formed, and they soon spread in south Ulster and north Leinster. Local sectarian tensions came to a head in an affray at the Diamond in Loughgall in 1795 that coincided with the formation of a new Protestant organization, the Orange Order.

By the end of the 1780s there was disillusionment in some Irish political circles about the failure of what had been billed as legislative independence to live up to expectations. In 1789 the Dublin Whig Club was founded as a political opposition group. By the early 1790s some wanted to go further, not only to win real independence for the Irish parliament but also to establish government on a more popular basis.[13]

Though reliant more on the thought of John Locke than of Tom Paine, the new radicals caught the enthusiasm which the French revolution had generated. In the autumn of 1791 they established both in Dublin and in Belfast an organization which they called the Society of United Irishmen, though by 1793 they were at odds with the Whigs over the latter's support for war with France.

The 400 Dublin members were professionals, merchants or textile manufacturers. At first it was a Protestant body, but Catholics soon joined in greater numbers. The Belfast Society was made up of linen drapers, tanners and merchants. It was Presbyterian in composition but of the tolerant, non-Calvinist, 'new light' variety. The Bastille-Day parades near Belfast in the early 1790s, for example, passed pro-Catholic resolutions. Rural Presbyterians tended to be Calvinist seceders and covenanters and were more anti-papist. They turned out to be more likely to join the Orange Order rather than the United Irishmen.[14]

During this first 'moral force' phase of their development, the United Irishmen were essentially a constitutional force, arguing for parliamentary reform and Catholic emancipation. They relied on such texts as Wolfe Tone's *An argument on behalf of the Catholics of Ireland* (1791) and William Drennan's addresses composed for the Dublin Society of United Irishmen. They were also keen to influence other bodies such as the Volunteers, whose 1793 Dungannon convention proved to be their last significant gathering.[15]

Meanwhile, the Catholic Committee was undergoing changes. By early 1792, with the departure of the deferential Lord Kenmare, it began to move in a more radical direction. A Catholic Convention of 210 members was elected, though new legislation forced it to dissolve. The 1793 relief act restored voting rights to some (few) Catholics and opened the military to them, but the removal of Earl Fizwilliam as lord lieutenant (representative of the crown and British

13 Curtin, *United Irishmen*, p. 39. **14** Dickson, *New foundations*, pp 202–4. **15** McBride, 'Nationalism and republicanism in the 1790s,' in Connolly (ed.), *Political ideas*, pp 159–84.

government) in February 1795 for supporting Catholic emancipation came as a great disappointment. As early as 1791 some leading members of the Catholic Committee had formed links with the Dublin United Irishmen.

The United Irishmen also forged ties with the Defenders, who were spreading beyond their original base. By 1795 there were Defenders in sixteen counties, mostly in Ulster, Connaught, north Leinster and Dublin. There were nearly 4,000 Defenders among the lower classes of Dublin, a city whose street politics had long been politicized and where there had been political riots in 1759, 1779 and 1784.[16] From being a mere faction, the Defenders had evolved into a fully-fledged political secret society, with a coherent, radical, middle-class leadership, especially in Ulster. Schoolmasters, innkeepers and middling farmers were prominent in its local leadership as, at regional level, were members of the handful of really successful Catholic families in Ulster.[17] These latter often provided links with the United Irishmen, which became closer as the Orange Order grew.

The year 1794 saw compulsory recruitment for a new government defensive force, the Militia, designed to replace troops withdrawn for the war with France. As many as 230 people died (the majority, Catholics) in riots associated with the recruitment. Because of its composition the loyalty of the new force came under question and, indeed, there was a certain amount of infiltration both by the United Irishmen and Defenders, provoking a series of courts martial in 1797.

In 1794 the Dublin United Irishmen were officially suppressed. The surviving organization moved into a second phase of development — one marked by radical journalism and popular politicization, with insurrection now seen as an option. The Society's Belfast newspaper, the *Northern Star* (1792–97) was the best known of a number of such papers and journals published in Belfast and Dublin. They included the Irish language *Bolg an tSolair, or Gaelic Magazine*, launched in 1795.[18] United Irish engagement with Gaelic culture extended to an interest in the 1792 Belfast Harp Festival, and the Gaelic poet Mícheál Óg Ó Longáin (1766–1837) combined Jacobite and United Irish thought in his work.[19] Nonetheless, the United Irishmen's activity was minimal in those large areas of the country where Irish was the vernacular.[20] The movement did engage with the popular culture of the English-speaking population, however, albeit often in terms of a bourgeois imposition on that culture. Because of limited literacy, there was a widespread use of ballads, prophecies, toasts, oaths and catechisms.[21] *Paddy's resource* (1795) was the first in a series of popular songbooks. Wearing shamrock, the green cockade or having a short haircut were signs of a radical

16 Smyth, *Men of no property*, pp 121–56. **17** Ibid., pp 118–20, 149; Whelan, *Tree of liberty*, p 39. **18** Theunte, *The United Irishmen*, pp 89–123. **19** Dunne, 'Subaltern voices?' *Eighteenth-century Life*, 22:3 (1998), pp 31–44. **20** Whelan, *Tree of liberty*, p. 95. **21** Ibid., p. 72.

allegiance as was participation in drilling and public rituals.[22] The movement did not have an interest in popular culture in itself, though it was intent on popular politicization. It thus failed to see culture as a basis for politics in the way later nineteenth-century radicals were to do.[23] This may have been one of the reasons why its influence did not extend much beyond its own day.

The second phase of the United Irishmen's development lasted until late 1796, when a French invasion fleet was dispersed by storms at Bantry Bay. Serious plans for a physical confrontation now began as the United Irishmen entered the third and final phase of their activity.[24] Initially, they only sought to mobilize an armed force to overawe the government into reform. They came to seek a separate republic only towards the end when no governmental reform seemed forthcoming.[25]

The ranks of United Irishmen increased greatly. Between October 1796 and May 1796 the numbers of United Irishmen in Ulster grew from 38, 567 to 117, 917.[26] But 84 per cent of this number were in Counties Down, Antrim and Derry.[27] The membership of the United Irishmen in general during this period remained overwhelmingly middle class with 41.5 per cent tradesmen, 13.4 per cent farmers, 18.7 per cent in commerce, 9.4 per cent clergy and 6.9 per cent professionals.[28] By the end of 1797 the United Irishmen had spread throughout the country with county directories in all Leinster and some Munster and Connaught counties. Ties were forged not only with the Defenders but also with southern Whiteboys and Rightboys, with farmers, urban traders and minor professionals.[29] Women were actively involved with the United Irishmen, often in ways other than as the supporters of men for which they have tended to be remembered in popular history.[30]

The government responded to the mounting crisis with the formation of the Yeomanry in 1796. This was a part-time, policing force organized by the gentry for local service. It had 40,000 members by June 1789, many of them in Ulster.[31] The government also established an informal alliance with the Orange Order. In its first two years the Order had garnered support mostly from the peasantry. By 1797 it was gaining gentry approval and permission was given for Orangemen to join the Yeomanry *en masse* and not simply as individuals.[32] At the same time it was spreading to the south of Ireland and, as it did so, gaining

22 Curtin, *United Irishmen*, pp 252–3. **23** Whelan, *Tree of liberty*, pp 62, 95. **24** McBride, 'Nationalism and republicanism in the 1790s,' pp 163–4. **25** Curtin, *United Irishmen*, pp 166, 283. **26** Ibid., p. 69. **27** Dickson, *New foundations*, p. 204. **28** Curtin, *United Irishmen*, p. 127. **29** Dickson, *New foundations*, p. 207. **30** Gray, 'Mary Anne McCracken,' and Anna Kinsella, 'Women of 1798,' in Keogh and Furlong (eds), *The Women of 1798*, pp 47–63 and 187–99. Equally, images of women were used in the iconography of the movement in complex and pluralist ways. See Thuente, 'United Irish images of women,' in Keogh and Furlong, *Women of 1798*, pp 9–25. **31** Dickson, *New foundations*, p. 210. **32** Blackstock, 'The raising of the Yeomanry,' in Dickson, Keogh and Whelan (eds), *The United Irishmen*, pp 234–43.

support further up the social scale. The Orange Order was to prove to be an invaluable, counter-revolutionary ally for the government, preventing radical infiltration of government forces, assuring the support of most Protestants for the government and frustrating communication between strongholds of the United Irishmen and Defenders.[33]

An insurrection eventually took place in the summer of 1798. There was rebel activity in eighteen counties, in seven of which it was quite significant. The rising around Dublin was soon dispersed. The north-east and Wexford saw the largest risings in May and June 1798, though they were eventually crushed. In Antrim a force of 4,000 Presbyterian United Irishmen captured several positions before being checked at Antrim town on 7 June. A week later a force of 7,000 United Irishmen was defeated at Ballynahinch. In Co. Wexford rebels captured Enniscorthy and Wexford town but failed to capture New Ross and Arklow and were eventually defeated at Vinegar Hill. In August a French force landed in Co. Mayo and progressed eastward until it was checked in Co. Longford. In October a final French fleet was captured at Lough Swilly, and with it the United Irishmen leader, Wolfe Tone.

Between twenty and fifty thousand people had actively supported the insurrection. Twenty thousand had died as a result, though only three thousand of these deaths were the responsibility of the rebels. The rest were due to the activity of the government and its allies during the insurrection and in reprisals in its immediate aftermath.[34]

Two incidents in particular during the insurrection in Wexford, in which large numbers of Catholic peasants took part, have from the beginning caused questions to be raised about the nature of the rising and the wisdom of United Irish tactics. The brutal massacres of Protestants at Scullabogue and Wexford Bridge might suggest that what happened in Co. Wexford was little more than a sectarian uprising. The politicizing propaganda of the United Irishmen had thus succeeded only in turning peasant anxieties into a blood-lust against the ruling Protestant class. Though espousing a secularist ideal, the United Irishmen had ended up reinforcing sectarian divisions.[35]

There was certainly a good deal of ideological hybridity as a result of the interaction between United Irish and popular mentalities, as the following Defender catechism illustrates: ' "Who sent you?" "Simon Peter, the head of the Church. Signed by order of the chief consul." '[36] There was also a good deal of sectarian tension, though some of it was engendered by the government and

33 Whelan, *Tree of liberty*, p. 124. **34** Dickson, *New foundations*, p. 214 and Whelan, '1798 rebellion in County Wexford,' in Keogh and Furlong (eds), *The mighty wave*, p. 28, both agree on the figure of 20,000. However, 'Insurrection of 1798' in Connolly, ed, *Oxford Companion to Irish history*, pp 260–1, puts it at 30,000. **35** Curtin, *United Irishmen*, pp 201, 284. **36** Dunne, 'Popular ballads,' in Gough and Dickson eds), *Ireland and the French Revolution*, p. 146.

its allies. The United Irishmen undoubtedly overestimated their capacity to unite disparate religious groups in a common cause. However, it is certainly possible to see the Wexford rising as being for the most part inspired by more positive United Irish ideas, and to argue that the two massacres, which were deeply regretted by the leaders of the rising, were the result of breakdowns in discipline. Equally, rebellion failed to break out in some other counties with strong sectarian tensions but with a lesser exposure to United Irish ideas.[37] In spite of this, though, it remains also possible to argue for a strong sectarian element to the rebellion.[38]

Some low-level rebel activity continued after 1798, most notably in Wicklow. The brief and abortive Robert Emmet rising in Dublin in 1803 had its roots in the United Irishmen, and the organization was still active in Leinster in 1804. There was even a brief revolt in Australia in 1804 by former participants in the Irish insurrection.[39] United Irishmen who fled to the United States helped to reinforce the Anglophobic strain in political culture there and, in their modes of political organization, paved the way for the Fenians in America half a century later.[40] Nonetheless, for the most part the decisive fashion in which the 1798 insurrection was suppressed definitively put paid to the United Irish movement.

Interpreting the insurrection quickly became a partisan pastime. Sir Richard Musgrave's *Memoirs of the different rebellions in Ireland* (1801) presented the insurrection as yet another proof of Catholic treachery in order to prevent further concessions to Catholics and to sunder the Catholic-Presbyterian alliance. Whigs, on the contrary, stressed the loyalty of many Catholics during 1798. Conservative United Irishmen such as Edward Hay in his *History of the insurrection in the county of Wexford* (1803) presented those who took part as reluctant rebels, forced into the field by government repression, while the more radical United Irishmen remained quiet but unapologetic. Watty Cox's *Irish Magazine* (1807–15) consistently blamed the landlord class for the rebellion. It was not until the middle of the nineteenth century, with the rise of new nationalist groups such as the Young Irelanders and the Fenians, and especially with the publication of the *Memoirs* (1863) of Myles Byrne that a more confidently positive account of the rebellion was given voice. Some time later Patrick Kavanagh's influential *Popular history* (1870) reinterpreted 1798 in terms of the struggle of the Catholic nation.[41]

Politically, the 1798 insurrection created a determination on the part of the British government to take Ireland more directly into its control. It led to the

37 Whelan, '1798 rebellion in County Wexford', pp 27–8. **38** Donnelly, 'Sectarianism in 1798,' in Geary (ed.), *Rebellion and remembrance*, pp 15–37. **39** O'Donnell, 'United Irishmen in New South Wales,' in Geary (ed.), *Rebellion and remembrance*, pp 38–50. **40** Wilson, *United Irishmen, United States*. **41** Whelan, *Tree of liberty*, pp 133–75.

passing of the Acts of Union in 1800 which amalgamated the legislatures of Britain and Ireland, to the opposition of Orangemen and with the support of many Catholics who both believed wrongly that it would lead to Catholic emancipation.[42] Ireland and Britain were among the few countries in Europe to fend off revolution in the 1790s.[43] Ruling elites survive best when they can absorb new groups in the face of changed realities. In some ways the United Irishmen's agenda had been one in favour of greater middle-class participation in government. For the future, though, the refusal of Catholic emancipation seemed to deny access by growing middle-class elements of Ireland's majority population to full participation in the life of the state, in a way which associated the new union of Ireland and Britain with that denial. For how long could Ireland's Anglican ruling class maintain its position under such circumstances?

42 Keogh and Whelan, *Acts of Union*. **43** Whelan, *Tree of liberty*, p. 129.

CHAPTER 2

The shaping of politics, 1801–47

The new state that came into existence in 1801 consisted in little more than the legislative grafting of Ireland onto Great Britain. British was the adjective applied to the two islands. The monarch's title in the nineteenth century was king or queen of Great Britain and Ireland. United Kingdom was rarely used as a name. Indeed, England was often blithely used in place of Britain and Ireland — with Ireland, and, indeed, Scotland and Wales being mostly thought of as regions of a greater England. It was not until the 1880s that the Liberal party began to move towards a four nations model of the islands.[1]

The 1790s had been very unsettling for the Protestant landed ruling class in Ireland, the term Protestant at the time generally referring to membership of the Anglican Established Church which under the union had become part of the United Church of England and Ireland. Now, in the early part of the nineteenth century, the anxiety of the ruling class was whether the loss of its parliament would mean the loss of its status as the ruling power in Ireland. Would the British government rule Ireland through it, or would it become merely another interest group to be ruled?

This anxiety became crystallized in the use of the term Protestant Ascendancy, or *the* Protestant Ascendancy. The phrase had first been used in 1787 in a non-contentious manner.[2] By 1792, and principally through its employment by John Gifford in Dublin civic politics, it had become a rallying cry for the Protestant interest in Ireland and for its right to be the dominant force in the running of the country.[3] From this middle-class origin the term would become identified with the owners of landed estates and would eventually by used by W.B. Yeats in the twentieth century to evoke a putative, high-culture civilization.[4]

The term took some time to establish itself, but what it stood for was well understood, not least by the Orange Order which set itself the task of defending Protestant interests in the new dispensation. In some respects the omens were good. For the first third of the nineteenth century the government was for the most part dominated by Tories, though there was no necessary link between Orangeism and Toryism. Many Tories who opposed Catholic emancipation, such as the duke of Wellington, held the Orange Order in abhorrence, though

1 Murphy, *Abject loyalty*, pp xii-xvi. **2** Hill, 'Protestant Ascendancy,' *Ireland after the Union*, p. 3. **3** Hill, *Dublin civil politics*, pp 234, 386. **4** McCormack, *Ascendancy and tradition* and *From Burke to Beckett*.

many extreme or ultra-Tories were sympathetic. Anglican religious identity was still fundamental to the British state, and sectarian tensions ran high in the early part of the new century not only in Ireland but also in Britain.[5]

The large British military presence in Ireland because of the 1798 insurrection gave an opportunity for the Orange Order to become the focus for such tensions.[6] Orange lodges were established in regiments in Ireland and continued in existence on their return to Britain. The movement took root in Britain in the military, in industrial areas, among the nobility and in the royal family itself. The duke of York, who at the time was heir to the throne, briefly served as grand master of the British lodges in 1821 until the legality of the position was publicly questioned. He helped to ensure the defeat of the Catholic emancipation bill by the House of Lords in 1825. His brother the duke of Cumberland became grand master in 1827. In 1835 there was turmoil in parliament when it became known that Cumberland had issued warrants for Orange lodges in the army. There were rumours that he had contemplated a coup, and his aide, William Blennerhasset Fairman, fled the country rather than co-operate with investigations into the order. Cumberland was eventually obliged to dissolve the lodges in Britain in February 1836, a move which was soon copied in Ireland.

In spite of the Protestant nature of the state, there were signs that in Ireland British governments and their Dublin-based representatives, the lords lieutenant and chief secretaries, were keen not only to maintain a distance from the Orange Order but to develop a neutral machinery of control. This was most clear when Whigs occupied key offices, but it also became true of the Tories. The statue of King William III in College Green, Dublin, was a focus for governmental and informal Ascendancy ritual, on the anniversary of the battle of the Boyne, 12 July, and on the king's birthday, 4 November. In 1806 and early 1807 a Whig-led government, 'the ministry of all the talents', was in office. An anti-government demonstration was held at the decorated statue on 12 July 1806. As a result the Whig lord lieutenant, the duke of Bedford, did not hold the usual state procession to the statue on the following 4 November. And, ominously for Orangemen, the state rituals were not reinstated by the successor Tory government.

In 1822 the lord lieutenant, the Marquess Wellesley, who was personally in favour of Catholic emancipation and who was to go on to marry a Catholic in 1825, banned the Orange demonstration at the statue on 4 November. A month later he was pelted with fruit and other items by Orangemen when he attended the Theatre Royal.[7] Then in 1825 the Orange Order found itself banned in

5 Bartlett, *Catholic question*, p. 273. 6 Senior, *Orangeism*. 7 Hill, 'National festivals,' *Irish Historical Studies* 24:93 (1984), pp 30–51.

Ireland, alongside the Catholic Association, by a Tory government. It re-emerged in 1828 but found its capacity to hold public demonstrations frustrated by the Party Processions Act of 1832.

Even Tories who opposed Catholic emancipation, such as Sir Robert Peel, Irish chief secretary between 1812 and 1818, wanted the state to adopt a neutral stance. Much of the administrative reform of the first four decades of the nineteenth century, which will be dealt with elsewhere in this book and of which Peel's own police reforms were a part, effectively side-stepped Ascendancy landowners in the governance of the country at local level.

Above all the maintenance of Protestant Ascendancy came to be symbolically associated with the denial of Catholic emancipation. That issue was of such political sensitivity that during Lord Liverpool's fifteen years in office as prime minister (1812–27) it was deemed to be an 'open issue' which the government would not attempt to resolve. Whigs, and indeed a number of Tories, supported emancipation. On the Whig side it was considered to be an important issue of liberty. This explains the unprecedented interest in Irish literature in Britain in the early nineteenth century, as will be seen.

From the Irish Catholic point of view the trouble with British sympathy for emancipation was that it was never high enough up the political agenda not to be the subject of delay in the pursuit of power. Neither Charles James Fox nor George Canning, two of the greatest supporters of Catholic emancipation, deemed it expedient to pursue the matter when they each attained high office, in 1806 and 1827 respectively, and within months each was dead. There was no early nineteenth-century Gladstone.

The Catholic response to the new political dispensation was initially to revert to organizing Catholic boards and committees and to the subservient petitioning of the late eighteenth century. Catholics also relied on friends in the Westminster parliament, such as Henry Grattan (1746–1820), former star of the Irish parliament, to present petitions, table motions and introduce bills for Catholic emancipation. This strategy was clearly not working, and it was left to a new generation led by Daniel O'Connell (1775–1847), barrister scion of an old Gaelic, land-owning family in Co. Kerry, to do something about it.[8] Though O'Connell was forever protesting his loyalty to the state and crown, he was equally strong in his demand for the rights of Catholics. Petition became demand, and a new form of politics was born in order to obtain that demand.

The new assertiveness was tested on the question of the veto. Some supporters of emancipation suggested that, in return for the reform, the government be given a right to veto episcopal appointments, so that the loyalty of the

8 Connolly, 'Aftermath and adjustment,' 'The Catholic question, 1801–12,' 'Union government, 1812–23,' 'Mass politics and sectarian conflict, 1823–30,' in Vaughan (ed.), *Union I, 1801–70*, pp 1–107.

Catholic clergy and hence the people might be guaranteed. O'Connell denounced this concession, even when it lead to a split among the supporters of emancipation in 1813 and in spite of papal approval for it in 1814–16. By the 1820s the demand for Catholic subservience in return for emancipation had been reformulated into moves on two fronts. The first was to have Catholic clergy salaried and hence controlled by the state, a proposition that was still being considered in the late 1840s. The second was to have most Catholic voters, who fell into the 40*s*. freeholder category, disenfranchised. Even before the era of parliamentary reform inaugurated by the 1832 reform act, only one fifth of the 105 Irish constituencies, as redrawn for the union parliament, did not have a real electorate of some sort. O'Connell was sanguine about the loss of the 40*s*. freeholder Catholic vote, however, and was much criticized when he agreed to it in the abortive 1825 emancipation bill. He believed that the freeholders were of little real importance as they would come under landlord control when voting in public. Ironically, their independence at a subsequent election was dramatically to increase the prospects for emancipation, though they were eventually to be sacrificed in the 1829 emancipation act.

Of much greater importance was O'Connell's mode of campaigning for emancipation. In 1811 the Catholic Committee moved to have itself elected but was subject to police raids and suppression. Pro-emancipation newspapers were regularly prosecuted by the government. O'Connell's solution was to invent a new form of mass politics. In May 1823 he and Richard Lalor Sheil (1791–1851) founded the Catholic Association. It became a mass movement with associate membership at 1*d*. per month. This so-called 'Catholic rent' raised £15,000 over the next five years. It was organized at parish level, often with the support of the new post-penal laws generation of priests. Its success was aided by the rise in mass literacy. Over the two decades to 1824 the numbers of children in elementary education had doubled and reached two-fifths of the total. The Association was strongest, as might be expected from the previous discussion of the Catholic core, in Leinster and Munster. Its principal aim, to gain for Catholics the right to sit in parliament, was of course of most interest to the middle class. And indeed its activists were generally comfortable farmers and shopkeepers. However, it also took a stand on popular grievances such as tithes so that it garnered enormous support from further down the social scale. Emancipation, though of no immediate benefit to them, thus became a symbol for a yearning to escape from poverty for the masses that supported O'Connell.[9]

The emancipation question came to a head with the election of a Protestant pro-emancipation candidate at Waterford in 1826 and then O'Connell's own election at Clare in 1828. The crisis brought on by O'Connell not being able

9 Connolly, 'Mass politics,' p. 94.

to take his seat in parliament was resolved when the government of Wellington and Peel, erstwhile opponents of the reform, induced the king to accept emancipation in 1829. The prolonged battle had opposing effects in the two parts of the kingdom, tending to reduce the centrality of religion in British politics, while securing it in Ireland. The refusal of emancipation for so long by the state had politicized the majority population in Ireland into an essentially Catholic nation. This might have happened anyway, but the denial of emancipation was a great encouragement.

By the early 1830s the days of Ascendancy rule in Ireland were effectively over. Dublin was dominated no longer by the Ascendancy but by the lawyers and doctors of the albeit still largely Protestant, upper middle classes.[10] Government control over the newspapers was gone and there were three openly nationalist papers, the *Morning Register*, the *Freeman's Journal* and the *Pilot.* However, Catholics were still mostly excluded from public office. Of the 3,033 crown offices in Ireland in 1828, only 134 were held by Catholics.[11]

If O'Connell thought of the Irish nation, it was not in terms of the transcendental ideals of romantic nationalism but as a shorthand for the individual people who lived in Ireland.[12] He was a utilitarian, as is evidenced by his unsentimental views on the Irish language:

> Therefore, although the Irish language is connected with many recollections that twine round the hearts of Irishmen, yet the superior utility of the English tongue, as the medium of all modern communication, is so great that I can witness without a sigh the gradual disuse of Irish.[13]

O'Connell saw the state as providing a practical mechanism for improving the condition of people's lives. He was to spend the decade and a half after emancipation promoting the interests of Irish people, especially Catholics, in the state. Catholics were appointed to crown offices in increasing numbers. O'Connell and his supporters in the Commons vigorously took part in political battles over tithes, parliamentary and municipal reform and the poor law. The Whigs were in power throughout much of the 1830s. They attempted to mollify Irish grievances and to replace fully the indirect rule of the Protestant Ascendancy with what they saw as rational, centralized, utilitarian government. O'Connell formed alliances with them, most notably in the Lichfield House Compact of 1835.

On the wider stage he supported civil rights for minorities such as the Jews and strenuously opposed slavery, firstly in the West Indies and then in the

10 MacDonagh, 'Ideas and institutions, 1830–45,' in Vaughan (ed.), *Union I, 1801–70*, p. 193. **11** Connolly, 'Catholic question,' p. 26. **12** MacDonagh, *O'Connell*, p. 311. **13** Ó Tuathaigh, 'Folk-hero,' in McCartney (ed.), *Daniel O'Connell*, p. 37.

United States, though it cost him valuable political support there. He was in favour of universal manhood suffrage, though he distanced himself from the English Chartists and their radical agenda. He supported liberal movements in Belgium, Poland and Spain, and when as a dying man he set out for Rome in 1847 he was acclaimed on the continent as a statesman of renown.

O'Connell's activities in the 1830s and 1840s took place under the umbrella of a call for the repeal of the Act of Union and the restoration of the Irish parliament. Throughout the nineteenth century this call proved a most convenient platform for Irish nationalist politicians. Apparently proposing something specific, it put the onus on the British political establishment to respond either with reforms or perhaps even with some form of self-government.[14] It was, after all, clearly impossible that the old Irish parliament could ever be restored in an age of greater democracy and increasing denominational and political fissures between Ulster and the rest of Ireland. The ill-conceived 'invasion' of Ulster by the O'Connellite, John Lawless, in 1828 and O'Connell's own uncomfortable visit to Belfast in 1841 were already illustrations of the cleavage between the two parts of Ireland.

O'Connell's call for repeal was in earnest, but there were occasions, which shocked some of his supporters, when he offered to drop it in return for justice for Ireland. Thus in 1836 or in 1844 he offered to trade his demand for repeal in return for a form of devolution called federalism. The continuance of Irish agitation dismayed many of the former supporters of emancipation in Britain who imagined that it marked a final concession that ought to have appeased Irish Catholics. Instead of being the end of a process, however, O'Connell thought of it as merely the beginning.

Throughout the 1830s he founded a series of often short-lived societies, such as the General Association and the Precursor Society, in order to provide a platform for himself and to put pressure on the government. In 1840, tired of the Whigs and anticipating the return of the Tories under Peel the following year, he founded the Loyal National Repeal Association. To balance his calls for repeal, he constantly sought to demonstrate his loyalty, especially to the young and popular Queen Victoria, who had Whig sympathies.[15]

O'Connell was opposed in Britain for seeking to alter the constitutional settlement of the union which had become sacred to a political establishment already fearful of the corrosive effects of Irish political self-assertion on the bonds that held the growing British empire together. In Ireland O'Connell embraced the Enlightenment title of 'Liberator', but was wary of the popular but politically dangerous appellation of 'uncrowned king'. In many respects he was more like an Irish chieftain reliant on personal loyalties, surrounded by

14 MacDonagh, *States of mind*, pp 57–8. **15** Murphy, *Abject loyalty*, pp 20–58.

lieutenants who were also relatives and financially supported by a periodic 'tribute' from his followers. For this reason his movement did not survive his death. Though O'Connell contributed much to the creation of Irish political culture and national identity, it would be forty years before a mass political movement could, albeit with difficulty, transcend the limitations of its leader and survive as a political system in spite of his departure. The promotion of O'Connell's son as the 'Young Liberator' was an absurdity and was part of the flamboyant, even burlesque, side of O'Connell's personality, which owed more to Regency than to Victorian manners. The *mise en scène* of his public appearances often involved over-sized vehicles, allegorical statues and large amounts of drapery.

Agitation for repeal began in earnest in the autumn of 1842 and O'Connell announced that 1843 would be the Repeal Year. Three million people enrolled in the Repeal Association and forty 'monster' meetings took place in that year, with perhaps 800,000 present at the meeting at Tara on 15 August 1843 alone. By even the most conservative estimates one quarter of the population of the southern provinces of Ireland attended one of O'Connell's meetings that year. They were spectacular participative occasions, with O'Connell's speech perhaps the least important element. There were bands, banners and coloured sashes for the different trades and a great procession to meet O'Connell that passed through triumphal arches. Greenery was carried and loaves of bread on poles as a symbol of poverty.[16]

In Britain O'Connell was feared and derided as an agitator for his appeal to and mobilization of the politically unenfranchized populace. The discipline and peacefulness of his mass rallies during the repeal years were particularly disturbing as they precluded the use of state force to suppress them. 'You can hardly overrate the gravity of the present moment. The peaceable demeanour of the assembled multitudes is one of the most alarming symptoms', the Irish lord chancellor, Sir Edward Sugden, told Sir Robert Peel on 28 May 1843, with no apparent irony.[17] O'Connell, however, in spite of his well-known abhorrence of violence was not above hinting that violence might be the consequence of a failure to grant reforms.

As with the emancipation movement, though, the repeal movement was essentially middle class at its core. It cost 1*s*. to sit on the speakers' platform during monster meetings, and several hundred people generally did so. After O'Connell's speech the crowds drifted away while the members of the middle class present, the 'popular elite' that had assembled and controlled the proceedings, accompanied him to a banquet.[18] A similar situation obtained in Dublin where the Repeal Association had its headquarters. In 1841 there were

16 Owens, ' "Monster meetings," ' in Donnelly and Miller (eds), *Irish popular culture*, pp 242–69.
17 Sir Edward Sugden to Sir Robert Peel, 28 May 1843, in Parker (ed.), *Peel*, vol. 3, pp 48–9.
18 Cronin, 'O'Connellite crowds,' in Jupp and Magennis (eds), *Crowds in Ireland*, pp 139–72.

roughly 35,000 professionals in Ireland, including teachers, clergy, lawyers and doctors. They constituted one per cent of the work-force. The Catholic representation in most professions ranged between one quarter and one third. Of the 509 supporters of the Repeal Association in Dublin in the 1840s, 164 were members of the intelligentsia (including professionals, clerics, military officers, writers, students, engineers and architects), 40 belonged to the gentry, 231 were merchants and there were 74 others. Of the members of committees the most active tended to belong to the intelligentsia. Nearly half the 114 intelligentsia committee members were lawyers, though only 14 per cent were identifiably Protestant. O'Connell's core activists therefore were drawn overwhelmingly from the still slender ranks of the Catholic professional classes.[19]

The government banned the monster meeting at Clontarf in October 1843 and O'Connell spent several months in prison the following year. However, it was Peel's apparent subsequent legislative concessions that really began to undermine the position of the ailing O'Connell. The Charitable Bequests Act and especially the legislation to establish provincial, non-denominational, third-level education in the Queen's Colleges or 'godless colleges', as they came to be known, split the Catholic hierarchy and Catholic opinion generally. It also sundered relations between O'Connell and the Young Irelanders, a group of radicals centred around the *Nation* newspaper, whose view of the nation was at once more secular and romantic than O'Connell's.

Peel had succeeded in stalling O'Connell's momentum and for the moment in fracturing the Catholic nation. That political formation, the creation of the denial of Catholic emancipation at the union, would nonetheless survive. So too would O'Connell's creation, the notion of a popular constitutional politics, often pushing out the restricting boundaries of a still essentially undemocratic state to the limits of their tolerance. This was an alternative both to subservience on the one hand and political violence on the other,[20] albeit an alternative in which bourgeois nationalist agendas would be preferred. Yet there were other modes of popular organization in early nineteenth-century Ireland than those which related to bourgeois nationalism. Their interaction with a centralizing state keen to put social control in the hands of dispassionate institutions and procedures, which will next be examined, was of great importance.

19 Hill, 'Intelligentsia,' *Studia Hibernica* 20 (1980), pp 73–109. **20** Thuente, 'Violence in pre-famine Ireland,' *Irish University Review* 15:2 (1985), p. 147.

CHAPTER 3

Ordering peasants, 1801–45

This chapter looks at some of the features of social life and popular culture throughout the nineteenth century. It also analyses popular discontents and the state's responses to the sometimes violent expression of those discontents in pre-famine Ireland. Organized religion will be dealt with in a later chapter but only because it was such a large and complex phenomenon and not so as to suggest that it was merely an extraneous imposition on popular culture or not integral to that culture. There were economic and social gradations within the peasantry which will be adverted to here where necessary and which will be explored in greater depth in a later discussion about economics. As for the term 'peasant' itself, for all its inadequacies when applied to Ireland it remains *faute de mieux* a useful shorthand. Finally, the ordering alluded to in the title of this chapter refers not only to the state's attempts to order the peasantry and society in general but also to the forms of order found within peasant social and cultural life. These were often dismissed by Irish bourgeois and British colonial commentators alike as signs of a lack of civilization and even barbarity. However, agrarian movements were a way of negotiating the economics of land tenure and, ironically, some of the practices of peasant social life served the same patriarchal purposes which were valorized in bourgeois life.

Perhaps the most striking feature of the period was the decline of the Irish language from the widespread vernacular of the Catholic peasant population to the daily language of a small minority. At the beginning of the nineteenth century just a little over half of the population used Irish as its day-to-day language.[1] The decline was well advanced by the middle of the century when only 23.3 per cent of people could speak Irish and 4.9 per cent could speak only Irish. This picture hides wide regional variations with the language very weak in Ulster and Leinster, though there were pockets of speakers in Donegal, Kilkenny, Louth and Meath. At that stage though Irish was still relatively strong in the other two provinces with half the population of Connaught and two fifths that of Munster being able to speak Irish. Forty years later, however, only 14.5 per cent could speak Irish nationally and 0.8 per cent could speak only Irish.

There was little encouragement for the Irish language from the Catholic Church, though the redoubtable archbishop of Tuam, John MacHale, published part of the Old Testament in Irish. Ironically, evangelical Protestants,

1 In 1799 Whitley Stokes estimated that 2.4 million of the country's then 4.75 million population used Irish. See Ó Bresláin and Dwyer, *Irish language*, p. 18.

intent on making converts, were often more likely to be exponents of the language. The processes of the state were also often hostile, and Irish speakers were sometimes ridiculed when giving evidence in court. Chairs of Irish had been established at third level institutions from the 1830s onwards. However, the use of Irish was discouraged in the education system until the late 1870s when it was allowed at both primary and secondary level in limited ways, thanks in part to the efforts of the Society for the Preservation of the Irish Language, founded in 1876.

There were poets of quality and sophistication with roots in the Gaelic tradition who wrote in the Irish language in the early nineteenth century and articulate historical popular grievances.[2] Among them were Antoine Raifthearaí (1779–1835) Mícheál Óg Ó Longáin, Máire Bhuí Ní Laoghaire (1774–1849) of Cork, Tomás Rua Ó Súilleabháin (1758–1848) of Kerry and Diarmaid Na Bolgaighe Ó Séaghdha (d. 1850) of Kerry.[3] Colm de Bhailís (1796–1906) of Connemara, whose life spanned the century, may have had the appearance of a peasant but spoke with the authority of the Gaelic poet.[4]

Popular culture was for the most part an oral culture. But popular literature both in Irish and in English was available. Broadside ballads and religious books were printed in Irish in the early part of the century. Peddlers sold chapbooks in English, the most popular types being romances and criminal biographies with *Irish highwaymen*, written in the 1730s, a favourite. Both sorts of story presented a world in which status and character were ancestral rather than personally achieved qualities. Far from confirming a sense of deference for the land-owning classes, however, these types of writing fulfilled a more subversive role, given what has been identified as the spreading sense among the members of the tenantry that they and not the landlords were the aboriginal inheritors of the land.[5]

Popular culture was characterized by a belief in magic and rituals. People did not move into new houses on a Friday, and the first day of the week, month or year was the best on which to begin a new task. Animal blood was smeared on homes and people on St Martin's feast, 11 November. Bonfires were lit on May Eve and on St John's Eve (23 June).[6] The year was punctuated by great seasonal festivals such as Lúghnasa, a late summer harvest festival associated with hill tops and water.[7]

Magic was socially connected with aggression. Supernatural aggression could be performed, it was believed, by people or by the fairies, the former

2 Dunne, 'Gaelic poetry and song,' in Geary (ed.), *Rebellion and remembrance*, pp 93–111. **3** Ó Cúiv, 'Irish language and literature,' in Vaughan (ed.), *Union II, 1870–1921*, pp 385–435. **4** Denvir, 'Language and literature in Ireland,' *New Hibernia Review*, 1:1 (1997), p. 56. **5** Ó Cíosáin, *Print and popular culture*. **6** Connolly, 'Popular culture,' in Byrne and Harry (eds), *Canadian and Irish essays*, pp 12–28. **7** Evans, 'Peasant beliefs,' in Casey and Rhodes (eds), *Irish peasantry, 1800–1916*, pp 37–56.

being associated with aggression outside the family, the latter with aggression within the family. Persons with 'the evil eye' could, often unwittingly, bring about malfunctions in agricultural equipment or illness and death in humans and animals. Milk and churn blinking involved depriving cows of their milk or ensuring that milk could not be turned into butter. These activities, which indeed were sometimes consciously practised by people who believed in them, were a means of choreographing on the supernatural plane actual interpersonal conflicts, envies and fears. Women who did not fit into the conventional familial category by being old, widowed, childless or independent, were often accused of being witches engaged in such practices.

Fairies, who supposedly lived in prehistoric raths or fairy forts, could take various forms from the leprechaun to the 'leannáin si' or vampire-like, fairy lover. Fairy or herb doctors were local people with the power to counteract the ill effects of contact with fairies by means of potions, prayers and other practices. Thus elf-shot cattle were ill because of an invisible fairy wound.

Fairies were unable to breed and so needed to abduct human children and adult women, replacing them with weak or sickly changelings. In some parts of the country boys were dressed in petticoats and long frocks into their teens in order to confuse fairies who might want to abduct them.[8] The diagnosis of a changeling, particularly in the case of a woman, was often the result of family tensions and was a means to reassert patriarchal authority. It allowed a victim to be treated as an aggressor. Women could be punished with alacrity and supposedly without damage to the structure of the family. When children were identified and punished as changelings, it was intended essentially as a rebuke to the parenting skills of the mother.[9] The best-known changeling case was that of Bridget Cleary who was burned to death by her husband and others near Clonmel in 1895. The Clearys were a modern, relatively prosperous couple without children and for these reasons were subject to the pressures of a climate of local suspicion which eventually occasioned the sudden and violent reversion to the simple certainties of tradition.[10]

Fairs, baptisms, weddings and wakes were occasions for communal celebration. The 'merry wake' was found not only in the countryside but also in the towns. It was a gathering in the presence of the body of the dead person characterized by drinking, singing and various games. It thus had a carnivalesque dimension and was a means whereby the community reordered itself in the face of the disruptive power of death.[11]

Wake practices mixed Christian and fairy world-views. For this reason they were generally condemned by ecclesiastical authorities. The clergy and sacra-

8 Fitzpatrick, 'Irish female,' in O'Flanagan, Ferguson, Whelan (eds), *Rural Ireland*, p. 164. **9** Jenkins, 'Witches and fairies,' *Ulster Folklife* 23 (1977), pp 48–56. **10** Bourke, *Bridget Cleary*. **11** Ó Crualaoich, 'The "merry wake" ' in Donnelly and Miller (eds), *Irish popular culture*, pp 173–200.

ments, especially marriage, were sometimes mocked, and there was usually a sexual element to the wake games. 'Making the ship', one popular game, culminated in 'erecting the mast', done by one of the women present using gestures. There were rare reports of men appearing naked at some wakes and of women dressing up as men. Wakes, however, were occasions for a comic bawdiness rather than for sexual activity.[12]

The wake games were organized by an old man who was thus the agent for the chaos out of which a new social order emerged. Of more importance was the 'bean chaointe' or keening women. She was the human equivalent of the banshee, the supernatural messenger of death.[13] She was a professional mourner and represented a rare opportunity for women to be centre stage, her words asserting the validity of women's experience and often articulating a rhetoric of resistance to violence and abuse.[14]

Whereas sacred trees, dolmens, stone circles and raths—of which there may have been as many as 40,000 in the country—were associated with fairies, the 3,000 holy wells were associated with local Christians saints. Pilgrims to holy wells often had to complete complex circuits of the area, a means of defending the sacred from the uninitiated. 'Patterns' were festive celebrations at such holy sites, usually on saints' days. They often involved drinking, with large-scale fighting echoing on the mortal plane the conflict between fairy groups for the crops.[15]

Wakes and patterns, which were both condemned by Church authorities, provided complements and perhaps even substitutes for more orthodox religious activities. Catholicism always had means for assimilating the miraculous as with the healings attributed to the intervention of the German aristocrat priest, Prince Hohenlohe in 1823.[16] A series of events, less susceptible to such assimilation, occurred during the panic associated with the cholera epidemic of 1832. Within six days in early June news spread by word of mouth from Co. Cork to Co. Derry, reaching three-quarters of Irish counties, that the Blessed Virgin Mary had prescribed the use of ashes or alternatively 'blessed turf' as a protection against cholera.[17]

Belief in fairies was held in common by Catholics, Anglicans and Presbyterians of the lower classes. Popular customs were often culturally hybrid and not necessarily the unchanged survivals of a Gaelic past. Patterns and pilgrimages may have been an innovation of the seventeenth century, encouraged by the landed classes, to prevent feuding kin groups having to encounter each

12 Connolly, 'Popular culture,' p. 23. **13** Ó Crualaoich, '"Merry wake,"' p. 192. **14** Bourke, 'Irish women's lament poetry,' in Radner (ed.), *Women's folk culture*, pp 160–82. **15** Ó Giolláin, 'The pattern,' in Donnelly and Miller (eds), *Irish popular culture*, pp 201–21. **16** Geary, 'Prince Hohenlohe,' in Malcolm and Jones (eds), *Medicine, disease and the state*, pp 40–58. **17** Connolly, 'Cholera and popular panic,' *Irish Historical Studies*, 23:91 (1983), pp 214–32; Robins, *Epidemic and panic*.

other at Sunday mass.[18] Christmas rhyming or mumming was found both in Ulster and Wexford and was of English origins. English May poles were erected in Ulster but also in Kilkenny. Bull baiting, another English pastime, was popular in towns.[19]

Many of the popular customs discussed here began to fall into disuse from the 1830s. The reasons for this included the opposition of the growing ranks of clergy, magistrates and police, the spread of the railways and national education system and the effects of the famine.[20]

The first three decades of the nineteenth century, marked as they were by minor famines and economic change, were also a time in which a variety of peasant agrarian societies flourished which were in broad continuity with their late eighteenth-century predecessors. Often dismissed as primitive forms of protonationalism or as unsophisticated predecessors of the Land League, David Lloyd has argued for them to be seen as forms of subaltern resistance free of bourgeois nationalist control.[21]

There was a wide variety of such movements, many in the midlands and southern part of the country and each with its own name, cause, and locality. There were at least twelve major outbreaks of agrarian agitation in different parts of the country over a total of thirty-five years in the first half of the nineteenth century. The conflict between the Caravats and Shanavests in Leitrim, Longford, Mayo, Sligo and Cavan, of 1806–11, for example, was clearly a class dispute between a lower-class syndicalist group and its middle class opponents.[22] The Rockite movement in Limerick, Cork, Tipperary, Clare, Kerry and King's of 1819–24 was fed by the millenarian ideas which were widespread at the time and which were communicated by handbills, broadside ballads or by teachers. In particular it was spurred on by the apocalyptic prophecies of 'Signor Pastorini', predicting as they did the triumph of Catholicism and defeat of Protestantism by 1825, which had been given widespread credence.[23]

In general, however, these movements have been grouped together under the heading of Whiteboys and attempts have been made to discern the commonalities between them.[24] Whiteboy groups were rural secret societies that enforced their will by means of oaths imposed on local communities and by punitive acts such as sending threatening notices and beatings and killings. When about their clandestine activities members often dressed in straw hats, white shirts or, though men, in women's clothes, and frequently used female sobriquets such as Lady Rock, Lady Clare, Terry Alt's mother or Molly Maguire.

18 Carroll, *Irish pilgrimage*. **19** Connolly, 'Popular culture.' **20** Malcolm, 'Popular recreation,' in MacDonagh, Mandle and Travers (eds), *Irish culture and nationalism*, p. 51. **21** Lloyd, *Anomalous states*, pp 125–62. **22** Roberts, 'Whiteboyism and faction fighting ,' in Clark and Donnelly (eds), *Irish peasants*, pp 64–101. **23** Donnelly Jr, 'Pastorini and Captain Rock,' in Clark and Donnelly (eds), *Irish peasants*, pp 102–39. **24** Beames, *Peasants and power*.

For the most part participants in these movements were from the less economically secure ranks of the peasantry, in counties where there were a large numbers of farms under 15 acres. Opinion has been divided over the objects or enemies of the Whiteboys. J.J. Lee's view is that they tended to represent rural labourers and cottiers, possessors of around five acres of land each. Essentially they were in dispute with somewhat more prosperous tenant farmers for whom they worked and from whom they rented small amounts of land under the conacre system to grow subsistence crops for their own families in return for labour.[25] Michael Beames's conclusion is that there was no hard and fast distinction between labourers and cottiers and small farmers. He believes that the Whiteboys represented the peasantry in general and were mostly in dispute with a new generation of commercial, improving landlords who were intent on rationalizing their estates in the years after the Napoleonic wars, a process which involved the clearing of land and consolidation of holdings.[26] Finally, James S. Donnelly Jr has argued that the composition of Whiteboy groups depended on economic conditions. When economic conditions were good, they tended to be composed of cottiers and labourers, fearful of rising rents and often in dispute with farmers. When economic conditions were harsh, the social base for the Whiteboys broadened to include not only the cottiers and labourers but also farmers higher up the social scale.[27]

Whiteboys flourished at the same time as another but very distinct group, the Ribbonmen.[28] They were the successors of the Defenders and had a nationalist and pronouncedly Catholic profile. Their membership was heavily urban, though it did include some farmers, and was composed of artisans, such as shoemakers and smiths, middle-class publicans and shopkeepers, and coal porters and brewery workers from the proletariat. They existed in south Ulster, north Leinster, north Connaught, along the eastern seaboard, especially in Dublin, and along arteries of communication such as the canals and were thus strongest in areas least affected by agrarian disturbances. They were intensively active in the early 1820s and throughout that decade lived in the expectation of a new revolutionary elite arising to call them to action. Divisions arose between the Ulster and Dublin groupings, however, and the latter was broken up by the police in the 1830s. Thereafter the Ulster Ribbonmen moved towards becoming a mutual help society with links in Britain and America. Ironically, Ribbonism came to be a generic term used in the later nineteenth century for agrarian societies.

25 Lee, 'The Ribbonmen,' in Williams (ed.), *Secret societies*, pp 26–35. **26** Beames, *Peasants and power*, pp 121–31. **27** Donnelly, 'Agrarian rebellions,' in Corish (ed.), *Radicals, rebels and establishments*, pp 151–69. **28** Beames, 'The Ribbon societies,' in Philpin (ed.), *Nationalism and popular protest*, pp 245–63; Garvin, 'Defenders, Ribbonmen and others,' *Past and Present* 96 (1982), pp 133–53.

Conflict can be about class but it can occur within families and between family factions.[29] Faction fighting was a significant feature of life in early nineteenth-century Ireland.[30] In 1822, 253 riots (including faction fights) were recorded. By 1827 the figure had risen to 1,001 though it fell in the 1830s due to greater police activity. Faction fighting was in some respects simply a particularly bloody form of popular recreation in an era before competitive games. Feuds between factions could develop for the most trivial of reasons. The decades-long feud between the Bootashees and Tubbers who were respectively the O'Brien family of Ballywilliam and the Kennedy and Hogan families of Kilmore and Youghal developed as the result of a quarrel over marbles between an O'Brien and a Hogan boy in 1794.

Fatalities were common during fights which were mostly prearranged rather than spontaneous affairs. In June 1829, for example, six men were killed and twenty-one men and women seriously injured at a faction fight at Borrisokane. In June 1834 at the 'Battle of Ballyeagh' in Co. Kerry 3,200 took part with twenty people dying and hundreds of injuries. English and bourgeois Irish commentators were accustomed to report faction fighting with horror as a sign of Irish barbarity. However, a form of recreational violence on the pretext of honour continued to be practised by the upper and middle classes into the 1820s, albeit in the more individualized guise of duelling.[31] Irish history might have been very different, one way or the other, if the arranged duel between Daniel O'Connell and Sir Robert Peel had been allowed to go ahead in 1815.

Faction fighting, Whiteboyism and Ribbonism tended to die away after the first third of the nineteenth century. One reason was changed social and economic circumstances. A second was the O'Connellite politicization of the 1820s which channelled energies in new directions. In 1828, for example, O'Connell called for an end to faction fighting, especially in Co. Tipperary, and encouraged mass gatherings of upwards of 30,000 persons, often with bands and quasi-military uniforms, in support of Catholic emancipation.[32]

The complex 'tithe war' against the payment of taxes to the Established Church of the early 1830s was an interesting example of an at times uneasy alliance between differing forms of popular action, some of them in the agrarian tradition and others in that of bourgeois nationalist politics. Since the 1823 Tithe Composition Act had brought pasture under the system, the collecting of tithes had become a source of grievance to substantial farmers, the Catholic clergy and O'Connellites as well as to poorer farmers. A campaign of non-payment and protest against tithes began in Graiguenamanagh, Co. Kilkenny, in October 1830 and eventually spread throughout Leinster and Munster. A solution was

29 Fitzpatrick, 'Class, family and rural unrest,' in Drudy (ed.), *Ireland, land, politics and people*, pp 37–75. **30** O'Donnell, *Irish faction fighters*. **31** Kelly, *Duelling in Ireland*. **32** Owens, 'Faction fights,' *Irish Historical Studies*, 30:120, pp 513–40.

eventually found in the Tithe Rentcharge Act (1838) which turned the tithe into a reduced charge payable by landlords. However, nationalist political leaders were not in control of the campaign and tended to withdraw from it as it descended into violence, with twelve demonstrators being killed in one incident in 1831 and eleven police and soldiers dying in another a few months later.[33]

O'Connell was to ensure that he controlled the mass mobilization of the Repeal movement in the next decade, but his was not the first successful attempt after the tithe war to mobilize mass gatherings. Indeed, he was effectively to cannibalize the organization which had done so, the temperance movement.[34]

Whiskey was the most popular alcoholic beverage because of the relative expense of beer. The period between the 1780s and 1840s was a time when illicit distilling flourished. The consumption of alcohol was actually not great among the poorer classes because of its expense. As a result poorer people tended only to engage in occasional periods of heavy drinking at events such as weddings, funerals, markets and patterns, though because of its public nature this created the false picture of a much higher rate of overall consumption. Until the late 1830s, though, campaigns against alcohol in Ireland were directed at better off and largely urban people and were part of a wider British movement.

Theobald Mathew was a Capuchin friar with an aristocratic background who joined the Cork teetotal society in 1838 and was soon beginning to turn temperance into a mass movement. By February 1839 he had enrolled 9,000 teetotallers in Cork. By the end of that year his organization had 66,000 members. Between 1840 and 1843 he conducted 350 major temperance missions, in Britain as well as in Ireland, facilitated by the advent of modern means of communication such as the railways. His greatest success was in the towns rather than in cities such as Dublin or, indeed, Cork, where the alcohol industry was based. In May 1841 he claimed that his movement had 4.3 million members and the consumption of whiskey may, indeed, have fallen by as much as a half.

Father Mathew's support among the Catholic clergy, however, was lukewarm in spite of his best efforts, with only around a third of bishops and priests taking the pledge when the campaign was at its height. Their suspicion was due among other things to the fact that movement had Protestant roots, though Mathew himself drew on the popular religiosity of his supporters and tacitly encouraged belief in his miraculous healing powers. In spite of such elements, the movement was anything but millennial. The bourgeois consolations of a happy domestic life were held up as the prize to be won by temperance.

O'Connell's public approval of Mathew was tinged with envy, and he was soon harnessing temperance supports, including temperance bands, for repeal

33 Jackson, *Ireland 1798–1998*, p. 41. **34** Kerrigan, *Father Mathew*; Malcolm, *Drink and temperance*; Townend, *Father Mathew*.

ends. Faced with O'Connell's interference, which alienated Protestant support, with Mathew's own health and financial difficulties and with the famine, the movement eventually foundered. Anti-drink campaigns later in the century focussed on restricting opening hours for public houses. These were government-regulated spaces for drinking which had only relatively recently exceeded outdoor drinking in popularity.[35] Meanwhile, at the end of the century, the Catholic Pioneers presented the alcohol abstinence pledge not as a safeguard for the drunkard but as an heroic sacrifice for the sober.[36] Overall levels of alcohol consumption in Ireland in the second half of the nineteenth century were, contrary to the stereotype, slightly below those of Britain and considerably below those of the United States.[37]

Both the temperance and repeal movements were attempts to discipline popular culture for ethical and political ends. The state, too, was making increasing attempts to exercise a similar discipline. This was especially true of the Whig governments of the 1830s which saw themselves as bringing much needed reform to Ireland. State discipline included the means both of restraining lawlessness through the legal, police and prison systems and of extending aid to those in need.

At the beginning of the nineteenth century policing was still largely in the hands of the military and much of it remained controlled by the Ascendancy rather than directly by the state. In 1813 there were 11,000 regular troops in Ireland, rising to 30,000 in 1847. There were 400 military posts and 100 barracks. The Ascendancy-dominated Yeomanry had 60,000 members in 1805, and 40,000 members four years before it was disbanded in 1830.[38] Militarization, however, did not always work in favour the Ascendancy. The militia, disbanded in 1816, had 12, 000 members in 1813, most of them Catholic. During the Napoleonic wars as many as 200,000 men or one sixth of Irish adult males saw service in the British Army or Royal Navy. The discipline of such experience was of undoubted assistance in the Catholic emancipation politicization of the 1820s.[39]

By the early nineteenth century there were police forces in Dublin (1786) and Belfast (1816) and a not very successful system of baronial constables (1787) around the country. However, Chief Secretary Peel was facing mounting agrarian activity. He was involved in 1814 in the passing of the Insurrection and Peace Preservation Acts which helped to restore order. The latter established a peace preservation force of around 1,000 men that could be sent to disturbed areas under the command of a stipendiary magistrate. Lord Lieutenant Wellesley established a County Constabulary in 1822, a force of upwards of

35 Malcolm, 'The rise of the pub,' in Donnelly and Miller (eds), *Irish popular culture*, pp 50–77. **36** Malcolm, 'Irish temperance movement,' *Irish Historical Studies* 23:89 (1982), pp 1–16. **37** Malcolm, *Drink and temperance*, p. 324. **38** Blackstock, *The Irish Yeomanry*; O'Donnell, *Irish faction fighters*, p. 42. **39** Bartlett, 'Militarization and politicization,' in *Culture et pratiques politiques*, pp 125–36.

7,000 men. By 1836 these two forced had been merged into a body designed to have 10,000 men called the Irish Constabulary or the Royal Irish Constabulary from 1867. Perhaps the most significant feature of it was that it was centralized and under government control. Local magistrates, whose reliability was a continuing source of anxiety for governments, were no longer involved in the running of the police. In spite of the establishment of a system of county lords lieutenant in 1831 to act as a link between the evolving state system and the gentry, this was a further blow against the Ascendancy.[40] Ireland was to have a much more centralized system of law and order, and indeed of government in general, than England, where the gentry were still to play a role for more than a hundred years.[41] The term 'bureaucracy' was first coined in 1818 by the novelist Lady Morgan in connection with the government of Ireland.[42]

As the years went on the Irish Constabulary took on many of the features of a civil police force. However, it remained essentially a paramilitary force. The state never fully succeeded in normalizing the administration of law in Ireland. For all but sixteen years of the nineteenth century Ireland was subject to special legislation, generally called 'coercion', which reduced a suspect's rights to the ordinary protection of the law. This gave ammunition to politicians who argued that Ireland was not being treated as an integral element of a united kingdom.[43] In fact Irish crime rates were not greatly different from those in Britain, but violent crime in Ireland was a cause of great anxiety because of the political context in which it often occurred.[44] Indeed, it was often in the interests of those in power who were resistant to social and political movements in Ireland to seize on what acts of violence there were as being characteristic of the people.[45]

In the eighteenth century there were three types of prison: debtors' prisons; county jails for persons awaiting trial; and houses of correction or industry which attempted to inculcate habits of industry in the poor. Capital punishment was prescribed as the penalty for many offences, though the number was reduced drastically as the nineteenth century wore on. Actual executions were fewer than might be imagined, however. Juries were slow to convict for capital crimes and many executions were commuted. Between 1826 and 1844 there were over 3,000 capital convictions but only 421 persons were executed. Transportation to Australia, either for life or a fixed term, was an alternative to execution. It was imposed for other crimes as well until it ended in 1853. Thus between 1837 and 1844 alone around 8,000 people were transported. Imprisonment was possible only for very short terms, though thousands of people were

40 Broeker, *Police reform*; Crossman, *Politics, law and order*. **41** MacDonagh, *The union*, p. 36. **42** W.J. McCormack, 'Language, class and genre (1780–1830),' in Deane (ed.), *Field Day*, vol. 1, p. 1080. **43** Appendix F 'Select list of statues relating to the preservation or restoration of order in Ireland, 1776–1923,' in Crossman, *Politics, law and order*, pp 199–230; MacDonagh, *States of mind*, p. 32. **44** Townshend, *Political violence in Ireland*, pp 6–14. **45** Lloyd, *Anomalous states*, p. 144.

thus incarcerated. A new Irish prisons system, however, came into operation in 1854 with nine prisons, four of them – Mountjoy, Grangegorman, Newgate and Smithfield – in Dublin, and with a remedial ideology consonant with current thought.[46]

The government's zeal for utilitarian reform extended to many other areas, administrative, educational, social and medical. Counties still continued to be administered by Ascendancy-dominated grand juries until the end of the century. The administration of towns and cities, however, was reformed and brought under slightly more popular control by means of various legislative measures, most notably the Municipal Corporations Act (1840). All but a dozen of Ireland's sixty corporations were abolished. Meanwhile, acts of 1828 and 1854 enabled the establishment of town commissioners in dozens of other urban areas.[47] A Board of Public Works was established in 1831 to co-ordinate state construction work. State-endowed education, which will be dealt with later, was another means of extending the discipline of the state, not least in the hope of reining in teachers, a hitherto subversive group, by paying for their salaries. No wonder that paying Catholic priests was also periodically considered as a serious proposition.

State control also extended to the medical and poor law systems. In 1838 the English poor law system of 1834 was effectively imposed on Ireland by the government in spite of the advice of the Whately commission which had been established to look into the matter and which had proposed schemes to alleviate poverty. The new system was intended to cater for 100,000, whereas the Whately commission had estimated that over two and a third million individuals needed assistance.[48] The new system did not allow for 'outdoor relief', state assistance to poor people in their homes, but required them to enter a workhouse in order to obtain state aid. This was intended to deter people from seeking state aid who had any prospect of finding work. The country was divided into territorial areas called 'unions'. Each was to have a workhouse run by a board of guardians that would raise a poor law rate to maintain it. A sum of £9,000,000 was spent over the next dozen years to implement the scheme, and by the end of the famine, there were 163 workhouses in the country. Outdoor relief was in fact allowed for a time during the famine and in August 1848 over 800,000 persons were receiving it. Workhouses regularly had a quarter of a million inmates during that period, though by 1872 it was less than 50,000. Overall, the Irish in fact received considerably less relief than those in Britain, as an enquiry in 1861 discovered.[49]

There was a variety of hospitals in existence at the beginning of the century.[50] There was also an extensive system of public dispensaries, 650 by the mid-

46 Carroll-Burke, *The Irish convict system*. **47** Crossman, *Local government*. **48** Geary, 'Mendicancy and vagrancy,' in Hill and Lennon (eds), *Luxury and austerity*, pp 121–36. **49** Burke, *The people and the poor law*. **50** Fleetwood, *History of medicine*.

1840s, and a board of health was established in 1820. Special provision was often made during epidemics, and in 1833 there were no fewer than seventy fever hospitals. In theory the Irish medical system was extensive and good.[51] Dublin, for example, had a large network of specialist hospitals and by the middle of the century was a centre of medical excellence of European reputation. Many of Dublin's hospitals, such as Jervis Street, St Vincent's and the Mater were voluntary institutions. In 1858 a General Medical Council was established to oversee the registration of doctors, who trained at five medical schools in Dublin and in the provincial Queen's Colleges. Women were admitted to the medical register in 1876.

In the early nineteenth century there were several lunatic asylums, institutions for persons with psychiatric disorders, in Ireland. There was the County and City of Cork Lunatic Asylum, the Richmond Asylum in Dublin, and an asylum founded by the Quakers at Bloomfield also in Dublin. However, between 1817 and 1830 a government system of district lunatic asylums was established with twenty-one such institutions in existence by the 1860s.[52] By 1870 there were 70,000 inmates, the number increasing threefold by 1914.[53] Women usually fared better than men in terms of frequency of discharge and living conditions.[54] After the famine, people committed tended to be young and unmarried, 'strident' members of the family. Having a family member in an asylum was not the disgrace that having a family member in a workhouse was. The state had provided the family with a convenient means of disciplining its recalcitrant members.[55]

The first half of the nineteenth century was a period of enormous transition with older patterns of social interaction giving way to but, to an extent, also continuing to coexist with a new and, by contemporary standards, highly sophisticated system of state control. Individuals interacted with national institutions and national movements to a greater and greater degree as the century wore on. Traditional patterns of life did seem to be on the wane. The Irish language was certainly in decline and was unmourned by utilitarians. By the end of the century, moves were afoot to revive it as a national vernacular. This new development, however, came at the end of over a century of interest and investigation in intellectual and literary circles into what was deemed to be the Celtic past.

51 MacDonagh, 'Ideas and institutions 1830–45,' in Vaughan (ed.), *Union I, 1801–70*, p. 210. **52** Robins, *History of the insane*, p. 75. **53** Finnane, *Insanity and the insane*. **54** Walsh, 'Gender and insanity ,' in Kelleher and Murphy (eds), *Gender perspectives*, p. 167. **55** Malcolm, 'The asylum, the family and emigration', in Malcolm and Jones (eds), *Medicine, disease and the state*, pp 177–91.

CHAPTER 4

Crafting Celts, 1760–1893

The debate about Irish history and the racial typology as Celts of the Gaelic-speaking people of Ireland was one of the key cultural debates of the nineteenth century, though less so for the poor rural speakers of the language than for the urban upper and middle classes. In the late eighteenth and early nineteenth centuries Ireland's Gaelic past was an issue taken up by certain elements of the Protestant ruling class of the country. It enabled the Patriots to establish a distinct identity for themselves over against that of England. Under the union, all radicalism now gone, parts of the Ascendancy embraced a Celtic cultural nationalism which they saw themselves as leading. They hoped it would be a way of retaining Ireland's position within the British empire by maintaining their own dominant position within Irish society, a position threatened, as they saw it, by the rise of the O'Connellite classes.[1]

By the middle of the nineteenth-century Catholic nationalist Ireland was well established. Reasons had to be found, in an increasingly democratic United Kingdom, for maintaining Britain's control over an unwilling Ireland. Irish national character, a long-established set of conveniently debilitating stereotypes, enabled such a continuance but was reinforced by a high doctrine of Celtic racial character, very similar to the Orientalist theories by which Europeans were justifying their rule in the east.

Towards the end of the nineteenth century a form of Celticism passed from the pro-union into the Irish nationalist camp as a programme for a distinctively Irish way of living and even speaking, as efforts were made to turn the hitherto dying Gaelic language into a flourishing vernacular. In its most inclusive form, Gaelicism, it was an invitation, transcending even racial origins, open to all who identified themselves as Irish to adopt what was identified as a Gaelic manner of living. Celticism, which began as an enquiry into Ireland's history, had turned firstly into a mode of delimiting Irish action before finally becoming a programme for building cultural cohesion.[2]

The activities of Celticists took place on two distinct though related levels, those of information gathering and theory formation. There were thus

1 Seamus Deane, 'General introduction,' in Deane, *Field Day*, i, p. xxiv. 2 There have been various attempts to periodize Celticism. John Hutchinson (*Cultural nationalism*, p. 50) writes of three cultural revivals, beginning in the mid eighteenth century, 1830s and 1880s respectively, each of which proceeds through stages of preparation, crystallization and articulation. Vivien Mercier (*Modern Irish literature*, pp 1–34) writes of three stages between the late eighteenth and late nineteenth centuries: the age of charlatans, the age of native scholars, and the age of foreign scholars.

attempts to find out more about the past and debates over the significance of that past. As time wore on investigation moved from the realm of antiquarianism to that of history, from interpreting ancient artefacts without a context to interpreting the past within an historical context.[3] Such as transition demands scholarship, and thus at its core Celticism was an activity of scholars or of people who passed as scholars or, at least, who passed themselves off as scholars in their own day. They worked as individuals or as members of societies. They collected, edited, translated and published ancient Irish texts.

The Scotsman James Macpherson's supposed translations from the Gaelic, *Fragments of ancient poetry* (1760), *Fingal* by 'Ossian' (1762), *Temora* (1763) and *Ossian* (1765) created a sensation and were highly influential throughout Europe. As early as 1761, Ferdinando Warner pointed out that there were many discrepancies in Macpherson's work. In 1787 Edmond de Harold published his own Ossian poems but made no pretence that they were anything other than an invention. In spite, or rather because, of their forged status Macpherson's writings spurred on the efforts of pioneering Irish scholars to produce something more authentic. This led to *Historical memoirs of the Irish bards* (1786) by Joseph Cooper Walker (1762–1810) and *Reliques of Irish poetry* by Charlotte Brooke (1740–93), the latter based on Bishop Thomas Percy's *Reliques of ancient English poetry* (1765). Brooke's work, designed to bring about conciliation with Britain by gaining its respect for Ireland, presents Gaelic poems in their original and in English translation, thus creating a novel parity between them.[4] Her godfather Sylvester O'Halloran (1728–1807) was both a scholar of Gaelic and a defender of the authenticity of ancient Irish civilization. His *Deirdre* (1808) continues her work and presents an Irish text and its literal English translation on facing pages.

In this early phase writing was dominated by people with an Anglo-Irish background who were often dependent for their information on the work of scholars from a Gaelic Catholic background who were themselves often financially insecure. It was to be the middle of the nineteenth century before Catholics were to secure professional positions to enable them to engage in such scholarship. Brooke and Walker were thus indebted to Theophilus O'Flanagan (1764–1814), who founded the Gaelic Society of Dublin in 1807. In the same way the English engineer and antiquarian General Charles Vallancey (1721–1812) was reliant on Charles O'Conor (1710–91) of Belanagare, an early advocate for the removal of Catholic disabilities and author of *Dissertations on the ancient history of Ireland* (1753). He assisted Vallancey with his *Collectanea de rebus Hibernicis*, a six-volume work published between 1770 and 1804.

The principal interpretative question at issue during this period was the historical status of the Gaelic Irish. Were they barbarians who had been civilized

3 Leerssen, *Remembrance and imagination*, p. 68. 4 Deane, *Strange country*, p. 101.

by first Norman and then English rule or had they once had a civilization of their own which had been destroyed by invasion? The question had obvious ideological significance for those keen to establish an Irish over against an English cultural identity in the present day. Curiously, the answer to this question was not sought in recorded history but in bizarre speculations about the origins of the Irish people in pre-history.

Irish antiquarians took up positions in a debate that had been raging since the seventeenth century about the origins of the Celts. The Phoenician explanation held that they had come from the middle east, via Carthage and Spain to the islands off north-west Europe. The opposing Scytho-Celtic explanation held that the Celts had come from northern and eastern Europe.[5] Scholars who favoured the notion of original Irish civility obviously leaned towards the Phoenician side; those who favoured the view that the English had civilized the barbaric Gaels to the Scytho-Celtic. One of the advantages of the Phoenician theory was that it allowed a comparison to be made between Carthage and Rome, on the one hand, and Ireland and Britain, on the other. Ireland, like Carthage, had an ancient civilization that had not only been defeated but obliterated by its conqueror Britain, as Carthage had been by Rome. It explained why so few traces of Irish civilization had survived.

Vallancey was a sturdy proponent of the Phoenician model in such works as *Essay on the antiquity of the Irish language* (1772) and *A grammar of the Iberno-Celtic or Irish language* (1773). At times he went even further and saw resemblances between Irish and other languages such as that of the Algonquin Indians. He was opposed by Edward Ledwich (1738–1823), author of *Antiquities of Ireland* (1790), though his own Viking theories were equally incredible. The Phoenician theory was revived in a literary fraud worthy of Macpherson by Roger O'Connor (1762–1834) in his *Chronicles of Eri* (1822). The book was a testament to his own supposed royal status, though his actual life as a former United Irishman and father of the Chartist leader Feargus O'Connor was more interesting. It purported to be a history of Ireland taken from ancient manuscripts. The central character Eolus is the wise king of Galicia around 1300 BC whose memory is later revered in Ireland by King Eocaid, the one a self-portrait of O'Connor himself, the other a display of the proper attitudes of respect which ought to obtain in the readers of that self-portrait.[6]

The early nineteenth century saw the foundation of a spate of Celticist societies: the Gaelic Society of Dublin (1807); the Iberno-Celtic Society (1818) for which Edward O'Reilly (1770–1829) produced *A chronological account of nearly four hundred Irish writers* (1820); and the Ulster Gaelic Society (1830). In a different league of course was the Royal Irish Academy (1785), a body for scholars

5 Leerssen, *Remembrance and imagination*, p. 72. 6 Tracy, *The unappeasable host*, p. 56.

in a number of different areas, which set about building up a library of Irish manuscripts, acquiring among others part of a copy of *The annals of the Four Masters*. In 1843 it received £600 from the government to buy the manuscript collection of Hodges Smith & Co. Government funding also enabled the commissioning of scholarly series such as the *Ancient laws of Ireland* (6 vols, 1865–1901).[7] Eventually the National Library of Ireland and the library of St Patrick's College, Maynooth, also built up substantial manuscript collections, and there were in addition many private scholarly collections throughout the country.

Throughout Europe at this time there was a new vigour and scholarly rigour about the recovery and publication of manuscript sources for cultures and languages that would soon be the objects of resuscitation attempts by cultural and political nationalists.[8] In Ireland the year 1831 saw the publication of *Irish minstrelsy*, an anthology of over one hundred Irish lyrics and folk songs with poetical translations, put together by James Hardiman (1728–1855). Hardiman's espousal of a Catholic nationalist view of the Celtic past occasioned a stinging rebuke from the Ascendancy-minded Samuel Ferguson in his four lengthy review articles for the *Dublin University Review* in 1834 and to his providing his own rather better translations. Ferguson's view of the Celts valorized their aristocratic loyalties, an admirable quality he felt for the current age in which the Ascendancy was being assailed by the more demotic forces praised by Hardiman.

The affair marked a transition not only to an age of a more professional form of textual scholarship but to a new ideological locus for the debate about the meaning of the past and its uses in the present. As a debate between the merits of British and Irish identities, Celticism was to become dormant at an academic level until Matthew Arnold took it up in England the 1860s. Within Ireland, however, it had become a complex debate between different versions of Irish identity—Catholic, nationalist and democratic or Protestant, unionist and aristocratic—and differing notions of scholarship, which did not allow for divisions into easily defined camps. Broadly speaking the lines of demarcation were between (pagan) primitivism and (Christian) medievalism in the realm of interpretation and between romanticism and positivism in the realm of scholarship.[9]

There was an early and, in some ways, decisive victory for positivism over the question of the provenance of the round towers, those tall edifices that still existed in significant numbers throughout the Irish countryside. In 1830 the Royal Irish Academy set up a competition for the best essay on the 'Origin and uses of the round towers of Ireland'. At that time the Academy itself and Irish scholarship in general was still heavily persuaded by the Phoenician theory. However, in 1832 it awarded its prize to George Petrie (1789–1866), whose

7 Ó Cuív, 'Irish language and literature, 1845–1921' in Vaughan (ed.), *Union II, 1870–1921*, pp 385–435. 8 Leerssen, 'European context,' in Stewart (ed.), *Hearts and minds*, pp 170–87. 9 See Leerssen, *Remembrance and imagination*, pp 68–156, and Murray, *Romanticism*.

Christian medieval interpretation that the round towers were ecclesiastical buildings formed the basis for his *Ecclesiastical architecture of Ireland* (1845) and has been accepted since as having essentially settled the matter. It displaced Phoenician fire temple and Danish theories of the origin of round towers and was not in the least disturbed by *The round towers of Ireland* (1834) by Henry O'Brien (1808–35), the runner-up in the competition, who fought for phallic and Buddhist interpretations. The Phoenician case, however, was still argued for years to come by Sir William Betham (1779–1853), but its day was now done.

Painter, folk music expert, manuscript collector and antiquarian, George Petrie was at the centre of Celtic scholarship in the second third of the nineteenth century. In the 1830s, at the invitation of Thomas Larcom (1801–79), he took charge of the topographical department at the Irish Ordnance Survey Commission (1824–41), with a brief to investigate local history, ancient monuments and place names. However, ambitious plans for publications had to be shelved when the government ended the project, though some of the material gathered was later published by other bodies. The work of the topographical department, which involved both field trips and library searches, was part of the contemporary flourishing of a cultural nationalism that eschewed a concomitant political nationalism. In fact Petrie and many of his colleagues, Ferguson among them, were supporters of the union with Britain. Petrie also made successful attempts to popularize the fruits of the new scholarship as an editor and contributor to the *Dublin Penny Journal* (1832–3) and the *Irish Penny Journal* (1840–1). He went on to publish books on Irish music and on the archaeology of the ancient site at Tara, though his latter years were somewhat marred by his acrimonious period as president (1857–9) of the artists' association, the Royal Hibernian Academy.

In some ways Petrie's relationship with his most distinguished scholarly colleagues on the Ordnance Survey project, the brothers-in-law John O'Donovan (1806–61) and Eugene O'Curry (1794–1862), was similar to that which had obtained between eighteenth-century Protestant antiquarians and their academically-unrecognized Gaelic advisers. However, both O'Donovan and O'Curry were eventually able to obtain senior academic positions. O'Donovan travelled the country between 1823 and 1841 in search of information on folklore, topography and place-names for the Ordnance Survey. He edited manuscripts for the Irish Archaeological Society between 1841 and 1844, and 1848–51 saw his six-volume edition and translation of the *Annals of the Four Masters*. In 1849 he was appointed professor of Irish at the new Queen's College, Belfast, at an annual salary of £100. It was a largely honorary position, however, as he had no students.

After his time at the Ordnance Survey O'Curry worked as a cataloguer of Irish manuscripts at the Royal Irish Academy and British Museum. In 1854 he was appointed professor of Irish history and archaeology at the Catholic

University, just established in Dublin, and in 1855–6 delivered a series of lectures which were published as *Lectures on the manuscript materials of ancient Irish history* (1861), a book which influenced Matthew Arnold. Another equally important work, *On the manners and customs of the ancient Irish* (1873), was published after this death. In 1853 O'Curry and O'Donovan were appointed co-editors of a government-financed project to publish the ancient Irish laws. It turned into an acrimonious task and was completed and published after both their deaths as *The ancient laws of Ireland.*

Celtic studies in the mid-nineteenth century centred round a second generation of scholarly societies such as the Irish Archaeological Society, founded in 1840, and the Celtic Society, founded in 1845. Among their activities was the publication of scholarly work on Irish antiquities and literature. Due to mutual financial difficulties, these societies merged in 1854 to become the Irish Archaeological and Celtic Society, which lasted until the 1870s. The two original societies had somewhat different social profiles. The Irish Archaeological Society was Ascendancy-dominated. The Celtic Society was more Catholic and middle-class with nearly half of its members being Catholic priests.[10] However, these were both socially conservative groups. The texts they had published tended to emphasize the role of the nobility, and there was consensus that medieval Christian Ireland, rather than pagan ancient Ireland, was what ought to be studied. Both Catholic and Church of Ireland clerics were anxious to claim medieval Irish Christianity as their own inheritance. Certain Anglican elements were especially keen to claim their church rather than the Church of Rome as the legitimate successor of the Celtic Church of St Patrick.

As a result of the predilection of these societies, the study of older forms of the Irish language tended to become the province mostly of foreign scholars. Among these scholars were Henry d'Arbois de Jubainville, John Strachen, Rudolf Thurneysen, Ernst Widisch, Whitley Stokes and Kuno Meyer. In 1853 the *Grammatica Celtica* by Johann Kasper Zeuss (1806–56) was published. In 1873 the journal *Revue Celtique* was established in Paris.

The Christian medievalists did not have it all their own way in mid-century Ireland, however. The interests of John O'Daly (1800–78) lay in pagan, primitive Ireland. He had begun his involvement in cultural matters as a publisher allied with the Young Ireland movement in the 1840s. He worked with Edward Walsh on *Reliques of Irish Jacobite poetry* (1844), with James Clarence Mangan on the first series of *Poets and poetry of Munster* (1849) and with George Sigerson on the second series (1860). In 1846 he issued *Self-instruction in Irish*. His interests were thus in the popularization of Irish literature, rather than in scholarship, and, unusually for this time, in the promotion of Irish as a living language.

10 Murray, *Romanticism*, p. 125.

He was initially involved with the Celtic Society but in 1853 helped found the breakaway Ossianic Society dedicated to the publication of the stories of the pre-Christian Oisín and the Fianna. The project ended in 1861 in acrimony between O'Daly, the Society's secretary, and the former revolutionary, William Smith O'Brien, its president.

Overall, scholarly positivism and Christian medievalism seemed to have won out over romanticism and pagan primitivism.[11] In the Irish revival of the late nineteenth and early twentieth centuries, however, the latter were to be more influential, especially with a new generation of post-Christian Ascendancy intellectuals. They rejected British Victorian progress and were keener on the aristocratic pagan Celtic Ireland of myth than on the bourgeois Catholic Ireland that confronted them. Disciples of the occult such as W.B. Yeats also drew on an Ascendancy tradition of interest in fairies that went back to Thomas Crofton Croker (1798–1854) and William Allingham (1824–89)

By the later nineteenth century, too, the revival of the Irish language was coming to the fore with a new generation of scholarly activists led by Douglas Hyde (1860–1949). The Society for the Preservation of the Irish Language was founded in 1878 and in 1880 the breakaway Gaelic Union. Hyde's 1892 address 'On the necessity for de-Anglicizing Ireland' led to the establishment in 1893 of by far the most successful of such bodies, the Gaelic League, which promoted the return of the Irish language to everyday use. Thus Irish folk culture and language, especially in the west of Ireland where it was most pronounced, could both be an escape from the modern and a source of national cultural renewal.[12]

Meanwhile abroad theories of race were in vogue and Celticism had become an international phenomenon. Ernest Renan (1823–92) had focused attention on the Celts as a race in his *La poésie des races celtiques* (1860). In England on the contrary the influence of the pro-German Thomas Carlyle (1795–1881) had created a fashion for a Teutonic view of English racial origins. Influenced by Renan and others, Matthew Arnold (1822–88) published his *On the study of Celtic literature* in 1867 in an attempt to moderate Teutonic excesses. He held that the English were a mixed race with elements of Saxon and the Celtic ancestry. The Saxons he associated with a Teutonic warrior masculinity, and the Celts with a cultured femininity. He praised the Celtic element as offering necessary corrective qualities to the racial mixture that had made the English so successful.

Arnold's Celticism was of relevance not only to the English but also to the Irish and to the relations between England and Ireland. He was thus breathing life into the use of Celticism as a means of negotiating the English-Irish relationship, a topic that had been alive at the popular level but effectively dormant at the level of theory for many years.

11 Ibid., p. 132. **12** Leerseen, *Remembrance and imagination*, p. 170.

The Celts themselves were, he believed, a beaten race which could never aspire to autonomy. However, in praising Celtic virtues and stressing their importance to the English, Arnold also hoped for a reconciliation between the Irish and English. Nonetheless, he believed that this could only be achieved through a continuing Irish political subordination. At their best the Irish, like Orientals, had child-like qualities and needed proper guidance.[13]

Arnold's ideas were in part positive about the Irish and were certainly moderate when compared with the more popular discourse about the Irish in Victorian Britain, which will be investigated in a later chapter. From the colonial point of view the apparent warmth of his views made them the more insidious. It is after all easier to want to rule a people whom one can think of as likeable and amenable that as unpleasant and resistant. In fact Arnold's views about the Celts were in some ways merely a cogent articulation of the more liberal English ideology of ruling Ireland.

In this regard the role of the royal family, the visits of whose members to Ireland were nearly always greeted with enormous popular enthusiasm, was of great significance and often caused considerable alarm among nationalists. It was held in elite circles in Britain that such enthusiasm showed the Irish could be loyal to the crown and connection with Britain if only they were paid enough attention, and that their political leaders, who demanded political autonomy, were after all not representative of their real views.[14]

Arnold's legacy of Celticism was a mixed one. On the one hand his racially-essentialist Celt provided part of the foundation on which the culturally-adaptable Gael of the Irish revival was constructed.[15] But on the other his views could be used to bolster an even sterner form of imperialist interpretation as was the case with *The English in Ireland in the eighteenth century* (1874, 1881) by James Anthony Froude (1818–94), a disciple of Carlyle. Froude's view of the Irish was that they were an inferior race whose undoubted capacity for loyalty had been spoiled by misrule and were therefore now best left alone.[16]

Conciliation had been one of Matthew Arnold's objects. Conciliation based on moderate reform was a constant theme in nineteenth-century Ireland, often among those interest groups who feared that the advancement of the Catholic masses would bring about monumental change. It was certainly a preoccupation of the literature of the early part of the century.

13 Cairns and Richards, *Writing Ireland*, pp 45–9; Pecora, 'Arnoldian ethnology,' *Victorian Studies* 41:3 (1998), pp 355–79. **14** Murphy, *Abject loyalty*. **15** Deane, *Strange country*, p. 109. **16** Brown, 'Saxon and Celt,' in Brown, *Ireland's literature*, pp 3–13.

CHAPTER 5

Whig and emancipation literature, 1800–29

Nineteenth-century Irish poetry and fiction is difficult to read today as a means of deriving literary pleasure in the way that the poetry of Keats and Tennyson or the novels of Austen and George Eliot, from Ireland's neighbouring island, still are. The reason for this is not just that much of such writing is not of high quality. There is still an essential continuity between the twenty-first century reader and the world depicted in the early nineteenth-century English novel which allows the latter to continue to be a source of aesthetic pleasure for the former. The role of the individual is to strive for fulfilment in terms of both public power and wealth, and private pleasure and relationships within a given society. Bourgeois realism conceals the economic and ideological processes that have gone towards the creation of such a society. Its purpose is to bolster stability at all levels and to act as a bulwark against social unrest.[1] Nineteenth-century Irish literature in English, on the other hand, was incapable of summoning up the ideological concealments of realism, thus aligning it more with the literature of modernism and, if anything, increasing its worth for the study of Irish culture.

The market for literature was overwhelmingly in England. Between 1800 and 1870, 13,000 books were published in Dublin, 26,000 in Edinburgh but 240,000 in London.[2] Irish literature in English was a literature written by Irish authors for English readers whom the authors thought ignorant of Irish realities and their responsibilities towards Ireland and possessed of a negative view of Irish character.[3] It was thus openly didactic and anthropological in purpose and often focused on the peasantry rather than on the middle class, as the Irish peasantry was the object of British concern and hostility.[4] All this had the effect, as Joep Leerssen has pointed out, of turning the Irish author into an exterior observer of Irish life, adopting a midway position between the English readership and the Irish topic. During the decades of high romanticism, Irish authors sought to interest English readers in Ireland by presenting it in anachronistic and exotic terms. Peripheral areas, because of their very remoteness, were represented as being most typical of Ireland.[5] Thereafter, Irish authors who were keen to deny the violent and unstable sides to Irish national character, which English discourse ascribed to it, tended to envision an Ireland of dull respectability.[6]

1 Eagleton, *Heathcliff*, pp 145–225. **2** Whelan, 'Writing Ireland,' in Litvack and Hooper (eds), *Regional identity*, p. 190. **3** Ibid., p. 189. **4** Deane, 'Irish national character,' in Dunne (ed.), *Writer as witness*, pp 100–3. **5** Leerssen, 'Irishness in romantic Anglo-Irish fiction,' *Irish University Review* 20:2 (1990), pp 254–84. **6** Deane, 'Irish national character,' p. 103; Dunne,

Another problem, particularly with Irish literature in English in the first half of the nineteenth century, is that it has long been categorized under the rubric of 'Anglo-Irish literature'. This was essentially a late nineteenth-century category, and the restrictive effects of its construction will be examined towards the end of this book in a general exploration of literature in nineteenth-century Ireland. For the moment it will be discarded as a category. The discussion of the literature of the first half of the century in this and subsequent chapters will be framed in terms of the various underlying ideologies which energized different literary versions of Irish society. These were later to be either smoothed out or distorted within the canon of Anglo-Irish literature. Whig, emancipationist, Tory and romantic nationalist are the four categories which will inform this and subsequent discussion, though a necessary exposition of the role of religion in nineteenth-century Ireland will precede the exploration of Tory literature.

In January 1812, Percy Shelley, the radical romantic poet, arrived in Dublin with his sixteen-year-old bride, Harriet Westbrook, and her sister Eliza. Ireland was briefly to be his cause, and he issued an *Address to the Irish people* in which he called for the victory of reason over intolerance of all kinds. By this he meant both the intolerance which refused Catholic emancipation and the intolerance which informed Catholicism.[7]

Given the triumph of a largely ethnic Irish nationalism by the end of the nineteenth century, it is sometimes difficult to take seriously alternative political and cultural formations that in their day seemed to be viable options. Ethnic nationalism existed in early nineteenth-century Ireland, but there were also other vehicles for the articulation and solution of Irish grievances which had Irish, British and European contexts. There was a continuum between French Jacobinism, English radicalism, the United Irishmen and English and Irish Whiggism. This continuum was both ideological and personal. Thus the United Irish leader Lord Edward Fitzgerald was a cousin of the English Whig leader, Charles James Fox. Yet there was also an essential difference between Whigs and their more radical associates. Whigs believed in liberty and progress but thought that they were best guaranteed by aristocratic rather than popular government. In Ireland Whigs agreed with Shelley to the extent that they hoped that the granting of Catholic emancipation would neutralize Catholicism as a political force and pave the way for a peaceful Ireland under their own benign rule. Their hopes were to be dashed with the rise of O'Connell and a Catholic nationalism that saw emancipation as the beginning rather than the end of a process.

This discussion will focus on the three key figures who illustrate the diversity even within Irish literary Whiggism itself: Sydney Owenson, Lady Morgan

'Irish romantic writing,' in Porter and Teich (eds), *Romanticism in national context*, pp 68–91.
7 Vance, *Irish literature*, p 109.

(1776-1859), a Whig with initial radical and Jacobin leanings; Maria Edgeworth (1767-1849), an Enlightenment reformer who moved towards a greater conservatism; and Thomas Moore (1779–1852), whose Whiggism eventually shaded into an ethnic nationalism.

Lady Morgan's father was an actor and Protestant convert from Co. Mayo, her mother an English Wesleyan. Her mother died when she was young, and her father had variable success with his career. Morgan began her own career as a governess before making writing her main focus. Early on she made an enemy of the Tory politician and critic, John Wilson Croker (1780–1857). However, with the success of her early novels she became a celebrity and was hailed as 'the Irish de Staël', embodying personal as well as authorial authority.[8] She found patrons in Lord and Lady Abercorn and married Sir Charles Morgan.[9] In *France* (1817) and *Italy* (1821) she produced accounts of contemporary Europe which were hailed by radicals such as Lord Byron. With the rise of O'Connell, however, she withdrew from politics, alienated from developments in Ireland, and eventually settled permanently in London where she was awarded a civil list pension of £300 per annum in 1837. By the time of her death she had produced twenty-seven different works in eight different genres, twelve of them about Ireland.[10]

History is important in Morgan's work. In her novels historical investigations change people's lives and bring about reconciliation.[11] During the height of her writing career she saw history in terms of three stages: the period before 1782; the period between the supposed legislative independence of the Irish parliament and the Act of Union which she thought of as the golden age of Irish Whigs; and the period after 1801 when Catholic emancipation would be championed by Irish Whigs.[12]

Morgan's principal claim to fame was *The wild Irish girl* (1806). It is the story of Horatio, son of the Earl of M——, who is banished to his father's Connaught estates where he meets the impoverished Gaelic prince of Inismore and his daughter Glorvina whom he eventually marries. The prince was an amalgam of Morgan's father and the prince of Coolavin, a real, impoverished Irish chieftan, whom Morgan had actually met. Glorvina was an idealized version of Morgan herself.

The novel went into seven editions in two years.[13] However, publishers had been initially fearful of political reaction which producing the book might create. What was radical about the novel was that it challenged accepted Enlightenment views about progress in which peoples moved from savagery, in

8 Connolly, ' "I accuse Miss Owenson," ' *Colby Quarterly* 34:2 (2000), pp 98–115. **9** For convenience she will be referred to as Morgan throughout, rather than as Owenson and then Morgan. **10** Campbell, *Lady Morgan*; Newcomer, *Lady Morgan*. **11** Dunne, 'Irish romantic history,' p. 74. **12** Dunne, 'Lady Morgan's Irish novels,' in Dunne (ed.), *Writer as witness*, pp 133–59. **13** Atkinson and Atkinson, 'Lady Morgan,' *Éire-Ireland* 15:2 (1980), pp 60–90.

which there is no concept of property, through barbarism, characterized by the clan system and moveable property, and finally into civilization, with fixed and heritable property guaranteed by the state. Each society was at a different stage in this progression. Regions were thus distinguished not only by space but also by time. They were chronotopes, differing from each other in their relative progress from past savagery to modern civilization.

The wild Irish girl was noteworthy in that it created a positive chronotope of the supposedly primitive west of Ireland as a place of plenitude set against the impoverished present of an Ireland that was supposedly being modernized by a civilizing, colonial Britain.[14] However, the novel ends in a withdrawal from radicalism and a retreat into Whiggism. It is represented by a reconciling compromise, the 'national marriage' of Glorvina and Mortimer, of the embodiment of ancient Irish culture and of governing English aristocracy, as a means of legitimating the rule of the latter.[15] Morgan had been reliant on Sylvester O'Halloran among others for her heavily footnoted novel. Thereafter she was to lean towards Protestant historical sources and never again to be so repentant about colonialism.[16]

In *The wild Irish girl* Morgan had inaugurated the 'national tale', depicting the regionalist chronotope which could draw cosmopolitan travellers back into it. Sir Walter Scott, in the more stable environment of Tory Scotland, was to supersede it with the historical novel in which different future possibilities are tested in the past.[17] However, the national tale was to enjoy a reasonable vitality in Ireland over the following several decades and Morgan herself wrote three more such novels.

She began *O'Donnel* (1814) attempting to write an historical novel but quickly turned it into the story of a contemporary character, Roderick O'Donnel. The novel's pro-emancipation argument turns on presenting him as being a Catholic gentleman, an almost revolutionary notion in Ascendancy-dominated days. O'Donnel's military service has been in aid of Austria and France because the wasteful penal laws have prevented his service to the British state until recently. He marries the pro-emancipation duchess of Bellmont, another version of Morgan herself, and thus recovers ancestral lands which she owns. Backtracking from *The wild Irish girl*, *O'Donnel* is somewhat critical of Catholicism and Protestant readers' fears that emancipation would undermine their economic position are allayed by O'Donnel's acceptance of the colonial settlement.[18]

Florence Macarthy (1818) is subtitled *An Irish tale.* Once more there is a national marriage, this time between the Gaelic noble, Florence Macarthy, and Fitzadelm who is of Norman descent. The villainous land agent, Conway Crawley, is a satirical portrait of Croker, though Morgan is more serious in

14 Whelan, 'Foreword,' in Morgan, *The wild Irish girl*, pp ix-xxiv. **15** Kelly, *English fiction*, p. 93; Whelan, 'Writing Ireland.' **16** Dunne, 'Irish romantic writing,' pp 74–5. **17** Trumpener, 'National tale and historical novels,' *ELH* 60 (1993), pp 685–731. **18** Dunne, 'Irish romantic writing,' p. 75.

arguing the need for the education of the peasantry if they are properly to participate in society. Finally, *The O'Briens and the O'Flahertys* (1827) is a complex and at times extravagant story of the radicalism of the 1790s as it affects two Gaelic families, one of which remained in poverty in Ireland during the penal laws while the other prospered on the continent.

Maria Edgeworth was the daughter of Richard Lovell Edgeworth (1744–1817), four-times married and father of twenty-two children. For a time he tried to raise his son Richard along the lines of Rousseau's *Émile*. While living in England he had been a member of the Lunar Society, a group of Midlands industrialists, which included Josiah Wedgewood, whose purpose was to bring science and technology together. R.L. Edgeworth was himself an inventor who during the 17890s unsuccessfully tried to develop a telegraph system. He was also a friend of the chemist and dissenter, Joseph Priestley. He returned to his family estate at Edgeworthstown, Co. Longford, in the 1780s, acting as an improving landlord and taking part in public life, which included supporting the Volunteers, the French revolution and Catholic emancipation. When he and his family were forced to take refuge in the heavily loyalist Longford town during the French invasion of the west of Ireland in 1798, he was almost lynched as a suspected French spy. He subsequently favoured the Act of Union on economic grounds, as an MP in the Irish parliament, though sometimes voted against it in protest at the way it was being forced through.

R.L. Edgeworth saw himself as an educationalist. Maria Edgeworth was to join her father in this endeavour, and much of her writing, some of which was undertaken in collaboration with him, can be seen in this light. It encompassed theoretical works, practical lessons, children's stories and, indeed, instructive fiction for adults. Together they wrote *Practical education* (1798) and *Professional education* (1809), key texts in their enterprise. With the popular success of her novel *Castle Rackrent* (1800), a favourite with King George III it was said, Edgeworth began to develop an independent reputation as a novelist which soon outstripped that of her father.

In 1802, during the brief peace between Britain and France, Maria Edgeworth was feted in Paris, refusing a marriage proposal from the Swedish scientist Edelcrantz. In 1813 she was lionized in London society. When Jane Austen sent her a copy of *Emma*, Edgeworth famously did not bother to read it. However, when her father died in 1817 and was criticized by reviewers of his memoirs, which she published in 1820, she felt discouraged from writing. Nonetheless, she enjoyed great success during her 1822 trip to London, making many friends among leading Whigs, and the next year visited Sir Walter Scott at Abbotsford. Wordsworth called to see her at Edgeworthstown in 1829, though she preferred scientists to poets. For a decade and a half from the mid 1820s she was forced to manage the family estate which had fallen into debt due to the incompetence of her brother Lovell. She died in 1849, having spent the last years of her life engaged in famine relief.[19]

Edgworth was essentially an Enlightenment figure who moved from her father's youthful radicalism to a conservative Whig position. She favoured Catholic emancipation but also the union of Ireland and Britain. She believed that Irish landlords had been remiss in their obligations, and sometimes used her fiction to admonish them. This was certainly the case with *Castle Rackrent*, her most important and successful novel with an Irish theme.

The novel is narrated by Thady Quirke, the professedly loyal servant of the landlord Rackrent family, whose history over several generations he recounts. It is in two parts, the first written between 1793 and 1796 and the second two years later. A glossary was later added to convey sociological information for the English reader. A preface was also included which makes clear that the story being told is that of an Irish past which will soon seem all the more remote with the coming into force of the Acts of Union.

Thady Quirke was based on R.L. Edgeworth's land steward, John Langan. Though Edgeworth used some of her own Anglo-Irish ancestors as a basis for the Rackent family, the novel identifies them as originally a Gaelic family called O'Shaughlin whose name was Anglicized so that they could inherit their estate. They are both bad landlords and dissolute individuals. Sir Patrick Rackrent is jovial but a drunk. Sir Murtagh is both litigious and a miser, refusing his tenants their customary rights. His younger brother, Sir Kit, is fashionable and a gambler. His imprisonment of his Jewish bride, until he is killed in a duel, because she will not hand over her jewels is based on the real-life story of Lady Cathcart who had been imprisoned for similar reasons by her husband Colonel Maguire at Tempo Manor, Co. Fermanagh. Finally, Sir Condy is weak, sentimental, unable to forge a successful marriage and gets into debt. He loses the estate to Thady's lawyer son Jason and dies on a drinking binge.

Edgeworth intended Thady's apparent whole-hearted approval of the Rackrents to be ironic. His conclusions are the opposite to the ones she wishes the reader to draw about the behaviour and responsibilities of landlords.[20] Edgeworth, however, was soon alarmed that the novel was being read as an affectionate threnody for a now defunct type of landlord who could command such loyalty.[21] She and her father produced *An essay on Irish bulls* in 1802 as a demythologizing corrective that argued for a hidden rationality in much apparently quaint Irish discourse.

Edgeworth wrote *Castle Rackrent* largely without her father's help and initially for amusement rather than publication.[22] For this reason it is a more multiva-

19 Butler, *Maria Edgeworth*. **20** Tracy, *The unappeasable host*, pp 11–23. **21** Kelly, *English fiction*, p 75.

lent text and escapes from the extreme didacticism of much of the rest of her work. Recent critics, especially those influenced by post-colonial studies, have read the novel in a new way and detected in Thady in particular a hostility for the Rackrent family and an eagerness for his son to unseat them which is masked by an apparent servility. Thady thus exhibits a typical strategy of covert resistance to colonial control.[23] Finally, the novel's teleology of progress towards the Acts of Union is problematized by the succession of failed marriage unions within it.[24]

Castle Rackrent was only one episode is Edgeworth's efforts to promote a society both in Britain and Ireland based on merit and money rather than on interest and patronage. Like her father, she advocated the professionalism of all classes.[25] Her *Popular tales* (1804) provided a fictional bolster to *Practical education* (1798) and was intended for those towards the bottom of the social scale. *Professional life* (1809) was for the higher classes and was followed by two series of novels, in 1809 and 1812 respectively, under the rubric *Tales of fashionable life*. This was a genre wherein English Jacobin criticism of aristocratic excess was turned into a conservative cause for reform that advocated the embracing of professional middle-class values and proper domestic and social practices.[26]

This agenda also permeated many of Edgeworth's other novels such as *Patronage* (1814), *Harrington* (1817) and *Ormond* (1817), and, indeed, is implicit in her second novel, *Belinda* (1801), a work which deals with issues of gender and race. In it Lady Delacour's choice of a public life involves her in embracing inappropriately male behaviour such as cross-dressing, and climaxes in a duel in which her breast is bruised. Her anxiety that she is actually suffering from breast cancer leads her back to her proper domestic sphere with her family, from where she can prevent the marriage of her protégée Belinda to a West Indian creole.[27] Edgeworth held to an Enlightenment belief in women's rationality and in the importance of their education but so that they could fulfil their role as equal partners in marriage and educators of children. *Belinda* is her retort to the more radical feminist views of Mary Wollstonecraft (1759–97) and Mary Hayes (1760–1843).[28] Lady Delacour's choice transforms her from fashionable to domestic woman.[29]

Ennui and *The absentee*, both of which have an Irish setting, occur in the first and second series respectively of *Tales of fashionable life*. However, within the professionalizing ambit of the series they touch on specifically Irish issues and effectively do so on Lady Morgan's national tale territory. In *Ennui* the bored and

22 Weekes, *Irish women writers*, p. 59. **23** Dunne, *Maria Edgeworth*, pp 7-8. **24** Graham, 'History, gender and the colonial moment,' *Irish Studies Review* 14 (1996), pp 21–4. **25** Kelly, 'Money and merit,' *Wordsworth Circle* 15 (1994), pp 89–93. **26** Kelly, *English fiction*, p. 72. **27** Greenfield, '"Colonial boundaries in Edgeworth's *Belinda*,' *PMLA* 112:2 (1997), pp 214–29. **28** Atkinson and Atkinson, '*Belinda* and women's rights,' *Éire-Ireland* 19:4 (1984), pp 94–118. **29** MacFadyen, 'Lady Delacour,' *Nineteenth-century Literature* 48:4 (1994), pp 423–39.

uneducated earl of Glenthorn is revealed as really being of peasant birth and loses his estate. He qualifies as a barrister and then marries Cecilia Delamere. Now actually ready for rule, he recovers through his wife his old estates which the restored real earl, who had been brought up as a peasant, and his son had been unable to manage. The novel's message that the capacity to govern depends on education and not on birth is consonant with the theme of the series. But it is also a commentary on *The wild Irish girl* inasmuch as the possibility of a 'national marriage' is raised early on but frustrated when Glenthorn's proposal of marriage to Lady Geraldine, a Glorvina-type character, is turned down.[30]

The absentee is a more thoroughgoing exploration of Irish life as Lord Colambre makes his way from a merchant-dominated Dublin to his absentee father's various neglected Irish estates, encountering Anglo-Irish life, ruinous Gaelic hospitality, the work of both good and bad land agents, and an eminent antiquarian en route. At the end he marries Grace Nugent, but the revelation that she is of English descent prevents it from being a Morganesque national marriage.[31]

Ormond (1817) was written as an addendum to the *Tales of fashionable life* and inhabits the same thematic Irish territory. Harry Ormond experiences various Irelands during his formative years. An orphan, he lives with the Anglicized Sir Ulick O'Shane, an eighteenth-century type, and also with his feudal, Gaelic cousin Cornelius O'Shane, 'King Corny' of the Black Islands. Once again the prospect of a national marriage is raised as Ormond falls in love with Corny's daughter, Dora. But Ormond is also influenced by the Edgeworthian Herbert Annaly, a rational and modern-minded landlord, and chooses to marry his sister Florence. However, when faced with a choice of buying Corny or Ulick's estates he chooses the Black Islands, where he is hailed as prince. He thus combines the role of improving landlord with that of traditional leader of the people.[32] Edgeworth's utilitarianism is thus adjusted to cope with the realities of an Ireland in which she recognizes that the Whig dream of a renewed leadership by the Anglo-Irish landed classes will need to take account of ethnic and cultural considerations as well as being based on rational improvement. She does so, however, without Morgan's relish for the Gaelic past.[33]

Edgeworth regarded *Belinda*, *Patronage* and her late novel *Helen* (1834) as her most important works.[34] Her famous remark in 1834 that 'It is impossible to draw Ireland as she now is in a book of fiction; realities are too strong, party passions too violent to bear to see, or care to look at their faces in the looking-glass'[35] reflected a similar disillusionment to that of Morgan, faced with the persistence

30 Tracy, *The unappeasable host*, pp 27-9. **31** Ibid., pp 31–6. **32** Ibid., pp 36-8. **33** Cary, 'Maria Edgeworth's hope,' *Éire-Ireland* 26:4 (1991), pp 29–37; Trumpener, *Bardic nationalism*, p. 63. **34** Kelly, *English fiction*, p. 78. **35** Maria Edgeworth to Michael Packenham Edgeworth, 14 February 1834, quoted in Butler, *Maria Edgeworth*, p. 453.

of O'Connellite nationalism in the aftermath of the granting of Catholic emancipation. Whig hopes to lead Ireland were dashed, and this was evidenced by the recent reluctance of the Edgeworths' tenants to vote for the family's candidates at elections.

Whereas the rise of O'Connellism caused Morgan and Edgeworth to despair, the Whig poet Thomas Moore was able to an extent to embrace the new reality of a more demotic religious and ethnic nationalism because he, unlike his novelistic Whig colleagues, was a Catholic. He was born into a Dublin merchant family and educated at the Protestant Trinity College where he knew United Irishmen such as Robert Emmet. Indeed, much of the imagery in his writing was derived from the literary tradition of the United Irishmen.[36] In 1799 Moore set out for a literary life in London, where he did well under the patronage of Lord Moira. He met Lord Lansdowne, became well known in Whig political circles and dedicated his first book to the prince of Wales. In 1803 he left for a government post in Bermuda and returned the next year, entrusting the position to a deputy, though he would have to live for several years on the continent after 1819 because of the debts which eventually mounted up in Bermuda in his name.[37]

Moore became most famous for writing the poetical lyrics for music which was arranged by John Stevenson and published by the Power brothers – James, who lived in London, and William, in Dublin. Much of the music was reliant on Edward Bunting's *General collection of the ancient music of Ireland* (1796) which had been inspired by the Belfast Harp Festival of 1792. Eventually there were ten issues of the very popular *Irish melodies* (1808–34) and, though there would be disputes with his publishers, Moore received a retainer of £500 per annum for many decades. Wordsworth once told Moore that he had earned less than £1,000 from writing in thirty-five years. Moore had earned £20,000.[38]

The *Melodies* are concerned mostly with loss and dispossession and strike an elegaic note, linking a personal sense of grief with a vaguely defined sense of Irish history.[39] The themes of memory and freedom, love and death which are introduced in the first two poems of the first issue, 'Go Whose Glory Waits Thee' and 'Remember the Glories of Brian the Brave', set the tone for all the volumes.[40]

The *Melodies* were very popular internationally. In France they were arranged by Berlioz and became so famous that 'melodie' replaced 'chanson' as the French word for song. French romantics did not have a base in French nostalgia because of the disruptions of the French revolution and so had turned to Scott, Byron and Moore with relish instead.[41]

36 Thuente, *The United Irishmen*, p. 177. **37** White, *Tom Moore*. **38** Brown, *Ireland's literature*, p. 18. **39** Campbell, 'Thomas Moore's Wild Song,' *Bullán* 4:2 (1999–2000), pp 83–103. **40** Davis, 'Thomas Moore's *Irish Melodies*,' *Ariel* 24:2 (1993), pp 7–26. **41** Vance, 'Anglo-Irish lit-

Placing the *Melodies* in the context of the interaction between British and Irish culture has been problematic, however. At one end of the scale is Terence Brown's view that Moore was simply using Irish history to provide British drawing-room audiences with images for their own sense of personal loss. An Ireland of lost battles and silenced harps can thus be seen to provide a sentimental correlative for individuals' griefs.[42] Tom Dunne's opposing perspective sees the *Melodies* in an authentic Irish tradition, that of the nostalgia of late seventeenth-century Gaelic poetry for the past, a nostalgia which passed into the eighteenth-century aisling and which is accompanied by a fatalism about the present and an appeal for the future.[43]

It is certainly true that the Ireland depicted by Moore is one which does not invite historical investigation much less political action. This was surprising in a Whig activist but was reassuring to the more conservative elements of Moore's audience.[44] William Hazlitt said Moore had turned 'the wild harp of Erin into a musical snuffbox'.[45]

In the 'Prefatory letter on Irish music' which introduces the third issue Moore argues that his work is not subversive, for it is not designed to 'appeal to the passions of an ignorant and angry multitude' but to be performed in the parlours of 'the rich and educated', those 'who can afford to have their national zeal a little stimulated without exciting much dread of the excesses into which it may hurry them.' Melodies about Irish freedom were framed without reference to contemporary events and with an understanding that such freedom had been deferred. Though supporters of Catholic emancipation could see the *Melodies* as an artistic resource to spur them on to political action, for the most part liberal British audiences saw them as celebrations of a universal romantic struggle for freedom.[46]

Moore's *Melodies* arose from his liberal Whig context. He created an image of Ireland which was co-opted both by the colonizers and the colonized.[47] His work comforted British, especially Whig, views of Ireland but as time went on also provided Irish nationalism with a new poetic vocabulary. It included a tradition of celebrating martyrs, such as Robert Emmet in 'Oh breathe not his name'[48], and of reformulating nationalist aspirations in terms of an abstract spirit of the nation which proved to be a useful device for covering over divisions within nationalist Ireland and imaging a united national community.[49]

Lallah Rookh (1817) was Moore's next great success, running into twenty editions by 1841.[50] A four-part narrative poem set in the east, it is also about

erary relations,' *Irish Historical Studies* 22:87 (1981), p. 233. **42** Brown, *Ireland's literature*, p. 19. **43** Dunne, 'Irish romantic writing,' p. 87. **44** Eagleton, *Crazy John*, pp 142–6. **45** Vance, *Irish literature*, p. 102. **46** Davis, 'Thomas Moore's *Irish Melodies*,' pp 16, 21. **47** Ibid., p. 7. **48** Campbell, 'Thomas Moore's wild song,' p. 86. **49** Davis, 'Thomas Moore's *Irish Melodies*,' p. 20. **50** Brown, *Ireland's literature*, p. 18.

Ireland, Moore's comment that 'the spirit that had spoken in the melodies of Ireland soon found itself at home in the East'[51] confirming a view of the continuum of British perceptions of the Orient and the Celt. Indeed, 'The fire-worshippers', one of the stories within the book, is a thinly disguised version of the story of Robert Emmet.

Moore spent part of the 1820s in continental Europe and later became embroiled in what to do with the potentially explosive memoirs which his late friend Lord Byron had left in his care. He eventually burned them. However, his interests also returned to Ireland and a new and more assertively nationalist Moore began to emerge in the era of agitation for Catholic emancipation. His satirical *Memoirs of Captain Rock* (1824) provided an historiographical corrective to the likes of Sir Richard Musgrave. It is a vindication of Irish Catholics and an indictment of British misrule in Ireland.[52] His *Life and death of Lord Edward Fitzgerald* (1831) is a defiantly nationalistic account which the latter's cousin and leading English Whig, Lord Holland, discouraged. *Travels of an Irish gentleman in search of religion* (1833) publicly attested Moore's Catholicism.

Like many others Moore was disoriented by the eventual granting of Catholic emancipation, confessing that 'I little thought I should ever live to see the end of my politics.'[53] He suspected O'Connell of being rather too dictatorial but remained on good terms with him and contemplated standing as an O'Connellite MP for Limerick in 1832. But he was also ever the Whig and was offered jobs when his friend and future biographer, Lord John Russell, who was to preside as prime minister over the parsimonious Whig government during the famine, first became a minister. Moore eventually accepted a civil list pension of £300 per annum and died in 1852, preceded by his five children.

Moore was the brightest star in a constellation, if not a galaxy, of early nineteenth-century Irish poets, some of whom will be considered again in a general discussion on literature towards the end of this book. Edward 'Pleasant Ned' Lysaght (1763–1810), who was Lady Morgan's godfather, wrote poems in support of the Irish Volunteers of 1782. James Orr (1770–1816) and William Drennan (1754–1820) were both from Ulster and United Irishmen. Sir Aubrey de Vere (1788–1846) was a friend and imitator of Wordsworth. Mary Balfour (1780–1819) was a poet and collaborated in the work of Edward Bunting. Thomas Furlong (1794–1827) wrote *The doom of Derenzie* (1829) and provided verse versions for James Hardiman's literal translations from the Irish. George Darley (1795–1846) spent his working life in semi-seclusion in London where he wrote mathematical textbooks. His major poem *Nepenthe* (1835), like much of his work, explores a myth of weakness. Its high romanticism is reminiscent

51 Ibid., p 25. **52** O'Sullivan, 'Irish rural insurgency,' in Geary (ed.), *Rebellion and remembrance*, pp 73–92. **53** White, *Tom Moore*, p. 235.

of Keats and Shelley.[54] J.J. Callanan (1795–1829) travelled around west Cork seeking to encounter nature and the Gaelic poetic world.[55] Noted for poems about marginal figures such as 'The Convict of Clonmel', 'The Outlaw of Loch Lene', and 'The Dirge of O'Sullivan Beare', his principal work was *The recluse of Inchydoney* (1830), a Byronic quest poem.

Romanticism influenced not only poetry but also what in early nineteenth-century Ireland was a rather fluid continuum of genres from journalism, sociological description and travel writing to anthropological collections of folk tales, didactic essays, religious tracts and fiction. Examples include *Collection of lives of the Irish peasantry* (1822) by Mary Leadbeater (1758–1826); *Tales of Irish life* (1824) by Michael James Whitty (1795–1878); *Researches in the south of Ireland* (1824) and *Fairy legends and traditions of the south of Ireland* (1825) both by Thomas Crofton Croker (1798–1854); *Today in Ireland* (1825) by Eyre Evans Crowe (1799–1868); *Sketches in Ireland* (1827) by Caesar Otway (1780–1824); *Cabin conversations and castle scenes* (1827) by Selina Bunbury (1802–82); *Irish priests and English landlords* (1830) by George Brittaine (1790–1847); and *Wild sports of the west* (1832) by W.H. Maxwell (1794–1850).

The doyenne of such writers was Anna Maria Hall (1800–81), author of *Sketches of Irish character* (1829), *Lights and shadows of Irish life* (1838) and *Stories of the Irish peasantry* (1840). She is best known for *Ireland, its scenery, character etc.* (1843) written with her journalist husband S.C. Hall (1800–89). Her books were very successful commercially, and their purpose was not only to make the Irish peasantry better understood in Britain but also to press for the reform of peasant life, a reform which she thought of as coming from without and involving the adoption of more English ways. The peasants were seen as essentially inferior though by the time she wrote her novel, *The Whiteboy* (1845), she had come to blame the authorities for Irish poverty. That work, however, recounts the ultimately successful attempts of a returned absentee landlord to improve his Irish estates.[56]

The work of these writers varies greatly in style and polemical tone. Many of them though evince a romantic concern with the picturesque, in addition to their realism. They are also largely concerned with the peasantry. Again this is consonant with romanticism but also with the political climate generated by the O'Connellite campaign for Catholic emancipation. Could Irish Catholics be trusted as loyal subjects and members of society? The principal beneficiaries of reform were to be the middle classes, but the debate focused on the peasantry, which loomed largest in the British imagination concerning Ireland, especially in the 1820s over the question of agrarian outrages. Not for the last time in

54 Brisman, *Romantic origins*, pp 183–223. 55 Welch, *Irish poetry*, p. 46. 56 Cahalan, *Irish novel*, pp 57–9; Keane, *Mrs C.S. Hall.*

nineteenth-century Ireland, middle-class Irish Catholic authors would seek to explain the Irish peasantry to British audiences and vindicate the respectability of the Irish. The most prominent Irish writers of the 1820s and early 1830s fit into this category. Through their realist novels Michael (1796-1874) and John (1798–1842) Banim and Gerald Griffin (1803–40) were cultural combatants on behalf of Catholic emancipation and of the accession of middle-class Catholics to the central political, social and economic position hitherto held by the Ascendancy.[57]

The Banims were born in Kilkenny. Michael had to abandon his legal studies to go into the family shopkeeping business. He remained in Kilkenny all his life and of the two had the deeper knowledge of the Irish peasantry. John, on the other hand, was allowed to complete his education. Richard Lalor Sheil, the playwright and prominent emancipation campaigner, helped him to have a play staged in Covent Garden, London, in 1821. He lived in London throughout the decade, thus having a greater knowledge of English reading tastes than his brother. After spending some time in France, a public subscription enabled him to buy a small home in Kilkenny, where he died of consumption in 1842.

In 1822 the brothers decided to form their own writing collective called 'The O'Hara family' and to begin to publish novels which they had written either individually or jointly. Their novels were published on their own or, as in the case of some of them, in the two series of *Tales of the O'Hara family*. They ranged over history, the supernatural and peasant life and often touched on the darker side of Irish life.[58] John Banim's biographer, P.J. Murray was clear about the overall purpose of the *O'Hara tales*. It was 'to raise the national character in the estimation of other lands, by a portrayal of the people as they really were; but at the same time to vindicate them from the charges of violence and bloodthirstiness' by explaining the conditions which gave rise to violence.[59] The assertion of authentic reporting innocently juxtaposed with a political or ideological purpose was to become a common refrain in Irish literature.

The ten novels which the brothers published in the years between 1825 and 1830 were their most important.[60] *The tales of the O'Hara family*, first series (1825) consists of three novels. *John Doe* was written mostly by John but with a contribution by Michael Banim. In it the violence of an agrarian group is set in the context of the actions of a bad landlord and the opinions of an intelligently reflective peasantry. John's *The fetches* and Michael's *Crohoore of the billhook* blend realism with varying degrees of otherworldliness. Fetches were banshee-like doppelgängers in peasant lore and foretold long life if seen in the morning and death if seen in the evening. In John Banim's novel several ill and distressed mid-

57 Dunne, *Maria Edgeworth*, p 5. **58** Cahalan, *Irish novel*, pp 34–40. **59** Murray, *John Banim*, p. 93. **60** Hawthorne, *John and Michael Banim*; Hayley, 'Speech in the nineteenth-century Anglo-Irish novel,' in Bramsbäck and Croghan (eds), *Aspects of language and culture*, pp 159–72.

dle class characters claim to see them. The novel remains elusive over the status of the fetches as real beings or psychological disturbances or both.[61] Supposedly superstitious peasant beliefs are thus seen to replay a deeper analysis.

Michael Banim's *Crohoore* is critical both of the tithe system and of the actions of the Whiteboys who oppose it. It thus explains but does not excuse Irish violence. At the same time it seeks to vindicate the probity of the Irish peasantry by foregrounding the story of Crohoore, an individual popularly convicted of murder and abduction who turns out to have acted virtuously all along.

The second series of the *Tales* (1826) consists of the jointly written *Peter of the castle* and of John Banim's *The Nowlans*, a novel which in its dealing with issues such as abortion, prostitution and clerical sexuality strikes a decidedly modern note, albeit subject to a censorious moral tone. It thus inaugurates the theme of the relationship between sex and religion in Irish Catholic writing. By contrast with this gritty analysis of the rising Catholic middle classes, John's anonymously published 1828 novel *The Anglo-Irish of the nineteenth century* is a bitterly satirical nationalist attack on the Ascendancy whose plot is a variant of Edgeworth's *The absentee*. However, its hero Gerald Blount does come to embrace his Irish identity, having initially determined to be 'English-Irish'.

The brothers also produced four historical novels during their most productive six years, in imitation of Scott. However, unlike Scott's fiction in which characters negotiate history by steering a moderate course, characters embroiled in the more turbulent history of Ireland find themselves moving from naivety to political commitment.[62] This process is most evident in the case of the Banims in John's *The Boyne water* (1825), in which the Protestant Robert Evelyn falls in love with the Catholic Eva McDonnell, while his sister Esther falls in love with Eva's brother Edmund. However, one couple is separated by death while the other settles into married life. Their romances take place against the background of what is to Banim the polarizing bigotry of the Williamite wars, ironically the key movement for establishing liberty in the Whig view of history. The accord which the couples reach is enabled by the partly otherworldly context of storms and fogs in which it is achieved. Robert's conversion to sympathy with the Catholic cause enacts the process which Banim hoped his English readers would undertake over Catholic emancipation.[63]

Michael thought *The Boyne water* too polemical. His own *The Croppy* (1828) about 1798 is more deferential to English sensibilities in its attempts to explain how noble aspirations can degenerate into sectarian brutality and was well received in England. John's final two historical novels, *The last baron of Crana*

61 Denman, 'Ghosts,' in Welch (ed.), *Irish writers and religion*, pp 62–74. **62** Cahalan, *Irish historical novel*, p. 15. **63** Ibid., pp 43–66.

and *The conformists*, which were published together as *The denounced* in 1830, were written while Catholic emancipation was on the horizon. Fearful of alienating opinion they are more subdued than *The Boyne water*. Each details the survival of Catholics during the penal laws, sometimes with Protestant help.

Gerald Griffin was born into a middle-class, Limerick, Catholic family. He and the Banims were thus representatives of the prosperous Catholic core area. His parents emigrated to America in 1820, but he remained with his brother, a doctor at Adare, Co. Limerick. He went to London in 1823 to pursue a literary career and was friends there with John Banim and other Irish littérateurs. Like Banim he first tried to make his name in the theatre but was unsuccessful and was only sustained by journalism. He returned to Ireland in 1827. That year he saw published two collections of stories. *Holland-tide* consists of a novella and six short pieces. *Tales of the Munster festivals* is made up of three long stories. In its introduction there is a dialogue between the author, whose aim is to increase Irish-British understanding, and a Gaelic antiquarian, who wants writers to deal with the past.[64] Griffin belonged to the generation of O'Connellite utiliatarians and had little time for Celticism. Like the Banims, Griffin's concern is in promoting a less negative view of Irish character, especially of the peasantry, but through a deeper analysis of social and cultural issues rather than through the comic trivialization which would hold such sway later in the century.[65]

In 1829 Griffin met Lydia Fisher with whom he fell in love. It was also the year in which *The collegians* was published. It was a novel whose great success was to be reprised when it was turned into a play *The colleen bawn* (1860) by Dion Boucicault and an opera *The lily of Killarney* (1862) by Julius Benedict. It earned Griffin £800 and was an influence on Dickens.[66] Based on a real murder, it is a tragic romance in which the necessities of the rural class system frustrate the possibilities of love.

Pressure on the volatile Hardress Cregan, of a marginal gentry background, to marry his prosperous cousin, Anne Chute, means death for impoverished Eily O'Connor, with whom he has contracted a secret, love-match marriage. Rather like Edgeworth with *Castle Rackrent*, however, Griffin was dismayed when readers preferred the romantic Hardress to the novel's other principal male character, the rational Kyrle Daly, of a Catholic, middleman family who eventually marries Anne Chute, in Griffin's version of a national marriage.[67] In this case though such a marriage is designed not to bolster Ascendancy rule but to herald that of the Catholic middle classes.

Two short novels by Griffin were also published in 1829. *The rivals* repeats the themes of *The collegians*. *Tracy's ambition* paints a picture of the decay of the

64 Dunne, 'Gerald Griffin's portrayal of Ireland,' in MacDonagh and Mandle (eds), *Ireland and Irish Australia*, pp 64–80. **65** Cronin, *Gerald Griffin*. **66** Moynaghan, 'Gerald Griffin', in Zach and Kosok (eds), *Comparison and impact*, pp 173–80. **67** Dunne, 'Irish romantic writing,' p. 84.

moral economy on which the Ascendancy's rule is reliant. In it Abel Tracy, a Protestant middleman, is persuaded to side with Dalton, a corrupt landlord and magistrate, in his battle with the Whiteboys, with disastrous personal consequences for Abel.[68] Eventually Griffin was to tire of writing. Burning most of his manuscripts he became a Christian Brother and died of typhus in Cork in 1840. By that time a newly resurgent Protestantism was marking out its own cultural territory.

68 Sloan, *Anglo-Irish fiction*, p. 130.

CHAPTER 6

A religious education, 1801–84

As we have seen the central political issue in the first third of nineteenth century Ireland was that of the position of the Catholic majority within society. It was a wide issue that was symbolized in the demand for the right of Catholics to sit in the Commons. In one sense it was a piece of hyperbole to call the winning of this limited measure 'Catholic emancipation'. In another it was an aptly dramatic image for the broader struggle, a struggle that had such important consequences for the Protestant Ascendancy. The defining of a political nation in largely ethnic and religious terms might have been avoided had the obstacle that caused its formation, the denial of 'Catholic emancipation', not mistakenly been kept in place at the time of the Acts of Union.

By the end of the nineteenth century the Catholic Church in Ireland had become large, powerful, cohesive and assertive, especially on such issues as its support for denominational education. It had begun the century largely quiescent, loyal and moderate. Many factors contributed to the transformation but not the least of them was the galvanizing effect of the vigorous proselytism to which the Catholic community was subjected for most of the century, largely from sections of the Established Church.

Surprisingly then, while the political agenda for the first half of the century was set by the rise of a Catholic nationalism led by Daniel O'Connell, the religious agenda was set by the Established Church. In 1801 the Established Church in Ireland became part of a new united church with the Church of England. Its dilemma was summed by in 1838 by the prime minister, Lord Melbourne, who told Queen Victoria 'that [in England] the Established Church was *generally* kept up for the poor, as the rich could afford that themselves; whereas in Ireland ... the Established Church is *only* kept up for the Protestant feeling of the United Kingdom and not for the poor who are almost all Roman Catholics.'[1] It was a parlous position to be in especially with the social, economic and political position of the Protestant Ascendancy now under attack. Whig and Liberal governments were ever anxious to be seen to be bringing reform to Ireland in their attempts to win over Catholic nationalist opinion. From the Church Temporalities Act of 1833, which reduced the number of its bishoprics by ten, to its disestablishment and disendowment by Gladstone in 1869, the Church of Ireland provided an easy target for them.

1 Esher, *The girlhood of Queen Victoria*, i, p. 327. **2** Akenson, *Church of Ireland*, pp 322–30.

From an early point in the century the church had sought to bring about a reform within its own ranks, which had the effect of extending its pastoral outreach. The number of benefices was increased from 1,120 in the 1780s to 1,395 in 1832 and 1,518 in 1867. In 1787 there were 1,001 churches. By 1832 the number had risen to 1,293. At the same time the opulence of clerical lifestyles was being curtailed. In 1830 the primate's annual income was £14,000. By 1867 it had fallen back to £9,000.[2] The number of clergy increased by a half in the first third of the century. At the same time the number of parishes without a resident clergyman was cut by a half. The numbers of both parish schools and residences for clergy more than doubled, and nearly seven hundred churches were built or enlarged.[3] But all of this was not enough to sustain the church's position as the establishment. Whereas in England the Established Church has maintained its position down to the present day in a secularized society by for the most part embracing liberalism, the strategy that some sections of the Church of Ireland embraced in the early nineteenth century was quite different. It was an attempt to convert the Catholic population.

There were two ideological driving forces behind this move which were eventually to dominate the Church of Ireland, in an alignment which in other circumstances was not an obvious one. The first was the 'high church' tendency which valued ecclesiastical structures and hence the establishment. The second was the evangelical tendency which put a premium on the inner experience of personal conversion.[4] This latter movement conveniently restricted the miraculous to the inner life and allowed believers to live their outer lives according to the empirical norms of modern society.[5] For many evangelicals, Catholics with their apparently externalized sacramental system lacked that element of personal conversion necessary for salvation and were thus the objects of particular pity and zeal.

Established Church evangelicals were generally less concerned with denominational boundaries and were prepared to co-operate with dissenters in their work of conversion.[6] Indeed, the first Protestant missionaries in Ireland were a group of Irish-speaking Methodists in 1799, though at the time Methodists were still attached to the Established Church and it would not be until 1816 that a significant number of them in Ireland broke away to form their own church.[7] For the most part, though, the prevailing evangelical theology of sections of the Church of Ireland ensured that many who might have become dissenters could remain in the establishment.[8] Power le Poer Trench, a recent evangelical convert, was made archbishop of Tuam in 1819. On the other hand the Church's

3 Brown, 'New Reformation,' in Brown and Miller (eds), *Piety and power*, pp 186–7. **4** Bowen, *Irish Protestantism*, p. 328. **5** Miller, 'Presbyterianism and "modernization,"' in Philpin (ed.), *Nationalism and popular protest*, p. 106. **6** Brown, 'New Reformation,' p. 188. **7** Hempton, 'Methodist crusade,' *Irish Historical Studies*, 22:85 (1980), pp 33–48. **8** Bowen, *Protestant crusade*, p. 38.

two senior clerics for most of the period, Lord John George Beresford, archbishop of Armagh (1822–62), and Richard Whately, archbishop of Dublin (1831–61), were not supporters of evangelicalism.

Over the first seven decades of the century as many as five major trends or phases can be detected in the evangelical campaign, focusing successively on education, polemics, colonies, English evangelism and charities. The period until 1822 was one of often low-key educational work by Protestant societies, some based in England and some in Ireland. Among them were the Church Mission Society (founded 1799), the British and Foreign Bible Association (1804), the Hibernian Bible Society (1806), the London Hibernian Society (1809), the Religious Tract and Book Society (1810), the Sunday School Society of Ireland (1811), the Irish Evangelical Society (1814), the Irish Society (officially 'The Irish Society for Promoting the Education of the Native Irish through the Medium of their Own Language'), (1818) and the Scripture Readers Society (1822).[9] As time went on these societies began to take on a more evangelical hue. In particular the Kildare Place Society (1811), which ran hundreds of schools throughout the country and which might have formed the basis for a national system of education, was taken over by evangelicals in the 1820s, causing those Catholics including Daniel O'Connell, who had supported it, to withdraw.

On 24 October 1822 the high church archbishop of Dublin William Magee took things a stage further when he publicly called for a 'second reformation'. Though he may have been thinking more of the internal life of the Established Church, his intervention has been taken as marking the beginning of the concerted effort to bring about the conversion of Ireland's Catholics. This led to a period of public polemics between Protestant and Catholic controversialists in which evangelicals came up against Catholic spokesmen who were their equal in energy, such as James Warren Doyle ('JKL'), the Catholic bishop of Kildare and Leighlin (1819–34), though his natural inclination was for moderation. A six-day debate took place in Dublin in April 1827 between Fr Tom Maguire and the Revd Richard T.P. Pope, which Maguire was reckoned to have won. In Carlow, 18–19 November 1829, three Protestant and three Catholic controversialists engaged in public debate.[10]

The supporters of the evangelicals included a number of landlords such as Lords Farnham, Roden and Powerscourt. Among the issues that were to haunt the second reformation were charges of economic and cultural imperialism and that conversion was tainted by financial inducement and landlord pressure. In the last months of 1826 some 250 persons were converted on Lord Farnham's Co. Cavan estate, an event which caused such consternation in Catholic circles

9 Brown, 'New Reformation,' p. 189; Hempton and Hill, *Protestantism*, p. 55; Mercier, *Literature*, pp 64–85. **10** Bowen, *Protestant crusade*, p. 107; Brown, 'New Reformation,' p. 192.

that five bishops were dispatched to investigate it. By spring 1827 some 1,340 converts were reported nationally. It was an aberration, however, and by the middle of 1827 the converts were returning to Catholicism.[11]

Nonetheless, it was now clear that it was possible to convert Catholics. The next two decades were to see the flowering of a new Protestant literature and journalism. They were also to see a focusing of efforts to convert Catholics in 'colonies' – specially financed areas in which converts could be gathered together. The two most prominent such experiments were in Achill and Dingle. The Revd Edward Nangle founded the Achill colony in 1831 and publicized his activities through the *Achill Missionary Herald and Western Witness*. His colony flourished for two decades and survived for more than four. The Revd Charles Gayer, an associate of the Irish Society, began working in the Dingle area in 1838, founding colonies and making over 800 converts by 1845. However, his work received a fatal blow in the early autumn of 1846 when a Catholic 'mission' was held in the area by the Vincentian Fathers. Such events represented the beginnings of a more effective resistance by the Catholic Church to evangelical incursions.[12]

During the traumatic years of the famine there were accusations of 'souperism' – that the provision of food relief had been made dependent on conversion.[13] The case of the well-meaning Revd William Allen Fisher of Kilmoe, Co. Cork, is illustrative of the difficulty in determining the truth. He provided a sacramental service which even included confession for the Catholic population of his parish who had been deserted by their priest and was later reviled as a 'souper'.[14] What was undoubtedly the case was that the famine was seen in the Protestant providentialist thinking of the time as a judgment by God against the Irish and as a new opportunity to convert them.[15] Evangelical activity intensified and in 1849 the Revd A.R.C. Dallas founded the Society for the Irish Church Missions to the Roman Catholics, with its headquarters in Exeter Hall, London. During this English-based phase of the second reformation, 125 stations were established in twenty-four parts of Ireland and it was claimed that 35,000 Catholics had been converted.[16] However, by 1863 it had run out of steam.

Meanwhile, in urban areas and especially in Dublin proselytism was often associated with charitable work. The most notable example was that of the Smylie Homes, founded by Ellen Smylie. Her schools and homes for poor Dublin children, which were partly funded by the Irish Church Missions, openly selected children from Catholic and mixed religion families in preference to

11 Brown, 'New Reformation,' pp 199–204. **12** Murphy, 'Vincentian parish missions,' *Irish Historical Studies*, 23:94 (1984), pp 152–71. **13** Bowen, *Souperism*. **14** Bowen, *Protestant crusade*, pp 186–9. **15** Miller, 'Irish Presbyterians,' in Hill and Lennon (eds), *Luxury and austerity*, pp 165–81. **16** Kerr, *Priests, people and politics*, pp 210–11.

Protestant children. Margaret Aylward helped to found the St Brigid's orphanage as a Catholic counter to Smylie.[17]

The second reformation petered around after disestablishment. The Church of Ireland turned into a ghetto church in the south of Ireland and embraced a common Protestant identity with the Presbyterian Church in Ulster.[18] From the early 1890s, in what came to be known as the Anglo-Irish literary renaissance, a group of Anglo-Irish writers made a bid for cultural dominance in Ireland in perhaps unconscious imitation of the ambition for religious dominance of their evangelical forbears.[19]

The Presbyterian Church enjoyed a very different trajectory from the Church of Ireland during the nineteenth century. The first four decades were spent in struggles over various theological disputes that resulted in the majority of Presbyterians embracing conservatism and effectively ending the radical tradition which had inspired the United Irishmen. Henry Montgomery was the leader of the liberal grouping that had Arian and unitarian tendencies. However, he was progressively outmanoeuvred by Henry Cooke, leader of the conservative faction, and Montgomery and his supporters left the Synod of Ulster to form their own Remonstrant Synod in 1830. Meanwhile Cooke worked for the unity of conservative Presbyterians, and in 1840 the Orthodox Seceders and most of the Synod of Ulster combined to form the General Assembly of the Presbyterian Church in Ireland on the basis of the Westminster Confession. Cooke was also a strong advocate of an alliance between the Presbyterian Church and Church of Ireland in the common Protestant cause.[20]

The Presbyterian Church was becoming more cohesive politically and theologically, but it was in danger of withdrawing from its earlier communalism into a middle-class identity. Two opportunities presented themselves mid-century to reverse the trend, but neither was fully embraced and the slide towards middle-class respectability was unchecked. The first arose from the same providentialist view of the famine that had spurred on Established Church evangelicals to redouble their efforts. The famine seemed to some to offer the Church the chance to move beyond its Ulster-Scots ethnic identity and to open its doors to Catholic converts. When nothing came of this possibility, there were experiments in the 1850s in returning to the open air preaching which had been a feature of the earlier communal phase in the Church's existence. This experiment prepared the way for the second opportunity, the 1859 revival in which 100,000 people were reported to have experienced religious conversion. However, the effects proved short lived, mostly because of the reluctance of many Presbyterian ministers to endorse the bodily manifestations and altered states of

17 Ibid., pp 212–13; Preston, 'Lay Women,' *Éire-Ireland*, 28:4 (1993), pp 74–85. **18** Bowen, *Protestant crusade*, p. 79. **19** Mercier, *Literature*, pp 64–85. **20** Hempton and Hill, *Protestantism*, pp 69–75.

consciousness which were reportedly part of the experience of many converts.[21]

In 1834 there were 664,940 dissenters in Ireland and 853,160 members of the Established Church but 6,436,060 Catholics.[22] Catholics constituted 81 per cent of the population, though in view of the disproportionate effects of the famine on the Catholic population this figure would drop to 78 per cent by 1861, 77 per cent by 1871 and 74 per cent by 1911.[23] In 1861 Catholics constituted 50.55 per cent of the Ulster population (nine counties) but ten years later the figure was 48.9 per cent.[24] In 1871 Catholics were over-represented among labourers (87 per cent) and shopkeepers (83 per cent). However, they were dramatically under-represented among the higher professions such as barristers (30 per cent), doctors (34 per cent), solicitors (37 per cent), civil engineers (34 per cent), architects (34 per cent) and bankers (27 per cent) and even among merchants (42 per cent).[25] The Catholic emphasis on education had its roots not only in a fear of proselytism but in an urgent desire to increase the middle-class Catholic base.

From the point of view of the Church as an institution both the absolute number and the proportion to the population of full time religious personnel—diocesan and regular clergy, nuns and religious brothers—was of great importance. The early nineteenth century in fact saw a relative weakening of institutional strength in this regard, with the dramatic rise of the pre-famine population and the loss of the continental colleges that had trained priests before the French revolution. Whereas in 1731 there was one diocesan priest for every 1,587 Catholics, by 1800 the ratio had worsened to one for 2,678. Even though the number of such priests rose from 1,614 to 2,183 between the years 1800 and 1840, the ratio continued to worsen. It was only in 1871 with the continuing rise in the number of priests and the post-famine decline in population that the ratio improved to one for 1,560 and returned to the level it had been at 140 years before.[26] On the other hand the number of nuns showed an exponential increase across the century from 122 in 1800 to 8,000 in 1900.[27] By contrast with their Established Church contemporaries, Catholic clergy lived modestly. Bishops were paid £300 per annum and parish priests £65.[28]

The closure of most of the continental colleges had been compensated for to a degree by the foundation of Maynooth College in 1795. It was financed by a government fearful of the influence of Jacobinism on the Catholic clegy. In 1826 there were 391 students at Maynooth, 120 at other Irish seminaries and 140 in the continental colleges which had managed to survive or reform after the Napoleonic wars. Maynooth had its critics in the early nineteenth century, not least among the Ascendancy, whose constant cry was that it was advancing per-

21 Miller, '1859 revival.' **22** Kerr, *Peel, priests and politics*, p. 2. **23** Connolly, *Priests and people*, p. 25. **24** Bardon, *Ulster*, p. 345. **25** Vaughan, 'Ireland *c.* 1870,' in Vaughan (ed.), *Union I, 1801–70*, pp 740–1. **26** Connolly, *Priests and people*, p. 33. **27** Larkin, 'Devotional revolution in Ireland 1850–75', *American Historical Review* 77:3 (1972), pp 625–52. **28** Keogh, *French disease*, pp 11, 15.

sons to the priesthood from a very low social and economic background and was thus socially and politically subversive.[29] Official investigations, however, showed that the students at Maynooth were mostly from the middle rank of the tenant farming class, though some were from more comfortable backgrounds while some were the sons of merchants or tradesmen. The cost of an education at Maynooth put it beyond the reach of the poor. Ironically, the middling farmers were to come to dominate post-famine Ireland and its nationalist politics, in tacit alliance with the majority of priests who came from similar class backgrounds.[30]

Clerical discipline was not universally strong. In 1785 John Butler, the Catholic bishop of Cork, left his ministry and converted to the Established Church on assuming the barony of Dunboyne. In 1835 Francis O'Finan was appointed bishop of Killala but did not remain in his appointment for very long because of the opposition of some of the younger clergy who felt that one of them should have been appointed. Around the same time, a Co. Monaghan curate, Edward O'Callaghan, was suspended by his bishop but stayed on in his parish, supported by an armed bodyguard.[31] There was, then, a certain laxity in clerical discipline often marked by disputes, drunkenness and avarice, though priests under ecclesiastical censure were generally credited by the peasantry with having some special power, such as the ability to heal. Discipline may indeed have deteriorated in the early nineteenth century due to the poor training of some priests ordained during the disruption caused by the French Revolution.[32]

Most debate among historians, however, has focused on the religious practice of the laity, specifically on the rate of Sunday mass attendance. Some have argued for a rate as low as 40 per cent, whereas others argue for a much higher rate, taking into account those excused from church attendance on grounds of age, illness, distance from the church and the need for someone to remain at home to mind the house. What is clear, though, is that mass attendance was highest in English-speaking towns and rural areas and lowest in rural Irish-speaking areas. Geographically, mass attendance was highest in the area south of a line between Dundalk and Killarney with its heart in the Catholic core area previously identified. Economically, it was the area of greatest Catholic prosperity.[33]

By the end of the century clerical discipline was strict and attendance at Sunday mass had risen to the nearly total levels it was to maintain in Ireland for most of the twentieth century. Clearly something had happened both in terms of the pattern of religious observance, as controlled largely by the clergy, and in

29 Connolly, *Priests and people*, pp 34, 38, 46–7: Kerr, *Peel, priests and people*, pp 226, 247. **30** Connolly, *Religion and society*, p. 41. **31** Connolly, *Priests and people*, pp 62–3, 65, 68. **32** I am grateful to Professor Emmet Larkin for this point. **33** Connolly, *Priests and people*, pp 265–6; Corish, *Irish Catholic experience*, p. 167; Kerr, 'Catholic Church in Ireland,' in *Ireland after the Union*, pp 38–9; Miller, 'Mass attendance,' in Brown and Miller (eds), *Piety and power*, pp 158–79.

terms of the embrace of that religious observance by the Catholic population. In addition expectations of what constituted a practising Catholic also changed because the relatively low levels of Sunday mass attendance in the early nineteenth century did not cause the clergy great anxiety, and foreign observers often commented on the religious fervour of the Catholic Irish.

Great efforts were made to reformulate religious practice strictly along the lines of the sixteenth-century Council of Trent. There was a boom in church building such that the finance for it has been considered a significant factor in the development of the Irish economy for the period.[34] Regulations were enforced to limit the administration of the sacraments to the church building. Marriages, for example, had hitherto been performed in people's homes.[35] The system of station masses, although of no great antiquity, was also frowned on. Stations were occasions when the people of an area would gather in a specified house for mass and were thought to be occasions where unseemly behaviour might occur. Patterns and wakes were of course equally frowned on. Thus Canon Michael Murphy of Upper Killeavy employed the South Armagh yeomanry to help him suppress a local pattern, known for drunkenness and fighting. However, some traditions such as the penitential pilgrimage to Lough Derg made the transition to the new era.[36] In place of the discouraged practices was a new emphasis not only on the sacraments but on more individualized devotions such as the rosary, the stations of the cross and adoration of the blessed sacrament. Religious confraternities of men and women were also encouraged to perform various religious and charitable functions, but they were clerically supervized bodies. Finally, an enormous investment was made in hospitals, schools and other institutions and religious orders were founded or imported to provide them with personnel. The Catholic Church came to match the state in its creation of new centralized institutions and regulated practices.

If all this answers the question as to what took place, then the questions when and why remain to be answered. There is some disagreement and a variety of views on when the institutional reform took place. Some hold that the reform occurred gradually in the century from 1775 to 1875.[37] Others believe that the 1790s were key years for reform, under the leadership of John Troy, archbishop of Dublin (1786–1823).[38] Another view is that the first half of the nineteenth century was the most important time, especially with the advent of new and zealous religious orders such as the Vincentians.[39] Finally, there is the view that the post-famine period, the years between 1850 and 1875, constituted what Emmet Larkin has seen as a decisive 'devotional revolution' in Ireland.[40]

34 Kennedy, 'Roman Catholic Church,' *Economic and Social Review* 10 (1978–9), pp 45–57. **35** Corish, *Irish Catholic*, p. 212. **36** Donnelly, 'Lough Derg,' in Nolan, Ronayne and Dunlevy (ed.), *Donegal*, pp 491–508. **37** McGrath, 'Tridentine evolution,' *Recusant History*, 20:4 (1991), pp 512–23. **38** Keogh, *French disease*, p. 219. **39** Murphy, 'Vincentian parish missions.' **40** Larkin,

These divergent views can to an extent be reconciled by bearing in mind the difference between laying the ground work for reform in theory and its practical implementation. Tridentine devotions were introduced in the eastern, English-speaking parts of the country, for example, at a much earlier date than in the western Irish-speaking areas. It was certainly the third quarter of the nineteenth century before they had taken definitive national hold.

Key figures in the reform included Daniel Murray, archbishop of Dublin (1823–52), who encouraged the foundation of several important religious orders. In politics he was generally moderate and co-operative with the government.[41] By contrast his successor, Paul Cullen, archbishop of Armagh (1849–52), and of Dublin (1852–78), who was created cardinal in 1866, was assertive in his advocacy of Catholic rights. Cullen presided over the synod of Thurles (1850) which codified much of the reform of the clergy and religious practice already introduced by individual bishops over the previous fifty years. Many of these reforms were resisted by the Gaelic nationalist, John MacHale, archbishop of Tuam (1834–81), who remained one of the few independent forces in a hierarchy which was increasingly dominated by Cullen.

By temperament Cullen was a nationalist but accepted the status quo of the union in his pursuit of the enhancement of the status of the Church and Catholic community. He maintained his distance from governments but was equally keen to keep priests out of politics and to condemn more extreme forms of nationalism such as the Fenians.[42] His own attempts to establish a political party under the influence of the hierarchy in the National Association (1864) failed.

Cullen was a keen supporter of the ultramontanism of Pope Pius IX and played a prominent part at the First Vatican Council (1870) at which seventy-three Irish-born bishops from Ireland, America and the British colonies were present.[43] Ironically, his unifying of the Irish bishops in fact reduced the openings for Roman interference in the Irish Church which was always suspect in Ireland because of the British government's attempt to influence papal policy towards Ireland.[44] Thus in the 1880s the bishops, under the strongly nationalist William Walsh, archbishop of Dublin (1885–1921), were very resistant to papal condemnations of the Irish land war.[45] The land war also coincided with the reported apparition of the Blessed Virgin Mary at Knock, Co. Mayo, in 1879. Her silence during the apparition enabled it to be embraced by Catholics of a variety of political persuasions and social classes.[46]

'Devotional revolution.' **41** Kerr, *Peel, priests and politics*, pp 16, 19, 27. **42** Kerr, *Priests, people and politics*, pp 340, 358. **43** Kerr, 'Catholic Church in Ireland,' p. 41. **44** Brown and Miller, 'Introduction,' in Brown and Miller (eds), *Piety and power*, p. 4; Kerr, 'Catholic Church in Ireland,' p. 28. **45** Larkin, *Fall of Parnell*, p. xviii. **46** Bew, 'Popular piety,' in Devlin and Fanning (eds), *Religion and rebellion*, pp 137–51; Donnelly, 'Marian shrine,' *Éire-Ireland* 28:2 (1993), pp 54–99.

In fact the Catholic Church's interaction with nationalist politics led to the creation of a stable, liberal-democratic political system in nationalist Ireland.[47] This reached its apogee in 1884 when, under the influence of the nationalist Thomas Croke, archbishop of Cashel (1875–1902), the bishops gave their support to the Irish Parliamentary Party in return for its support for their policy on education. It was a consensus between the Catholic Church and Irish nationalism that survived the traumatic fall of the Irish nationalist leader C.S. Parnell in a divorce scandal.

As for why Tridentine Catholicism was embraced with such alacrity by the majority of Irish Catholics, the reasons must be more speculative. It has been suggested that Catholicism acted as a substitute for the dying Irish language as a marker of national identity or that the strict sexual mores of Tridentine Caholicism suited the economic priorities of the rising farming class, centring on the accumulation of capital. As farming families could now only afford one heir, celibacy or emigration was the only options for non-heirs, a choice reinforced by the Catholic prohibition on extra-marital sexual activity.[48]

The sexual puritanism considered so characteristic of Irish Catholicism may thus have fulfilled economic ends, as well as being an acquiescence in a desire for middle-class Victorian respectability.[49] Such considerations qualify the picture of an oppressive Church imposing its views on an unwilling population, believed by later generations of urban intellectuals intent on individual self-realization.[50] They also explain the relative failure of the clergy in imposing its will in other areas of life such as the excessive consumption of alcohol[51] and the practice of late marriage and emigration, all of which met with clerical disapproval. In particular, clerical power in areas of agrarian violence[52] and political agitation was definitely limited. Priests developed strategies to mitigate the effects of official ecclesiastical condemnations of revolutionary violence, so as not to alienate their congregations. The activities of historical revolutionaries could safely be praised. Symbolic nationalist gestures, such as the boycotting of state occasions, could be made, and a humanitarian sympathy could be extended to imprisoned revolutionaries such as the Fenians, whose actions had been condemned.[53]

The issue that preoccupied the Catholic Church above all was that of education. Seen by evangelicals as a means of converting Catholics from superstition to Biblical Christianity and by governments as a means of converting Catholics

47 Larkin, 'Church, state and nation,' *American Historical Review*, 80:5 (1975) pp 1244–76; *Modern Irish state*; *Plan of campaign*; *Fall of Parnell*; *Making of the Roman Catholic Church*; *Consolidation of the Roman Catholic Church*; *Home rule movement*; *Modern Irish political system*. **48** Larkin, 'Devotional revolution;' Hynes, 'The great hunger,' *Societas* 8 (1978), pp 137–56; Hynes, 'Farmers' ideology,' in O'Toole (ed.), *Roman Catholicism*, pp 45–69. **49** Connolly, *Religion and society*, p. 55. **50** Connolly, *Priests and people*, pp 217–18. **51** Connolly, *Religion and society*, p. 55. **52** Connolly, *Priests and people*, pp 260–3. **53** MacDonagh, *States of mind*, pp 98–9.

from disloyalty and backwardness to loyalty and progress, education was an issue over which Catholic leaders became more and more convinced of the need for denominational control.

Education transformed the population. The illiteracy rate in Ireland dropped from 53 per cent in 1841 to 33 per cent in 1871 and 14 per cent in 1901.[54] Even in the first quarter of the century two fifths of children went to school. The Kildare Place Society was in receipt of government grants and by 1831 was educating 140,000 pupils. Most children who attended school, however, were pupils at small private schools somewhat misleadingly termed 'hedge' schools.[55] Much of this educational provision was inter-denominational.

In education as in other areas the perceived backwardness of Ireland paradoxically paved the way for the creation, at considerable government expense, of one of the most modern and centralized of experimental systems in educational provision, far ahead of anything available at the time in Britain.[56] In 1831 the government introduced a system of national education at primary level which was intended to be multi-denominational with shared secular and separate religious education. Presbyterians came out against it but by 1840 had won concessions. The Established Church was disgruntled at what it saw as a Whig attack on its position. By 1839 its Church Education Society had been set up to rival the national schools system, and Established Church opposition continued until 1860. Catholics were divided and would have preferred a denominational system. Archbishop Murray supported it but was opposed by MacHale. Nonetheless, after some suspicion, Rome allowed the Church to embrace the new system,[57] though schools run by the Christian Brothers continued outside the system for many decades. In fact the national schools developed in practice into a system of denominational education with clerical managers. Thus by 1870 only 5 per cent of the Catholic children attending national schools were at truly multi-denominational schools.[58]

Third-level or university education was the next battleground when in 1845 Sir Robert Peel announced the establishment of three colleges at Cork, Galway and Belfast, which were eventually to form part of the Queen's University. Though non-denominational they were obviously intended to meet the needs of Catholics in the case of the first two and of Presbyterians in the case of the third, Anglicans already having Trinity College Dublin to meet their university needs. Quickly dubbed the 'godless colleges' by the O'Connellites, the colleges had their supporters among the Catholic hierarchy, including Murray once again. Attempts to gain concessions such as multiple denominational chairs for religiously-sensitive subjects failed, however. The colleges were opposed by

54 Akenson, *Education experiment*, p. 376. **55** Adams, 'Hedge schools,' in Donnelly and Miller (eds), *Irish popular culture*, pp 97–117; McManus, *Hedge school*. **56** Coolahan, *Irish education*. **57** Kerr, *Peel, priests and politics*, pp 59–62. **58** Connolly, *Priests and people*, pp 86–7.

MacHale and eventually by Cullen, the new power in the land. Though the Belfast college was a success, those in Cork and Galway were relative failures.[59] Cullen founded his own Catholic University in 1854 with the idealistic educationalist and Anglican convert, John Henry Newman, as rector. Because its qualifications lacked state recognition this, too, was a failure, apart from its Medical School, whose students could take exams in state-recognized institutions.

An impasse had been reached, with the hierarchy demanding denominational endowment and British governments adamantly resisting it. In 1868 Lord Mayo's plan for a non-endowed charter for the Catholic University failed. Gladstone's 1873 scheme to amalgamate all existing university institutions in Ireland led to the downfall of his government. An unsatisfactory but workable compromise was found in 1879 by the Tories, who established the Royal University as a qualifications body whose examinations could be sat by men and, indeed, women, from any institution or none. Fellowships of this university were awarded to the staffs of a variety of educational institutions including the Catholic University, now reconstituted as University College Dublin, under the direction of the Jesuits. This was a form of indirect endowment. The eventual, partial moderation of the hierarchy's demands led to a final solution in 1908. Two government-funded, teaching universities were established, the Queen's University of Belfast and the National University of Ireland. The latter subsumed the Queen's Colleges at Cork and Galway and UCD into an unofficially Catholic grouping.[60]

By contrast with the university sector, secondary or intermediate education was tackled with a slightly less protracted struggle. It was a much smaller sector compared with that of primary education. In 1871 there were 587 'superior schools' in Ireland with 24,170 pupils, compared with nearly half a million national school pupils.[61] Only half the pupils in secondary education were Catholics. There was a relatively large endowed sector under the control of the Church of Ireland, though there were a number of prestigious Catholic secondary schools such as Castleknock, Clongowes Wood and Blackrock colleges. The solution hit on to accommodate the needs of Catholics in secondary education in the 1878 Intermediate Education Act was a system of indirect endowment similar to that applied to the university question the following year. Pupils were paid scholarship money and their schools fees based on their performance at public examinations. The payment-by-results element, however, which was also introduced into national schools in 1879 had a deleterious effect on the quality of education, with pupils focused on cramming for examinations.

59 Kerr, *Priests, people and politics*, pp 91–2, 233, 309. **60** Murphy (ed.), *Castleknock College*, pp 68–80. **61** Akenson, 'Pre-university education, 1870–1921,' in Vaughan (ed.), *Union II, 1870–1921*, pp 523–38.

The nineteenth century thus ended with the state having entrusted considerable patronage and financial power into the hands of the Irish Churches in the educational arena. It was an outcome unforeseen by the Whig utilitarians of the 1830s who had begun the process or by their enemies, the new Irish Tory littérateurs who saw the written word as a prime weapon against Catholic superstition.

CHAPTER 7

Tory journalism and romantic nationalism, 1825–72

By the second third of the nineteenth century a Tory unionism, often with an evangelical hue, was coming to dominate Irish Protestantism, eventually eclipsing liberalism and radicalism and uniting Anglicans and Presbyterians in a common identity. It was to remain to the fore until repeated defeats, such as disestablishment, led southern unionism to develop a garrison mentality by the 1880s, and Ulster unionism began to assert itself with a semi-independent vigour. In parallel with the evangelical battle on the religious front, Irish Tory propagandists and writers waged a variant battle for cultural leadership in Ireland, rightly sensing that only in this way could the social, economic and political position of Protestantism be maintained in face of the rising Catholic classes. The Protestant Ascendancy based on law and force which had been defeated by Catholic emancipation had to be replaced by one based on hearts and minds if all was not to be lost. The 1830s were to be years of a Tory cultural nationalism which was wedded to Ireland's union with Britain and place in the empire, just as the 1840s were to be years of a romantic political nationalism, in Young Ireland and the *Nation* newspaper, which aspired to political independence. This chapter will explore the cultural nationalism of the 1830s and trace its links with later realist and Protestant Gothic strands in literature before turning to Young Ireland which, though politically different, was also influenced by it.

A central intellectual foundation for much Irish Tory thinking at the time was the work of Edmund Burke (1729–97).[1] This was ironic as Burke's view of the state was in the Whig tradition and one of the groups he had despised most was the Protestant Ascendancy in Ireland. A Protestant with some Irish Catholic links, Burke spent his political career in England and was ever a strong defender of the British constitution. He formulated the notion that there was a need for a match between the habits and customs of a people and their mode of government. Ignoring or removing those customs opened the way to despotism. This was the perspective which was to lead him not only to condemn the French Revolution but also to castigate British rule in India and north America and the rule of the Protestant Ascendancy in Ireland. A third of a century later, however, Irish Tories were using Burke for their own purposes and were gathering to themselves the mantle of long-established custom as a defence against the supposed neo-Jacobinism of the O'Connellite classes.[2]

1 Deane, 'Edmund Burke,' in Kearney (ed.), *Irish mind*, pp 141–56. 2 Gibbons, ' "Shadowy narrator," ' in Brady (ed.), *Ideology and the historians*, pp 99–127.

Literary journalism was the central forum for the campaigns of Irish Tories. In Britain the early nineteenth-century had seen the proliferation of a series of important journals, the Whig *Edinburgh Review* (1802), the Tory *Quarterly Review* (1809) and the dissenter *Eclectic Review* (1804) among them. John Wilson Croker, Lady Morgan's enemy, was to edit the *Quarterly Review*. Eventually, several Catholic journals were to join them, including the *Dublin Review* (1836). Though sponsored by O'Connell and written for by Maynooth professors, such as the scholarly Charles Russell, the *Dublin Review* was always based in London and was essentially a British publication.[3]

At a less grand level were metropolitan-based magazines such as the *London Magazine*, *Fraser's* and *Blackwood's*, which provided career opportunities for a number of Irish writers. Several of them were from Cork, most prominently William Maginn (1793–1842), founder of *Fraser's Magazine* in 1830, and Francis Sylvester Mahony (1804–66), a wayward Catholic priest, who adopted the pseudonym 'Fr Prout'. Their humorously cynical Toryism may have been in reaction to the utilitarianism and bourgeois nationalism of the Cork they had left. It was certainly popular in London. Their work often involved questioning the provenance of other writers' works and charging favourite targets such as Thomas Moore with plagiarism.[4]

Meanwhile in Ireland the political press was moving from a position where it was expected to endorse government policy, often in return for much needed subsidies, to a position of greater independence. The *Morning Register* was an O'Connellite organ. However, the *Dublin Evening Post*, which supported Catholic emancipation, was prosecuted for seditious libel as a result on a number of occasions. In 1853 advertisement tax was repealed, and the newspaper stamp tax was abolished in 1855. Thereafter many newspapers were able to publish at the cost of one penny. In 1852 there were one hundred newspapers publishing at least weekly, seventeen of them in Dublin. Among the three Dublin dailies, the *Freeman's Journal* was to emerge as the central voice of moderate nationalism.[5] In Belfast the *Northern Whig* became the standard-bearer of Ulster liberalism. However, many papers, such as the influential *Dublin Evening Mail*, took a strong pro-Tory position.[6]

Evangelicals were active in the world of popular magazines. The Revd Caesar Otway (1780–1842) founded the *Christian Examiner and Church of Ireland Gazette* in 1825 and with George Petrie the *Dublin Penny Journal* in 1832. This latter lasted until 1837. The *Catholic Penny Journal* (1834–6) was established as a rival, and there were numerous other competitors in the market often with

3 Edwards and Storey, 'The Irish press,' in Swift and Gilley (ed.), *Victorian city*, pp 158–78. **4** Eagleton, *Crazy John*, pp 167–88. **5** Comerford, 'Ireland 1850–70,' in Vaughan (ed.), *Union I, 1801–70*, pp 372–95. **6** Inglis, 'The Press,' in McDowell (ed.), *Social life*, pp 92–105.

similar sounding titles but differing ideological standpoints. By the 1840s the publisher James Duffy had emerged as the major sponsor for popular Catholic magazines such as *Duffy's Irish Catholic Magazine* (1847–8).[7]

Of central importance to the Protestant intellectual project was the *Dublin University Magazine* (1833–77) which was founded by a number of students at Trinity College Dublin, though it had no formal link with the university.[8] Over the years it had eleven editors and ten proprietors, including such luminaries as Isaac Butt, Charles Lever and J.S. Le Fanu. It was at its zenith in the years before the famine, enjoying a significant reputation at home and abroad and a circulation as high as 4,000 copies per month.

The tenure of Isaac Butt (1813–79) as second editor (1836–41) saw the *Dublin University Magazine* at its most evangelical, with attacks on Catholicism and calls for greater efforts at conversion. Butt was an active organizer of the new Tory political structures that were then coming into being in groupings such as the Irish Protestant Conservative Society and the Irish Metropolitan Conservative Society. He believed in the opportunities which Ireland's union with Britain afforded it in the empire. Over the years, however, both as an economic commentator on the famine, in works such as *A voice for Ireland—famine in the land* (1847), and as a lawyer who defended Irish nationalists Butt's ideas began to change. In 1848 he was briefly involved with the Protestant Repeal Association and he was eventually to lead a home rule movement in the 1870s. Like many Irish Protestants he had been equivocal in his support for British governments. His later views were thus in as much continuity as discontinuity with his early views.[9]

'A dialogue between the head and heart of an Irish Protestant' by Samuel Ferguson (1810–86) was published in November 1833 in the *Dublin University Magazine*. It was an early and cogent expression of the dilemmas of Protestants, disillusioned with British governments and seeking cultural leadership in a country, the religion of whose majority they disliked and suspected. Ferguson's four review articles of James Hardiman's *Irish minstrelsy* (1831) in 1834 faulted Hardiman's Catholic nationalist perspective on Irish culture as well as the quality of his translations. Ferguson offered a vision in which the positive emotions and loyalty supposedly characteristic of native Irish character could be saved from O'Connellism and moulded by Protestant Ireland's traditions of enlightenment, enquiry and representative government.[10]

Ferguson had been born and educated in Belfast and apart from a brief flirtation with repeal in 1848 was a life-long unionist. He was a lawyer, the first

7 Hayley, 'Periodicals,' in Hayley and McKay (eds), *Irish periodicals*, pp 29–48. **8** Hall, Dublin University Magazine; Tilley, '*Dublin University Magazine*,' in Litvack and Hooper (eds), *Regional identity*, pp 58–65. **9** Spence, 'Isaac Butt,' *Bullán* 2:1 (1995), pp 45–60. **10** Ó Tuathaigh, 'Ferguson,' in Brown and Hayley (eds), *Samuel Ferguson*, pp 3–26.

head of the Public Records of Ireland (in 1867), was knighted in 1878 and ended his life as president of the Royal Irish Academy.[11] Later generations were to portray him as a bridge between the literary nationalism of the 1830s and the literary renaissance of the 1890s, eliding their differing political agendas.[12] Ferguson was certainly an advocate of an Irish literary as opposed to political nationalism. He believed that Celtic models would provide a cultural common ground for Irish Catholics and Protestants and drew on Gaelic legend and newly available translations of ancient manuscripts in his fashioning of a new sort of poetry in English which he hoped would achieve this.

Ferguson also wrote poems about contemporary events. As late as the 1880s, 'The curse of the Joyces, 15 December 1882, at Galway', about the Maamtrasna massacre, and 'At the polo ground' and 'In Carey's footsteps', about the Phoenix Park murders, deal with murder and politics. Nor are his Gaelic poems free from direct political agendas. 'Conary', published in *Poems* (1880), was based on a ninth-century Irish story. In it a British pirate ignores pleas not to destroy the Irish tradition, pleas which resonate with those of Ferguson's own cultural nationalism against the deleterious interference of the British state in Ireland.[13]

Ferguson's central text *Congal* (1872) has also often been read in terms of a contemporary political allegory. It is based on *The banquet of Dun na n-Gedh and the battle of Magh Rath* (1842) edited by John O'Donovan. Ferguson's long narrative poem, which had parallels with Tennyson's *Idylls of the king*, is the story of the conflict between the pagan king Congal of Ulster and the Irish Christian king Domnal. Allegorical readings of the conflict between the free Protestant spirit and clericalized Catholicism, between Ulster and Ireland or even between Ireland (Congal) and Britain (Domnal) suggest themselves.[14] Alternatively the poem, which consistently emphasizes how everyone in Ireland comes from a group which entered or invaded the country at some point, may be attempting to dissolve altogether that opposition between dominating invader and dominated native which Ferguson found such an obstacle to his own vision for Ireland.[15]

Evangelical crusades rely on the zeal of converts to give them added impetus. Mortimer and Samuel O'Sullivan were two Protestant converts from Catholicism who themselves became strenuous advocates of evangelism and a distinct early influence in the *Dublin University Magazine*. Another convert was the peasant novelist William Carleton (1794–1869).[16] Though he allowed himself to work for literary propagandists in his early career, such as Caesar Otway, his work never degenerated into mere propaganda and he himself was a very secular sort of Protestant.

11 Denman, *Samuel Ferguson*. **12** Mercier, *Literature*, p. 95. **13** Welch, *Irish poetry*, p. 141. **14** Eagleton, *Scholars and rebels*, p. 66; Mercier, *Literature*, p. 87. **15** Graham, *Ideologies of epic*, pp 104–10. **16** Wolff, *Carleton*.

Carleton was born into a Catholic peasant family at Prillisk, Clogher, Co. Tyrone and educated at a hedge school. He decided he wanted to be a priest but his chances for acceptance at Maynooth seem to have ended when a cousin called Keenan, who was a priest and with whom he had been studying, was suspended by the bishop of Clogher. This was a blow to his Catholic loyalties that were loosened even further by a pilgrimage to Lough Derg in 1817. Carleton began to move around the country, finding work as a teacher, learning of the work of agrarian groups and in 1817 seeing the hanged bodies of those who had been executed for the fire at Wild Goose Lodge in which eight members of a Co. Louth family had died for opposing an agrarian group. By 1819 Carleton was in Dublin, had work as a teacher and was moving in Protestant circles. He was being paid £60 per annum by the Sunday School Society. In 1827 he met Otway, who published his first story in the *Christian Examiner*. A dozen more stories of peasant and clerical life were to follow over the next few years, though, when re-edited for publication in Carleton's book collections of stories, their anti-Catholicism was often toned down.

Carleton's most significant collection of peasant stories, *Traits and stories of the Irish peasantry*, was published in two series, in 1830 and 1833 respectively. The first series is more focused on folk language and custom and the second more on plot. Carleton has his narrators mediate between the peasant world of the stories and the world of their Ascendancy and English readers, by generally arranging for them to have a foot in both camps. They often grow up in peasant society but receive an education and rise to the ranks of gentlemen elsewhere which allows them to be trusted by middle-class readers as they relate stories of peasant life.[17]

Carleton began publishing full-scale novels and continued also to publish in journals and magazines such as the *Dublin University Magazine* and the *Nation*. His reputation was growing and the aged Maria Edgeworth wrote to Lord John Russell that she had read all his works and found them very illuminating of Irish life.[18] In 1848 he was awarded a government pension of £200 per annum. The same year, however, he had also apparently toyed with extreme Irish nationalism by writing for the *Irish Tribune*. By 1850 he had moved to London, his best writing years already behind him.

Carleton died in 1869 with a Protestant rector and local Jesuit appropriately disputing his death-bed religion.[19] The tenor of his novels depended to a degree on for whom he was writing. William Curry, owner of the *Christian Examiner*, was one of his publishers. Another was James Duffy, at the other end of the religious spectrum, who published three novels of Carleton in his library of Ireland

17 Chesnutt, *Carleton*, p. 141; Hayley, *Carleton's 'Traits and stories'*, pp 390–3. **18** Wolff, *Carleton*, p. 112. **19** Ibid., p. 128.

series. Nonetheless, Carleton was not strongly religious, was never part of the establishment and always retained a sense of Catholic grievance.[20]

The ten years from 1839 were the high point of Carleton's career as a novelist, as opposed to a short story writer. His analysis of the ills of Irish society found much blame to lay both politically with the various organized interest groups in the country and morally in personal behaviour. *Fardorougha, the miser* (1839) is both sympathetic and comic in its portrait of a man who loses everything.[21] *Art Maguire* (1845) is about temperance and is dedicated to Fr Mathew. *Rody the rover* (1845) attacks Ribbonmen and *The tithe proctor* (1849) Whiteboys. *Parra Sastha* (1845) is about peasant squalour and its possible reform. *Valentine McClutchy* (1845), *The black prophet* (1847) and *The emigrants of Ahadarra* (1848), perhaps Carleton's three greatest novels, deal with land, famine and emigration, the key issues of the famine decade.

Valentine McClutchy changed perceptions of Carleton with its pro-Catholic, anti-evangelical and anti-Orange tone, though Carleton claimed in the preface that he had not changed his principles and remained a liberal conservative. In it the corrupt rule of a land agent is reversed by the return of the absentee landlord in the manner of the age of Edgeworth and Morgan. Though set in the famine of 1817, *The black prophet*, which was dedicated to the prime minister Lord John Russell, is an indictment of the land system then currently facing the cataclysm of the famine. Some critics, however, have found its lasting value to reside in its socio-political rather than in its literary merits. Finally, *The emigrants of Ahadarra*, set in 1808, is about a much put-upon and unjustly treated tenant family, the McMahons, who are saved from emigration by the return of the landlord.

Carleton went on to write another eight novels in the remaining two decades of his life. But his moment had passed, not least because the English appetite for serious Irish fiction and poetry had declined even further. Ferguson, indeed, had hardly ever been a great commercial success. The tendency had been apparent from the 1830s as had its mirror image, a growing British desire to consume non-threatening, humorous images of Ireland, reliant on a very crude version of national character. This issued will be explored further later on. Here, however, it forms the context for examining the literary careers of Samuel Lover (1797–1868) and Charles Lever (1806–72). Lover's *Rory O'More* (1837) and *Handy Andy* (1842) were highly successful exercises in comic stereotype.[22] Popular in England they were denounced by Irish nationalists. Lover is often linked with Lever because of the similarity of his novels with the latter's *Harry Lorrequer* (1839), *Charles O'Malley* (1841) and *Jack Hinton* (1843). Lever's early success also damned him with nationalists and others. In 1842 Carleton accused

20 Vance, *Irish literature*, pp 141–7. **21** Sloan, *Anglo-Irish fiction*, p. 191. **22** Ibid., p. 187.

him of 'selling us for pounds, shillings and pence'.[23] However, the more serious and sombre turn that his fiction took after 1845 all but lost him his English audience where he had previously been compared with Scott and Dickens.[24]

Lever had qualified in medicine in 1831 and worked as a doctor at Kilrush, Co. Clare, and at Portstewart on the north coast.[25] Between 1837 and 1842 he and his family lived at Brussels. He returned to Dublin to edit the *Dublin University Magazine* for £1,200 per annum. He lasted in the post until 1847 when he moved to Florence. He remained in Italy for the rest of his life, holding a number of diplomatic posts which culminated in that of consul at Trieste in 1867, dying in 1872.

From the mid-1840s Lever's novels began to become more critical of British rule in Ireland. This is true of *Tom Burke of 'Ours'* (1844), *The knight of Gwynne* (1847), *Roland Cashel* (1850), *The confessions of Con Cregan* (1850) and *Sir Brook Fossbrooke* (1866). Equally, there is a sympathy for the Irish peasantry in *St Patrick's eve* (1845), which deals with the 1832 cholera epidemic, and an understanding of the collapsing power of the Ascendancy in *The Martins of Cro' Martin* (1856) and *Barrington* (1863). In a change from his early novels Lever's later books are populated by outsiders rather than insiders. Thus, Mary Martin of *The Martins of Cro' Martin* runs her family estate as an apparently marginal member of her family, unaware of her true identity as daughter of the heir.[26]

The O'Donoghue (1845), a novel set in 1798, is a major and critical analysis of the Irish land situation. It won Lever no new friends for neither the representative of rational English rule nor the native aristocratic O'Donoghues succeed as landlords, the latter veering between Anglicization and extreme nationalism, though Kate O'Donoghue holds out hope for a reasonable course between the two.[27] In *Luttrell of Aran* (1865) the differing economic and aesthetic positions of life in Ireland and England are revealed. Whereas in England the pursuit of a simple life can lead to the prize of aesthetic contemplation, in Ireland wealth is necessary to create the leisure needed for contemplation.[28]

Lever's final novel *Lord Kilgobbin* (1872) is one of his most important but least known.[29] An array of characters, representing everything from British rule in Ireland, in the person of Cecil Walpole, on the one hand, to its Fenian alternative, represented by Daniel Donogan, on the other, converge on the castle of the Kearney family. The most despised presence in the novel, however, is undoubtedly that of the newly prosperous Catholic commercial class, much disliked by Lever. Reactions to the nearby Bog of Allen determine the level of social and

23 Jeffares, *Irish writing*, p. 158. **24** Haddelsey, *Charles Lever*; Morash, 'Novels of Charles Lever,' in Rauchbauer (ed.), *Ancestral voices*, pp 61–76. **25** Bareham (ed.), *Charles Lever*. **26** Bareham, 'Charles Lever and the outsider,' in Bareham (ed.), *Charles Lever*, pp 96–122. **27** Rix, 'Lever,' in Kosok (ed.), *Studies in Anglo-Irish literature*, pp 54–64. **28** Morash, 'Lever's post-famine landscape,' in Bareham (ed.), *Charles Lever*, pp 94–5. **29** Ibid., pp 86–95.

political integration into Irish culture, with Walpole experiencing it as a nightmare and Donogan seeing its beauties. Kate Kearney represents a middle way between English rule and nationalism and the hope for a continuing role for the propertied classes. Her position, however, is overtaken by that of Nina Kostalergi, the half-Irish niece of Lord Kilgobbin and a Lever self-projection. She returns from continental exile to Ireland, is won over to patriotism, loved by the people, marries the rebel Donogan, and flees with him to the idyll of the new world.[30]

In spite of this ending Lever's is a realistic engagement with Irish life, albeit one over time that has moved from a conservative stance to one somewhat more sympathetic to nationalism. Poetry as well as fiction was a vehicle for such a generally political engagement. Aubrey de Vere (1814–1902), son of Sir Aubrey de Vere, became a Catholic in 1851 and wrote Catholic devotional poetry, such as *May carols* (1857). His politics as a liberal Tory did not change, however. *Inisfail: a lyrical chronicle of Ireland* (1861) is a sequence of 132 lyric poems, the longest poem by an Irish writer in English, which explores Irish history, is often critical of England, and employs dramatic voices in the manner of Browning.[31]

Even more focused on social and political realities is *Laurence Bloomfield in Ireland* (1864), a poetic rendition of the Irish land question by William Allingham (1824–89).[32] He was born in Ballyshannon, Co. Donegal, and worked in a bank and the customs service while making friends with such British literary luminaries as Leigh Hunt, Tennyson, Carlyle, Coventry Patmore and the pre-Raphaelites. Allingham was eventually able to settle in England and in 1874 became editor of *Fraser's*. *Lawrence Bloomfield in Ireland* is the 5,000-line story of a young landlord who returns to manage his estates, dismissing his bad land agent and successfully offering a new deal to his tenants, who have been partially enticed by the Ribbonmen. The poem embodies a liberal humanist hope for Ireland's future.[33]

If the Tory cultural nationalism of the 1830s had in part issued into the steady, sociological realism of the former *Dublin University Magazine* editor, Charles Lever, in the 1860s the less steady and more anxious side of Irish Protestantism had already found an outlet in the tradition of 'Protestant Gothic'. This was pioneered by Charles Robert Maturin (1780–1824) and later exemplified by the *Dublin University Magazine* owner, Joseph Sheridan Le Fanu (1814–73). A variety of explanations have been put forward for the Anglo-Irish

30 Cahalan, *Irish novel*, p. 70. **31** Chris Morash, 'Aubrey de Vere,' *Canadian Journal of Irish Studies* 20:2 (1994): pp 45–52; Schirmer, *Irish poetry*, p. 175. **32** Warner, *William Allingham*. **33** Brown, 'Allingham's Ireland,' *Irish University Review* 13:1 (1983), pp 7–13; Hughes, 'Allingham's *Laurence Bloomfield*,' *Victorian Poetry* 28:2 (1991), pp 103–17; Schirmer, *Irish poetry*, p. 124; Sheeran, 'Anglo-Irish literature,' *A Yearbook of English Studies* 13 (1983), pp 97–115; Welch, *Irish poetry*, p. 178.

interest in Gothic in the nineteenth century. It may have been a function of the repressed guilty of the Ascendancy at being in possession of another race's land or an attempt to find a magical equivalent to the supernatural power of Catholicism, a notion complemented by the later interest of the Yeats generation in the occult.[34] A third view sees it as copper-fastening the coherence of the isolated Anglo-Irish family. A final version argues that the Gothic interest in the destruction of survivals of the past in the present, such as vampires, expresses an antagonism to the perceived threatening anachronism, from a certain Anglo-Irish perspective, of an Irish identity based on a racial Celtic self-identification.[35]

Maturin was born in Dublin and was an Established Church clergyman, serving in Dublin from 1805. His clerical career was somewhat blighted by his love of dancing and fine clothes. He was the author of plays as well as of novels, and his tragedy *Bertram* was a success at Drury Lane, London in 1816. Issues of gender preoccupy Maturin's fiction, unsurprisingly for a male writer in a *genre* then dominated by women. *The wild Irish boy* (1808) is a commentary not only on Lady Moragan's similarly entitled novel but also on Edgeworth's *Belinda*.[36] *The Milesian chief* (1812) mixes some of the material of a 'national marriage' novel with an account of 1798. *Women* (1818) moves towards the Gothic area in a story of a man who falls in love with both a mother and her daughter.

His most significant work, however, was *Melmoth the wanderer* (1820). In it John Melmoth, a contemporary student, learns of an ancestor who a century and a half before had extended his life in return for his soul and still lives. He reads of the accounts of Melmoth by a traveller called Stanton and meets a shipwrecked Spaniard, Moncada, who has experienced the Inquisition and learned stories of Melmoth from the Jew Adonijah, in the 'The tale of the Indians', in which Melmoth tries to seduce a young castaway, and two other embedded stories, 'The tale of Guzman's family' and 'The lovers' tale'. Before all the stories can be fully told, however, Melmoth himself appears and finally expires.

In spite of having an apparent mission to entice others into a similar fate to himself, Melmoth often shows little interest in doing so. Indeed, the real interest in him as a character is the variety of supernatural and not so supernatural guises in which he appears in the various layers of the novel. Sometimes he is like a ghost and at other times more like a sinful human being. There is a similarly large catalogue of Biblical, mythical and literary templates of evil which are summoned up in connection with him. He appears both as Satan or the servant of Satan and as an evil Adam, as a Byronic Cain, a Prometheus and as both a Faust and a Mephistopheles. Evil is diffuse in the novel and, indeed, is at its most

34 Eagleton, 'The Anglo-Irish novel,' *Bullán* 1:1 (1994), pp 17–26; Eagleton, *Heathcliff*, pp 187–92. **35** Backus, *The Gothic family romance*; Morash, 'Supernatural narrative,' in Stewart (ed.), *Supernatural and the fantastic*, i, pp 123–42. **36** Pearson, 'Maturin's *The wild Irish boy*,' *Studies in Romanticism* 36:4. (1997): pp 635–50.

menacing in 'Guzman's tale' whose Gothic obsessions are located in the family rather than in a supernatural source.[37]

Voyeurism features in *Melmoth*, and the novel is interested in how people behave under stress but in doing so also probes the reader's motives for sharing in such an interest. Those under stress are often men reduced to a female passivity by being imprisoned or subject to abuse, a theme which links *Melmoth* into the concerns with gender that pervade Maturin's writings.[38]

Melmoth was written in the Godwinian tradition of Gothic with first-person testimony, flashbacks and stories within stories. It is often discussed in terms of marking the end of the great movement in English Gothic writing that had begun with Horace Walpole. In terms of its subsequent importance it was certainly an influence on Blazac, Baudelaire, Poe and Stevenson and was a major influence on the tradition of Irish Protestant Gothic from Le Fanu to Bram Stoker.[39]

Le Fanu was also from an Established clerical family, though of Huguenot descent.[40] He grew up in Co. Limerick during the tithe war when his father saw his income much reduced. He was a young Tory zealot, though he briefly flirted with political nationalism in the 1840s, and his stories for the *Dublin University Magazine* were posthumously published as *The Purcell papers* (1880). He had interests as owner and editor in a number of papers, most notably the *Dublin Evening Mail*, before buying the *Dublin University Magazine*, largely as a vehicle for his own novels. After he sold it, he serialized some of his works in *All the year round*, which had been founded by Dickens.

Some of Le Fanu's novels, such as *The cock and anchor* (1845) and *The fortunes of Col. Torlogh O'Brien* (1847) deal with relations between Catholics and Protestants in Ireland in the conventional setting of the historical novel. *The house by the churchyard* (1863) is a murder story set in eighteenth-century Ireland. Le Fanu's next publisher's contract stipulated that any new novel should be modern and set in England. His Gothic masterpiece *Uncle Silas* (1864) is indeed set in England and in the context of a Swedenborgian world-view, which interested Le Fanu, though it is customary also to read the work as an Irish novel. It is the story of Maud Ruthyn who goes to live with her uncle Silas, after her father's death. He first tries to have her marry his son Dudley and then to kill her to inherit her property. Her father's and uncle's houses represent various forms of Anglo-Irish life, alienated both from English and Irish realities, though the novel also celebrates a redemptive element in female experience.[41]

37 Baldick, 'Introduction,' in Maturin, *Melmoth the wanderer*, pp vii-xix; Smith, 'Maturin's *Melmoth the wanderer*,' *English Studies* 74:6 (1993), pp 524–35; Stott, '*Melmoth the wanderer*,' *Études Irlandaises* 12:1 (1988), pp 41–52. **38** Ellis, *Gothic novels*, pp 166–78. **39** Coughlan, 'The Recycling of "Melmoth," ' in Zach and Kosok (eds), *Comparison and impact*, pp 181–91; Punter, *Literature of terror*. **40** Begnal, *Joseph Sheridan LeFanu*; McCormack, *Sheridan Le Fanu*. **41** Milbank, *Gothic in Victorian fiction*, p. 195.

In a glass darkly (1872) is a collection of three short stories, followed by two longer ones, represented as the cases of Dr Hesselius, a device of sceptical narration in Gothic fiction which would be used by Bram Stoker in *Dracula* (1897).[42] In the three shorter stories the possibility of a natural explanation remains open. The monkeys who haunt the central character in 'Green Tea' may be supernatural in origin or not but they carry the symbolic resonance of the Irish who were regularly linked with simians in the hostile caricature of the times. The pursuit of the innocent Laura by the vampire Carmilla in Styria, in the longer story 'Carmilla', may also touch on Anglo-Irish fears of a resurgent Catholicism, with Carmilla presented as a sort of banshee. She belongs to an ancient family but can be countered by a baron with antiquarian knowledge, suggesting the Anglo-Irish antiquarians who sought to use knowledge of Ireland's past to their own community's cultural advantage.

An instructive parallel in the lives of Butt, Ferguson and Le Fanu is their flirtation with political romantic nationalism in the 1840s, especially with the Young Ireland movement. Though in some ways an adjunct to O'Connellism, the Young Ireland movement and romantic nationalism in general can be seen as a third channel for Tory cultural nationalism, in addition to realism and Gothicism. Indeed, the sobriquet 'Orange Young Ireland' was sometimes jokingly and anachronistically applied to Butt, Ferguson and others. The world of Young Ireland, however, was also in many ways quite different from 1830s cultural nationalism

In October 1842 a weekly newspaper, the *Nation*, was founded by Charles Gavan Duffy (1816–1903), a Co. Monaghan Catholic journalist, John Blake Dillon (1816–66) of a Co. Mayo Catholic shopkeeper family, and Thomas Osborne Davis (1814–45) of English and Anglo-Irish Ascendancy ancestry.[43] It was founded with O'Connell's blessing, and he hoped that it would attract, younger, Protestant and more liberal elements to support Repeal. The *Nation* soon ran into conflict with the *Pilot*, another O'Connellite paper that advocated an explicit Catholic nationalism and did not like the *Nation*'s apparently greater cultural and religious pluralism. The fact that the *Nation* became the more popular paper, eventually reaching a readership of perhaps 250,000,[44] and that it was soon distrusted by the Catholic clergy meant that O'Connell had to seek to keep it under control.

By the middle of 1845 tensions between O'Connell and Young Ireland, a term which had first mockingly been coined in 1844, reached a head over the question of the Queen's Colleges which O'Connell opposed and Young Ireland supported. During the course of a debate Davis's reference to one of his oppo-

42 Tracy, 'Introduction,' in Le Fanu, *In a glass darkly*, pp vii-xxviii. **43** Davis, *Young Ireland*. **44** Cairns and Richards, *Writing Ireland*, pp 32–7.

nents as 'my very Catholic friend', allowed O'Connell to question the impartiality of his own credentials.[45] By the autumn of 1845 Davis was dead and John Mitchel (1815–75), a new leader of the group, of Ulster unitarian background, was writing in the *Nation* of how railways could be prevented from being of use to the government during a rebellion. Duffy, the paper's editor, was prosecuted as a result. Eventually, in July 1846 Young Ireland split off from the O'Connellites over O'Connell's demand that everyone subscribe to 'peace resolutions' which renounced the use of violence for political ends. At the end of the process the Young Irelanders found they had a new ally and, indeed, leader in William Smith O'Brien (1803–64). Of gentry background and a one-time Tory, he had tried to mediate between Old (O'Connellite) and Young Ireland as a 'middle-aged Irelander' but now found himself siding with the more radical group.[46]

In January 1847 the Young Irelanders founded an organization called the Irish Confederation. Within the next eighteen months a network of 224 Confederate clubs had been established in twenty-six of the thirty-two counties with approximately 45,000 members. Apart from Dublin with fifty-six clubs, the movement was at its strongest in east Munster, especially Tipperary with forty-nine clubs and Cork with thirty-three clubs. These clubs appealed mostly to young men in search not only of patriotic commitment but also of comradeship and good times and established a pattern for such organizations that would be repeated later in the century.[47]

By early 1848 the new French revolution was radicalizing Irish nationalist opinion and seemed to hold out the prospect for an insurrection in famine-torn Ireland. Meanwhile splits were developing within Young Ireland itself between moderates such as Duffy and the radical Mitchel, who broke away from the *Nation* to found his own *United Irishman*. Eventually Mitchel was to be convicted of treason-felony and transported to Tasmania, from where he escaped to America in 1853 where he ran into trouble with the Catholic archbishop of New York and later controversially supported the Confederate States during the civil war. Meanwhile, Smith O'Brien lead a brief and abortive rising in Co. Tipperary in July 1848, being sentenced to death and subsequently transported to Australia when the sentence was commuted. This effectively ended Young Ireland, though the sonorous Duffy, who was one of the least revolutionary of the Young Irelanders and was eventually to become premier of Victoria in Australia, endeavoured to manipulate its historical reception in his numerous subsequent writings on the period.[48] Nonetheless, the achievement of Young Ireland was considerable, effectively complementing, if not entirely replacing, the utilitari-

45 Ibid., p. 40. **46** Davis, *William Smith O'Brien*. **47** Owens, 'Clubs of the Irish Confederation,' in Geary (ed.), *Rebellion and remembrance*, pp 51–63. **48** Knowlton, 'Charles Gavan Duffy,' *Éire-Ireland* 31:3 and 4 (1996), pp 189–208.

an O'Connellite notion of the nation with the transcendental nation of romanticism.

Of the Young Ireland leaders Thomas Davis most closely approximated to the cultural profile of someone who might have been a Tory cultural nationalist as easily as a political romantic nationalist.[49] In July 1840 he had addressed the Historical Society at Trinity College Dublin with the arresting assertion, 'Gentlemen you have a country!' His father was English and his mother a member of the rather disreputable Atkins family of Mallow, Co. Cork, whose members were given to internecine murder. Seizing on the existence of a remote Gaelic ancestor, Davis adopted the pseudonym 'The Celt' for much of his writing.

Davis had begun his intellectual development as a utilitarian Benthamite.[50] Like J.S. Mill, though, he discovered the need to supplement such a position with a cultural dimension. His growing bourgeois nationalism would be based on a cultural agenda, albeit that of an Irish culture in the English language. He believed that before a national epic, the product of a heroic national culture, could be created the prior stages of literary development had to be passed through. In particular, the epic required a basis in ballad and folk song.[51] Among the early influences on Davis in this regard was the French historian Augustin Thierry who had written sympathetically of Ireland. Thierry in turn had been influenced by Thomas Moore and wrote of Moore's lyric Irish world of song and harp as if it really existed. Davis was so influenced by Thierry that he came to believe that such a society could actually be brought into existence. The trouble was that Irish ballads were not in a healthy condition. The *Nation* would have to supply the deficiency.

It was Duffy who first proposed ballads in the *Nation* and in May 1843 *The spirit of the nation*, a collection of ballads, was published.[52] Meanwhile, in the *Nation* itself there was an intense discussion about ballads. Of the three traditions of Irish ballads, the Gaelic ballad, the street ballad and the Anglo-Irish ballad, the third was the form which the *Nation* sought to rehabilitate, believing the other two have become degraded in various ways. The Anglo-Irish ballad was of course the tradition of Thomas Moore, whom Davis praised in December 1844, though he felt that more forceful popular ballads than Moore's were now needed. Between November 1844 and January 1845 two articles in several parts entitled, 'A ballad history of Ireland' and 'Irish songs', were published. These laid down a romantic theoretical basis for the ballad and projected the launch of two new undertakings, 'Songs of the Irish nation' and 'Songs for the street and field', though few ballads were actually written as a result.

49 Molony, *Thomas Davis*; Sullivan, *Thomas Davis*. **50** Brown, *Irish literature*, pp 46–56. **51** Lloyd, *Anomalous states*, p. 91. **52** Kenny, 'Ballads,' *Cahiers du Centre d' Études Irlandaises* 3 (1978), pp 31–45.

Davis's views were a mixture of utilitarianism, a bourgeois emphasis on moral improvement—at one stage the *Nation* campaigned strongly in favour of temperance—and a genuine romanticism.[53] He was the most secular of the Young Irelanders, seeking to relegate religious belief to a matter of private conscience in the hope of inserting Protestants into a cross-class, cross-religious alliance.[54] His secularism was thus similar to evangelicalism to the extent that both saw Catholicism as a problematic force that had in some way to be neutralized. Davis was always torn, though, between wanting to be a Celt and wanting a new Irish nationality embracing Celtic, Norman and Saxon elements. Davis's admonition to his fellow Trinity students that they had a nation was part of an address in which he warned that Protestants would have to adapt in the face of the rising number of educated Catholics. In his 'Letters of a Protestant on repeal', published in the *Nation* in 1842–3, he argued that Catholics needed Protestant help and leadership, in terms not dissimilar from those in the *Dublin University Magazine*. The difference was that Davis believed that Catholics ought to be trusted. His *The patriot parliament of 1689* (1843) argued that Catholic Jacobites had behaved well when in power.

Davis's early death enhanced his romantic image, even though romanticism was only one of the influences in his complex intellectual formation. Living until 1875, John Mitchel turned himself into a living romantic icon of Irish nationalism, largely on account of his autobiographical *Jail journal* (1854), in which he used the expression of his intense hatred of England to fuse his own identity with that of Ireland.[55] Mitchel was in the radical dissenting tradition of Joseph Priestley and Thomas Jefferson, believing in liberty and fairness though not necessarily in complete equality of opportunity.[56] With other Young Irelanders he was an admirer of Carlyle's 'might and right' doctrine, if not of his conclusions about England. Mitchel believed that Ireland needed to seize its opportunity for freedom.[57] His influence on nationalism extended beyond his own self-creation as a nationalist hero suffering for Irish freedom and into the nexus of historical myths that sustained that nationalism. His British genocide interpretation of the famine, advanced in his *The last conquest of Ireland (perhaps)* (1861), proved a powerful influence both in Irish America and in Ireland.

An early essay of Thomas Davis's entitled 'Udalism and feudalism' (1842) advocated tenant ownership as a solution to Ireland's land difficulty. The *Nation* itself went through an early phase of advocacy of agrarian reform until it turned more fully towards cultural nationalism. Agrarian radicalism reappeared in the

53 Dunne, 'Irish romantic writing,' pp 77–8. **54** Cairns and Richards, *Writing Ireland*, pp 32–41. **55** Flanagan, 'John Mitchel,' *Irish University Review* 1:1 (1970), pp 1–29; Ryder, 'John Mitchel and James Clarence Mangan,' *Irish Review* 13 (1992–3), pp 70–7. **56** Knowlton, 'John Mitchel,' *Éire-Ireland* 22:2 (1987), pp 38–55. **57** Morash, 'Mitchel's *Jail Journal*,' in Leerssen, Weel and Westerweel (eds), *Forging in the smithy*, pp 207–18.

Nation in the contributions of James Fintan Lalor (1807–49), the physically-disabled son of a Catholic middleman from Queen's Co., who called for a rent strike and for popular and social revolution, though his attempts to found a Tenant's Association in Co. Tipperary failed. His methods of argument relied on using the principles of English law to decide property claims to undermine the whole English position in Ireland. Though never a significant activist himself, Lalor became an important influence on Mitchel.[58]

Poetry featured widely in the *Nation* and much of it was written by women such as Speranza (Jane Elgee), Eva (Mary Eva Kelly), Finola (Elizabeth Treacy), Eithne (Marie Thompson) Mary (Ellen Mary Patrick Downing) and Thomasine (Thomasine Olivia Knight). Margaret Callan was briefly editor of the paper when Duffy was arrested in 1848.[59]

The greatest poet to write for the *Nation*, however, was James Clarence Mangan (1803–49), whose extravagant sartorial appearance, possible addiction to drugs and tragic life made him a symbol of romantic suffering to later poets such as Yeats. Like Carleton, he resisted complete assimilation to one or other side of the political and religious divide and refused to conform to the role of nationalist poet, as he refused himself final definition and identity.

Mangan grew up in Dublin, becoming an apprentice scrivener before turning to writing.[60] He had several romantic attachments in his life but never a serious relationship with a woman. In 1831 he became involved in journalism through the *Comet* newspaper, and later published his work in the *Dublin Penny Journal*, the *Irish Penny Journal*, the *Dublin Satirist*, the *Dublin University Magazine* and, eventually, the *Nation*. He was employed in the Ordnance Survey Office and then as a cataloguer in the library at Trinity College Dublin. Eventually, he died of cholera.

Mangan produced a significant body of enduring poetry, 'Dark Rosaleen', 'A vision of Connaught in the thirteenth century', 'O'Hussey's ode to the Maguire', 'Siberia' and 'The nameless one' among them. Some of Mangan's poems are entirely original. Others are versions of poems in Irish for which Petrie, O'Curry and O'Donovan provided literal translations. Yet other poems are translations from German, or supposed translations from Persian, Arabic, Turkish or Persian.[61] Some of his poems in these categories were collected in Oriental, German and Irish anthologies of his poetry.

Mangan saw himself in the great tradition of romantic poets.[62] However, because of his Catholic devotion and lack of sexual experience he was unable to

58 Buckley, *Lalor*. **59** Anton, 'Women and the *Nation*,' *History Ireland* 1:3 (1993), pp 34–8; Davis, *Young Ireland*; Melville, *Jane Francesca Wilde*. **60** Lloyd, *Mangan*; Shannon-Mangan, *Mangan*. **61** Donaghy, *Mangan*; Flanagan, 'Literature in English, 1801–91,' in Vaughan (ed.), *Union I, 1801–70*, p. 505; Welch, 'Mangan,' *Éire-Ireland*, 11:2 (1976), pp 36–55. **62** Andrews, 'Mangan,' *Irish University Review* 19:2 (1989), pp 240–63.

deploy those elements of blasphemy and eroticism on which the kind of high romanticism he aspired to depended. Nonetheless, he adopted three stereotypes in his writing to enable his romantic elevation. In his prose stories he tended to write in the Gothic mode. In poetry, on the other hand, he identified himself firstly with the persona of the forsaken lover and later on with the figure of the outcast, living in a lifeless wasteland. Some of his last pieces, such as 'Siberia' and 'A vision of Connaught in the thirteenth century', embody the wasteland motif to a very effective degree. Whereas for the most part his commitment to a tragic romanticism is never fully realized in his work, in these poems he does achieve a more searing personal integration of a key romantic motif. In this Mangan's life and death coincided with a wasteland experience being undergone by several million Irish people at the time, in the great famine.

CHAPTER 8

Catastrophe, 1801–51

The early nineteenth century saw the arrival of government censuses that provide unrivalled information on the economic and social structure of the Ireland of the time. In 1841 there were 10,000 large landowners. Among the tenantry there were 50,000 rich farmers with an average of around eighty acres each, 100,000 comfortable farmers with around fifty acres, 250,000 family farmers with twenty acres, 300,000 cottiers with five acres and 1,000,000 labourers with around one acre.[1] Two in five people lived in single-room mud cabins and a similar number in mud cabins with several rooms. In the more prosperous area bounded by Dublin and Cork and in parts of Ulster, however, two in five people lived in houses of five to nine rooms.[2]

This latter point illustrates the differing economic strengths of different parts of the country. Various models have been proposed for understanding the situation. Lynch and Vaizey's view of the economy saw it as divided between a commercial maritime zone, running from Belfast to Cork and including Limerick and Galway, and the poorer remainder of the country. Kevin Whelan's more recent view identifies four major economic archetypes at work in the regions of Ireland outside the cities. They were, firstly, a pastoral area in two zones, one in the northern parts of Leinster and Connaught and the other in a band between Kilkenny and Limerick. Secondly, there was a tillage triangle between Dundalk, Cork and Wexford, dominated by farmers and middlemen. Thirdly, came an area of small farmers in Connaught, west Munster and west Donegal, in which the rundale system, by which tenants' land might be dispersed in many different fields, was in partial operation. Fourthly, there was the Protestant industrial north and north-west in Ulster and surrounding regions in which families engaged both in farm and in home-based manufacturing work.[3]

Around one in five of the landowners was resident in Britain, absentees being most common in Ulster and Connaught. However, in spite of its importance in the novels of the time, non-residence was not itself the key issue in the relationship between landlords and tenants, as land agents were being increasingly employed to run estates in the name of the landlord.[4] What was important was the degree to which landlords were able and willing in invest in their estates in

1 Ó Gráda, 'Poverty, population,' in Vaughan (ed.), *Union I, 1801–70*, p. 114. **2** Freeman, 'Land and people,' in Vaughan (ed.), *Union I, 1801–70*, p. 253. **3** Ó Gráda, *Economic history*, pp 32–4, 41; Whelan, 'Settlement and society,' in Dawe and Foster (ed.), *Ulster literature*, pp 45–67. **4** Ó Gráda, *Economic history*, pp 124–9.

agricultural improvements and it was in this area that they were most open to criticism.

Because of legal changes and the way in which the poor law rate was levied on landlords, large-scale subletting was no longer so attractive to landlords. The middleman system therefore began to disintegrate. Cottiers were at the greatest disadvantage in the land system, however. They held their small 'conacre' plots for eleven months of the year from tenant farmers who could demand a cash or labour-in-kind payment as it suited them. They tended to demand cash when the harvest was poor, and they did not need so much labour, at times when the cottiers were themselves in even greater difficulties. Tenant farmers were often criticized by observers for their primitive farming techniques, relying on spade husbandry and customary labour processes such as the 'meitheal' or gathering by which neighbouring farmers would help each other out when ploughing or harvesting. In fact this was the result of a landlord-tenant relationship still operating within an essentially feudal framework, by which an economic surplus was effectively extracted by coercion, rather than within a capitalist competition framework.[5] The feudal relationship acted as a disincentive to investment in technical improvements in agriculture, though eventually there were moves to replace wooden with iron ploughs and sickles with scythes and to introduce crop rotation and better livestock strains.[6]

The French revolution and Napoleonic wars had been a boom time for Irish agriculture, with Britain effectively cut off from the continent and maintaining a large army in the field. Grain exports increased nearly thirteen-fold between 1780 and 1815. In the decade after the culminating battle of Waterloo, cereal prices declined by one third. On the other hand, the once accepted view that after 1815 there was a major shift away from tillage and towards pasture in Ireland is now treated with caution. Before the famine, tillage still accounted for 60 per cent of agricultural output.[7]

The population of Ireland had been growing dramatically. In 1740 it stood at two million, in 1800 at five and in 1845 at eight and a half. Seven in every eight people lived in the countryside.[8] However, the rate of population increase was declining. Between 1790 and 1821 it had varied between 1.4 per cent and 1.6 per cent per annum. In the 1820s it had declined to 0.9 per cent and in the fifteen years thereafter to between 0.5 per cent and 0.6 per cent.[9] The potato was the staple food of one third of the population. Poorer people ate between ten and twelve pounds of potatoes daily but also had access to milk and to turf for heating. The notion that Ireland was a country spiralling downwards into a cycle

5 Slater and McDonough, 'Feudalism,' *Research in Political Economy* 14 (1994), pp 63–118. **6** MacDonagh, 'Economy and society,' in Vaughan (ed.), *Union I, 1801–70*, pp 220–1. **7** Ó Gráda, *Economic history*, pp 28, 117–18. **8** Ó Gráda, 'Poverty, population,' p. 118. **9** Ó Gráda, *Economic history*, p. 69.

of overpopulation and poverty and that the famine was the necessary corollary is not now as strongly asserted as it once was.[10]

The infrastructure of communications was undergoing significant change.[11] The Ordnance Survey was engaged in map-making under Larcom and others. Sir Richard Griffith (1784–1878) was charged with land valuation. Road transport was improving with new roads and coach systems, provided by Charles Bianconi (1801–40) and others, which cut travel times by one third and fares by a half in the first four decades of the century. There was a huge government investment of one million pounds in the six hundred miles of canals, though they were never to be the complete success hoped for.[12] By 1845 there were less than seventy miles of railway in operation, though this was to increase to two thousand miles by 1870, when trains were carrying fourteen million passengers. At the same time sixty-five million letters were being delivered annually by the post office.[13] Apart from roads, the most significant transport development in the early part of the century had been the development of steam ship transport across the Irish Sea. This had begun in 1818, and by the 1840s there were one hundred crossings between Britain and Ireland per week.[14]

Banking had been in a precarious condition until an act of 1824 opened the way for joint stock operations. The previous fifteen years had seen a number of bank failures. After 1824 a more reliable system developed, but it still did not prevent a further banking crisis from occurring in 1836. More legislation followed, and by 1845 there were 173 bank branches in ninety towns. There were some two dozen banks, though the Bank of Ireland enjoyed a pre-eminence on account of its central banking role and because it was the issuer of notes. The client base for banking was a small one, however, being mostly made up of members of the upper and middle classes.[15]

In spite of Ireland's rural profile, a significant number of people were engaged in industry. In 1821 two-fifths of workers were employed in manufacturing, often in a rural, cottage industry setting, though this system's days were numbered. The cotton industry was in decline by the 1820s. Linen, however, which was concentrated in the north-east, was to survive, but it was increasingly to be concentrated in linen mills. The woollen industry was slower to be absorbed into the factory system than cotton and linen. Shipbuilding was another industry that was to flourish in the north-east. By the beginning of the twentieth century, Belfast was to be responsible for 8 per cent of world output. Industry did not fare so well in the rest of Ireland. However, alcohol was a sig-

10 Connolly, 'New work on the Irish famine,' *Victorian Studies*, 39:2 (1996), pp 205–16; Ó Gráda, *Before and after the famine*, pp 50–1, 122; Ó Gráda, *Economic history*, pp 12–23. **11** Freeman, 'Land and people.' **12** Ó Gráda, 'Industry and communications,' in Vaughan, ed.,*Union I, 1801–70*, pp 137–57. **13** Comerford, 'Ireland 1850–70,' in Vaughan (ed.), *Union I, 1801–70*, pp 372–95. **14** Ó Gráda, *Economic history*, p. 138. **15** Barrow, *Banking system*.

nificant Irish export, though Scotch dominated the world whisky market. Brewing trebled in size in the second half of the nineteenth century, with Guinness eventually becoming the largest brewing company in the world.[16]

The legislative union of Britain and Ireland had brought about an economic union, too. Import duties between the two countries were abolished by the 1820s. The two exchequers were united in 1817, and the British and Irish currencies assimilated in 1825. Ireland was to pay two seventeenths of United Kingdom expenditure.[17] In 1894 a royal commission on Irish finances concluded that Ireland had been over-taxed because poorer than Britain and thus more susceptible to indirect taxation.[18]

Throughout the nineteenth century and since, a debate has raged on the relationship between the union and Ireland's economic, especially its industrial, decline in the period. Ironically, having argued that Britain had inhibited Irish industry in the eighteenth century by the imposition of trade tariffs, nationalists now argued that industrial Britain was damaging Irish industry because of the lack of trade barriers. There was never been a definitive conclusion to a debate in which lack of resources, physical peripherality, a dearth of enterprise and even the absence of the supposed Protestant work ethic have been adduced as reasons for Ireland's industrial failure. Ireland's one advantage, low wages, did not help because it was a symptom of low productivity.[19] In recent times, opinion has moved towards a neutral if not a positive view of the union's economic effect on Ireland. Indeed, during the nineteenth century itself nationalist calls for economic protection tended to fall away.[20]

The greatest vulnerability in Ireland, however, was to famine, especially with the possible failure of the potato crop, on which such a large proportion of the population depended. There were significant famines in 1800–1 and 1817–19 in which 40,000 and 60,000 people respectively died, and lesser famines in 1822 and 1831. Nothing could compare though with the catastrophe of the Great Famine, which began in 1845 and lasted until the early 1850s. One million people died and a further million emigrated during the period, initiating a haemorrhage in the Irish population which declined in approximate terms from 8,500,000 in 1845 to 4,700,000 in 1891. Only six of Ireland's thirty-two counties lost less than 15 per cent of their populations during the years 1845–51. Eleven counties lost 25 per cent. Of those who died of starvation or disease between 1846 and 1851, two in five died in Connaught, one in five died in Ulster and three in ten in Munster, but only one in twelve in Leinster.[21]

16 Ó Gráda, *Economic history*, pp 272, 295, 308, 320, 323. **17** Ibid., pp 43–6. **18** Kennedy and Johnson, 'Union,' in Boyce and O'Day (eds), *Revisionist controversy*, pp 34–70. **19** Mokyr, *Why Ireland starved?* pp 2–3; Ó Gráda, *Economic history*, pp 307, 330, 338, 342. **20** Kennedy and Johnson, 'Union,' pp 49, 58. **21** Donnelly, *Potato famine*, pp 169, 176.

In 1845 two and a half million acres of land were planted with potatoes and half the crop was lost because of the appearance of potato blight. The next year only two million acres were planted and the blight extended to all parts of Ireland. Ironically, in 1847 the blight did not have a major impact on the crop. However, by then the effects of the famine meant that only one quarter of a million acres had been planted. In 1848 three times the 1847 level were planted but the blight returned in strength.

The first year of the famine coincided with the last year in power of Sir Robert Peel.[22] Indeed, Peel's determination to repeal the corn laws, which prohibited the importation of foreign corn into the United Kingdom until domestic prices had reached a predetermined level, was a response to the famine and brought about, albeit indirectly, the downfall of his government. It also brought about a split in his party which caused a widespread realignment in British politics and effectively kept the Tories out of power for nearly twenty years. Peel established a relief commission in November 1845. One hundred thousand pounds worth of Indian corn was purchased and was sold on to nearly seven hundred local relief committees, most of them in the west and south of Ireland, for resale to the people. By the summer of 1846 98,000 people were also being employed on public works programmes.

Peel's government saw its efforts as being of a temporary nature in the hope of stimulating the private importation of grain and of goading Irish landlords (who were subject to much criticism in Britain) into taking responsibility for relief. Peel's measures were subsequently often praised when compared with those of the successor Whig government under Lord John Russell. However, he thought of them as temporary, and had he remained in office his actions might not have differed greatly from those of the Whigs.

Russell's government undoubtedly proved to be less than sympathetic to interfering with the processes of laissez-faire economics.[23] Nonetheless, a certain amount of Indian corn was imported, though its release was delayed and the government refused to prevent the export of Irish grain. Its main emphasis changed to public works under the control of the Board of Works. Five million pounds was to be raised from local taxes on landlords. Payment to the starving was to be on the basis of work completed. Average pay was supposed to be one shilling per day, but with grain prices rising it bought less than hitherto. In fact many people were unable to earn more than seven pence per day. Bad weather meant no work, though eventually people were issued with half wages on bad days. In the course of one week in March 1847 nearly three-quarters of a million people were being employed in public works.

22 Ibid., pp 41–56; Kinealy, *Great calamity*, pp 31–70. **23** Donnelly, *Potato famine*, pp 65–80; Kinealy, *Great calamity*, pp 71–135.

Then in the spring of 1847 government policy changed again. Soup kitchens were to be set up and the poor law used to provide for famine relief.[24] Public works were to be phased out. Meanwhile, in England public opinion was growing restive with what it saw as the failure of the Irish to help themselves and with its exaggerated perception of the violence which was accompanying the famine, particularly as a result of the murder of Major Denis Mahon in 1847.[25] By this time mortality was very high, hundreds of people were dying daily and disease was spreading throughout the workhouses. People appeared emaciated and listless. By the summer of 1847 three million people were receiving soup, made of Indian meal, rice and oat meal. Mortality declined, though scurvy increased because the soup did not contain all the necessary elements for nutrition. With prices falling and large amounts of grain now being imported into the country, the soup kitchens were closed in the autumn of 1847.

In addition to government relief, there were a variety of private relief organizations in Ireland – the Quaker Central Relief Committee, the Mansion House Committee, the Irish Relief Committee and the General Relief Committee. The British Relief Committee was supported by Queen Victoria, who wrote a public letter on its behalf. Overall, it raised nearly half a million pounds, though British charity tended to diminish towards the end of 1847. Donations came form abroad, from the pope, the sultan of Turkey and the Choctaw tribe of Oklahoma, among others.

In the autumn of 1847 the government placed the burden of famine relief on the poor law system, unusually allowing outdoor relief as well as workhouse accommodation. However, the notorious Gregory clause in one of the enabling acts limited outdoor relief to those with a quarter of an acre or less, in an attempt to reduce the number of small-holders and to use the famine as an opportunity for land reform.[26] It caused many individuals to risk death rather than seek aid by giving up the security of their land. New workhouse and fever hospital provision was eventually put in place, with 250,000 places available by autumn 1849. Financial pressure was mounting on the poor law system. By 1849 twenty-two poor law unions in the west and south were effectively bankrupt. In response, the government instituted in June 1849 an Ireland-wide tax to support the poor law system, to the chagrin of many who saw this Irish only measure as a betrayal of the notion of a united kingdom of Ireland and Britain.

By early 1848 there were 120,000 people in the workhouses. In February 1848 about half a million people were receiving outdoor relief. In the autumn with a new system in operation the number receiving outdoor relief had risen to one and a half million, though the government was now determined to bring

24 Donnelly, *Potato famine*, pp 81–100. **25** Kerr, *Priests, people and politics*, pp 92–6. **26** Kinealy, *Great calamity*, pp 136–264.

relief work to an end. The same year the government introduced the first Encumbered Estates Act to enable, it was hoped, the transfer of bankrupt estates to new and more financially solvent landlords. Within a few years five million acres, a quarter of the land, had changed hands.

Blight, however, reappeared in 1848, and the treasury was forced once more to support the impoverished west of Ireland poor law unions. The next year 1849 was the last of wide-scale distress and death, though there was a change in the outbreak of disease from fever and typhus, associated with famine, to cholera. That year the harvest was good in the autumn, and the government arranged a visit from Queen Victoria to Cork, Dublin and Belfast to draw a symbolic end to the famine years. Nonetheless, there continued to be blight in Clare, Kerry, Limerick and Tipperary. Government policy now sought to end outdoor relief and to concentrate relief in workhouses. In 1850 the harvest was good, though distress continued in some areas such as Co. Clare, particularly in Kilrush.

In 1851 there were roughly 6,500,000 people in Ireland. Had population growth not been interrupted by famine and emigration, there ought to have been 9,000,000. The annual taxation revenue for the United Kingdom for the 1840s was around £53 million. The cost to the British treasury of famine relief amounted to £8 million over seven years. Some time after, around £69 million was spent on the Crimean War, a medium-scale conflict, though it has to be remembered that expenditure on war was considered a duty of governments at the time, whereas relief expenditure was not.[27]

As well as being a catastrophe causing enormous human suffering in its own right, the famine and the myths it generated had a fundamental effect on subsequent Irish attitudes especially to Britain and to landlords. Among the issues that arose were the questions of the export of food during the famine and of famine evictions. Whereas just before the famine almost half a million tons of grain were exported from Ireland annually, in 1847 only 146,000 tons were exported. During the famine imports of grain exceeded exports by a ratio of three to one. Banning exports of grain, for the failure to do which the British government was later much criticized, would have made some difference but probably not a decisive difference to the course of the famine.[28]

Over half a million people were evicted during the disaster.[29] The overall effects of the famine caused a dramatic change in the structure of land holding. One quarter of all farms disappeared, most of them under fifteen acres. Nearly three quarters of holdings of one acre or less vanished, half of those between one and five acres and over one third of those between five and fifteen acres.[30] The famine had the effect of restructuring the social configuration of the rural com-

27 Donnelly, *Potato famine*, pp 118–19. **28** Ibid., pp 214–15. **29** O'Neill, 'Famine evictions,' in King (ed.), *Famine, land and culture*, pp 29–70. **30** Daly, *Famine*, pp 120–1; Donnelly, *Potato famine*, pp 132–68.

munity and in many ways making what was left of it into something more prosperous and homogeneous than it had been before. This new cohesion reduced the opportunity for conflicts within the tenant community distracting from conflicts with landlords.

The famine was often mediated to the wider world through images of women. Women in fact fared somewhat better than men during it. The allocation of official relief in workhouses, for example, favoured women among younger adults, though males among children and the elderly.[31] Images of women in the famine were prominent among those that appeared in the *Illustrated London News*.[32] In famine texts, women often function as bearers of meaning with the emaciated maternal body in particular signalling a shocking lack of nourishment and the failure of the most basic form of shelter and protection. At the same time as images of women expressed the breakdown inherent in the famine, they also enabled an evasion of an analysis of the political and economic causes of it by focusing on moral and emotional registers.[33] Claims of the indescribability of the famine, which frequently occur in accounts, are part of a familiar literary trope and do not indicate a genuine inability of conventional discourse to deal with what was happening.[34]

The popular memory of the famine, as recorded much later by the Folklore Commission, focused on the export of food and bad landlords but not on British politicians and workhouses. The characterization of Queen Victoria as the famine queen was for the most part a creation of nationalists towards the end of the nineteenth century who wished to puncture the continuing popularity of the monarchy in Ireland. The popular memory of the famine was a constructed amalgam of personal memory and public discourse. In this regard, the influence of the Young Ireland group was key. Its members argued that there was enough food to feed the populace. As they wished Ireland to govern itself, it was in their interests to emphasize the maladministration aspects to the calamity.[35]

John Mitchel's view of the famine as a British genocide proved influential, especially in Irish America. The late twentieth-century revisionist view that the government essentially did all that was in its power to do, given the prevailing laissez faire ideology, has given way to a more critical assessment. This sees the government as callous and wilfully blinkered in its desire to purse economic and social reform in Ireland rather than to effect a humanitarian response to the crisis.[36]

31 Fitzpatrick, 'Women and the great famine,' in Kelleher and Murphy (eds), *Gender perspectives*, pp 50–69. **32** Crawford, 'Famine,' in Gillespie and Kennedy (eds), *Ireland: art into history*, pp 75–88. **33** Kelleher, *Feminization of famine*, pp 29, 39, 56, 74. **34** Morash, *Writing the Irish famine*; Ryder 'The famine and the *Nation*,' in Morash and Hayes (eds), *'Fearful realities,'* pp 151–63. **35** Donnelly, *Potato famine*, pp 37–40, 209–45; Murphy, *Abject loyalty*, pp 63–5, 282–4, 291–2. **36** Davis, 'Irish famine,' in O'Sullivan (ed.), *Meaning of the famine*, pp 15–39.

Political economy, with its belief in market mechanisms, certainly produced a strong ideological atmosphere against more interference in the market, both in Britain and in Ireland.[37] Richard Whately had been professor of political economy at Oxford before becoming the Estabished Church's archbishop of Dublin in 1831. The next year he founded the Whately chair of political economy at Trinity College Dublin, whose occupants had a five-year tenure, ensuring a succession of professors would eventually become an influential group. In 1847 the Dublin Statistical Society was founded and became an institutional redoubt for political economy. By removing the lower elements of the rural Irish social structure, the famine was achieving one of the goals which political economists thought necessary if Ireland was to be modernized. Though too late for its victims, it did have the effect of modifying the views of some political economists, most notably in Ireland John Elliot Cairnes (1823–75) and others such as Thomas Edward Cliffe Leslie (1827–82) and John Kells Ingram (1823–1907). Their new moral perspective on political economy led to a historicization of the discipline and to the realization that England did not provide an absolute model for all economic progress.[38] In England John Stuart Mill (1806–73) came to believe that Irish conditions required a special form of land reform. His influence on British politicians paved the way for remarkable concessions to Ireland during and after the land war.[39]

Of more importance than theories of political economy, though often allied with it in the complex world of British attitudes to the famine, was Christian providentialism. Lord John Russell and Lord Clarendon, the lord lieutenant, for example, were influenced by Liberal moralists who had a negative view of Irish character, wanted to reform Irish society and saw the famine as the opportunity to do so. They combined an optimistic version of political economy with a providentialist theodicy of 'natural laws'. God, through nature, was forcing Ireland into modernity, and the human suffering which the transition to the new era was producing was inevitable and often the result of human folly.[40] Of course, there were more extreme forms of providentialism, though not as influential in government, which saw the famine as a punishment for the moral failings of the Irish, for their Catholicism and for their political recalcitrance.[41] Queen Victoria was horrified by the sermon she heard on the national fast day for the famine. In it Bishop Wilberforce of Oxford effectively blamed the famine on the political agitation of the late Daniel O'Connell.

37 Boylan and Foley, *Political economy*; Boylan and Foley, ' "A nation perishing " ' in Morash and Hayes (eds), *'Fearful realities,'* pp 138–50; Eagleton, *Scholars and rebels*, pp 100–21. **38** Foley, 'Gender and political economy,' in Kelleher and Murphy (eds), *Gender perspectives*, pp 21–35. **39** Kinzer, *England's disgrace*. **40** Gray, *Famine, land and politics*, pp 331–7. **41** Miller, 'Irish Presbyterians,' in Hill and Lennon (eds), *Luxury and austerity*, pp 165–81; Murphy, *Abject loyalty*, p. 65.

The net effect of providentialism, political economy and the less than inclusive embrace of Ireland in the United Kingdom was to make the British response to the crisis far from creditable. Though the charge of genocide cannot be sustained, the moral outrage against the British government of the time that goes with it is now acknowledged by historians as valid and warranted. The impact of the famine was felt not only by those who were its direct victims. It was a factor in coalescing Irish nationalism in a more pronounced Anglophobic groove than ever, not least because such an attitude absolved Irish people from examining their own often less than virtuous efforts at self-preservation during the famine, at the expense of others.[42] In Britain the famine undermined the certainty, though in certain quarters only, that the British political establishment necessarily knew what was best for Ireland and fed one line of thought about Ireland which was that it required special, concessionary measures which would never have been considered for other groups. This came to a head in Gladstone's twenty-year crusade to pacify Ireland, which culminated in the land war and home rule crises of the 1880s. These in turn had themselves only been rendered possible on the Irish side by the narrowing social effect which the devastation of the famine had on rural Irish society. Such changes facilitated a greater ideological convergence around a notion of the nation conducive to an essentially bourgeois rural society. They bolstered Tridentine Catholicism and allowed the tenant classes to show a more united front against the landlords in the 1880s than had been possible in the more fissiparous days of the agrarian conflicts of the early nineteenth century. Finally, the changes in Irish society were facilitated by the continuing emigration that the famine had reinforced, an emigration which also profoundly shaped destination countries such as Britain, the United States, Canada and Australia.

42 Donnelly, *Potato famine*, pp 207–8.

CHAPTER 9

Dispersal and reinvention, 1815–91

In the eighteenth century one quarter of a million people left Ireland for America.[1] Between 1783 and 1812, when travelling was restricted by the revolutionary and Napoleonic wars, 100,000 still managed to depart for north America. Two thirds of them were Ulster Presbyterians, confirming the trend of the eighteenth century. In the years between Waterloo and the famine, one million went to north America, half a million to Britain and 30,000 to Australia. The annual rate of emigration rose from 40,000 in 1828–37 to 50,000 in 1838–44. If that trend had continued nearly half a million would have emigrated between 1845–51. As it happened, over twice that number emigrated during those famine years, and the number for the decade 1845–55 was 2.1 million, of which 1.5 million went to north America and nearly 300,000 to Britain. By 1870 at least five million had left, with several million more leaving before the end of the century. In 1871, 3.5 million Irish-born persons were living outside the country, constituting 3 per cent of the British population, 5 per cent of that of the United States, 6 per cent of that of Canada and 13 per cent of that of Australia. The Irish-born diaspora was at its greatest extent at that time.

In the run-up to the famine, there was a good deal of emigration from south Ulster because the industrialization of the linen industry caused a degree of unemployment.[2] During the famine itself, emigration was heaviest from the north-central and south-central regions of the country. The highest rates of emigration were from areas which were poor but not destitute and where people had the means to emigrate. In counties such as Clare, Kerry, Kilkenny, Limerick and Tipperary emigration rates were between 16 per cent and 18 per cent during the famine, whereas in Mayo it was only 8 per cent. Thus there was an inverse relationship between famine deaths and emigration. People died in greater numbers in areas where they were poorer and therefore unable to afford emigration. There were two exceptions to the trend: in Ulster emigration was inhibited by the relatively low rate of destitution; in north Connaught, where there was a high rate of destitution, remittance money from previous emigrants enabled emigration.

The remittance system of financing emigration through sending pre-paid tickets home eventually contributed to the establishment of patterns of emigra-

1 Donnelly, *Potato famine*, pp 178–86; Fitzpatrick, 'Emigration, 1801–70,' in Vaughan (ed.), *Union I, 1801–70*, pp 562–622; Fitzpatrick, 'Emigration, 1871–1921,' in Vaughan (ed.), *Union II, 1870–1921*, pp 606–702; Kinealy, *Great calamity*, pp 297–341. **2** Collins, 'Proto-industrialization,' *Social History* 7:2 (1982), pp 127–46.

tion from particular parts of Ireland to particular parts of other countries. A culture of emigration also began to develop in Ireland with ritualized leave-taking, including the 'American wake', during which the departing person was mourned as though he or she had died. Remittance money also enabled various forms of uneconomic existence to survive in Ireland longer than they otherwise might have. In 1867, for example, it was estimated that $120 million had been sent from America to Ireland in the previous twenty years.[3]

For a time, seasonal migration had been viewed as a serious alternative to emigration, especially in the west of Ireland. Before the famine, work in the textile industry in Britain had enabled individuals to retain their subsistence plots of land in Ireland. When this was no longer possible with contraction in the textile industry and the famine in Ireland, many of those who emigrated permanently to north America were former seasonal migrants.[4] Other forms of seasonal migration, principally in agriculture, retarded emigration from the west of Ireland until the end of the century, for from the 1880s openings for seasonal migrants in Britain went into steep decline.[5]

There was some state assistance for emigrants, particularly to Australia. One in twenty emigrants in the seventy years after 1800 was helped in this way at a cost of £2 million. In the 1880s individuals, such as James Nugent, John Sweetman, James Hack Tuke and Vere Foster, devised planned emigration schemes, which were generally unsuccessful.[6] It cost £3 to travel to America in the middle of the nineteenth century but £10 to £15 to go to Australia. By 1883 the fare between Liverpool and New York was four guineas and to Australia sixteen guineas. Until 1850 the Atlantic crossing took one month. Thereafter with the introduction of iron-hulled screw steamers, the journey was reduced to two weeks. Fifty-nine passenger ships between Britain and America were wrecked between 1847 and 1853. The death rate on ships crossing the Atlantic during the famine was 2 per cent. However, mortality on the so-called 'coffin ships' making for Quebec in 1847 was high, with one in six dying at sea or in reception centres such as Grosse Île.

During and after the famine, emigrants had generally to travel to England and to ports such as Liverpool in order to move onwards to America. However, by the 1870s only two in five emigrants were following this traditional pattern. Most emigrants left directly from Ireland, from Queenstown (Cobh), if they were from Munster and Connaught; from Belfast or Derry, if they were from Ulster; and from Dublin, if from Leinster. In 1881 Charlotte Grace O'Brien (1845–1909) publicized the deficiencies of the White Star Line which took passengers from Queenstown. She set up a boarding house there and was especially

3 Kenny, *American Irish*, p. 100. **4** Harris, *Irish labour migration*. **5** Ó Gráda, 'Seasonal migration,' *Studia Hibernica* 13 (1973), pp 48–76. **6** Moran, 'Connemara colonization,' *Éire-Ireland* 31:3 and 4 (1996), pp 130–49.

sedulous concerning the welfare of young women emigrants. In 1894 the Merchant Shipping Act introduced greater regulation.

The experience of Irish women emigrants has been the object of much recent attention. What is most noteworthy is that many of them were young, unmarried women who went into domestic service in America and elsewhere and eventually married in their countries of adoption. An assessment of their motivation in emigration depends on the view that is taken of their position and prospects in Ireland. Assessments as to why they emigrated vary from seeing them simply as the objects of male oppression in Ireland, in search of economic independence abroad, to an assessment of their priorities as being to recover abroad the lost opportunities which had been available in pre-famine Ireland.[7] In particular, emigration gave women greater control over when and whom they married. As for their position in Ireland, it was true that there were now reduced opportunities for their economic activity with the rationalization of agriculture and cottage industry after the famine. Women were increasingly confined to the domestic sphere as the family underwent a psychological embourgeoisement. However, married women at least exercised a new and greater influence over their husbands and children.[8]

Most emigrants, male and female, were unmarried adults, and two in five were in their early 20s. Most male emigrants described themselves as labourers, though many were from farming rather than labouring backgrounds. Nonetheless, emigration did contribute to the decline of the labouring and cottier classes in Ireland.[9]

Emigration to America was affected by economic patterns there. A recession in the United States in the late 1870s, for example, reduced emigration and may have intensified the early stages of the land war in Ireland. Heavy renewed emigration in the early 1880s may have then tended to dissipate it. In addition to the phenomenon of emigration was the matching, but much more minor, phenomenon of returned emigrants. However, 'returned Yanks' often found reassimilation difficult. If successful they were stereotyped as being in search of land or a spouse; if unsuccessful they were generally despised.

As for those who did stay abroad, a debate has ranged over how well different Irish groups did relative to one another. Kerby Miller has argued that Irish Catholics suffered from a cultural disability based on their religion and Gaelic background. They were more communal, dependent, fatalistic and passive than Irish Protestants, who were more individualist, independent and optimistic.[10] Emigration was seen as exile and the result of British oppression and not as a

7 Diner, *Irish immigrant women*; Nolan, *Women's emigration*; Miller, Doyle and Kelleher, 'Irish women, migration and domesticity,' in O'Sullivan (ed.), *Irish women and Irish migration*, pp 41–65. 8 Bourke, *Husbandry to housewifery*. 9 Fitzpatrick, 'Irish emigration,' *Irish Historical Sudies* 22:86 (1980), pp 126–43.

freely chosen option for the future. 'Poor Pat must emigrate' was the title of one popular song. The exile motif had Gaelic roots and was bolstered by the rhetoric of certain political exiles such as John Mitchel.[11] As a result, Irish Catholics tended to huddle together in cities and to have a lower occupational profile than Irish Protestant emigrants. Donald Akenson has used a close investigation of the information available in a number of countries to query this line of argument, however. Much of the original argument had been based on impressions of the Irish experience in the United States and on the fact that Irish Catholics did not appear to take to farming, which was deemed to be an occupation requiring individualism and self-reliance. However, in Ontario, Canada, and in Australia where Irish Catholic immigrants encountered less hostility than they did in the United States, they did embrace farming as an occupation.[12]

Irish emigration to north America began in the seventeenth century when as many as 100,000 crossed the Atlantic, three quarters of them Catholic.[13] In the eighteenth century, over a quarter of a million people emigrated to north America, three quarters of them Ulster Scots Presbyterians. In 1790 10 per cent of the United States population was of Ulster Scots origin, while 4 per cent was Irish Catholic. Many early Catholics emigrants to the United States were converted to various forms of Protestantism because of the weakness of the Catholic Church structure there at the time. Ulster Scots emigration continued in the nineteenth century, but Irish Protestants in general tended to integrate early into Protestant American life and not to form a distinct religious-ethnic community. In contrast, Irish Catholics chose a distinctive identity in an initially hostile environment. As a result, Irish American identity today is associated with Irish American Catholicism, whereas in fact most descendants of Irish immigrants into the United States are probably Protestant.[14] As in other countries, the history of Irish emigration and settlement has tended to be written in a distorted fashion as if it only concerned Catholics. Indeed, Church of Ireland members were frequent emigrants, as were Presbyterians, and in the mid-nineteenth century there was even the phenomenon of Irish gentry emigration to Australia.

Until 1835 most Irish emigrants travelled to the United States via British North America (later to be called Canada). Thereafter most Irish Protestant emigrants went to Canada and, indeed, the Orange Order because a feature of Canadian life. Between 1800 and 1845 there were 450,000 Ulster emigrants to Canada, though Catholics who reached Canada tended to go on to the United States. Thus between 1815 and 1861 0.9 million Irish people arrived in Canada

10 Miller, with Boling and Doyle, 'Irish emigration,' *Irish Historical Studies* 22:86 (1980), pp 97–125. **11** Miller, *Emigrants and exiles*, pp 556, 564. **12** Akenson, *Small differences*. **13** Kenny, *American Irish*. Much of the following discussion on the Irish in America follows this book. **14** Akenson, *Irish diaspora*, p. 250.

but in 1861 there were only 286,000 Irish in Canada.[15] In 1872, 60 per cent of Canadian Irish were Protestant.[16]

In the United States, Irish emigrant men tended initially to gravitate towards menial labour and women to domestic service or to the needle trades and sweat shops.[17] In the south, Irish labour was often used for dangerous work in preference to that of valuable slaves. Often equated with African Americans in an intentionally unflattering comparison, many Irish workers felt themselves to be in competition with ex-slaves, and this helped to foster an Irish racial antipathy towards them. Irish hostility to African Americans was a route to establishing themselves as fully 'white'.[18]

The nineteenth century saw a takeover and expansion of the existing Catholic Church structure in the United States by Irish Catholics, reversing its previous congregationalism and imposing an authoritarian style. Between 1815 and 1850 the number of American Catholics rose from 90,000 to 1.6 million, mostly due to Irish and German immigration. By 1900 two thirds of American bishops were Irish, though 'liberal' clergy who favoured Americanization and labour rights won out over conservatives who saw American culture as a threat to religion.

In 1850 one third of Irish people in the United States lived in cities over 25,000. New York, Philadelphia, Boston, Chicago and San Francisco were the chief cities for the Irish. Three in ten Irish people were to be found in the states of New York, Massachusetts, Pennsylvania and Illinois. In the anthracite region of Pennsylvania, the Molly Maguires were an active group in the 1860s and 1870s and were a hybrid of trade unionism and old-style Irish agrarianism. Twenty Irish people were eventually executed for the murder of sixteen men.[19]

In the 1830s and 40s, American nativism flourished as a movement opposed to Irish Catholics. There were riots and church burnings, and Orange lodges were founded in cities such as New York and Philadelphia. Irish Catholics began to organize politically and joined the Democratic party in increasing numbers. Nativism eventually led to the formation of the Know Nothing political party which flourished briefly in the 1850s, and nativists questioned the Americanism of Catholics and thus led the Catholic Church to respond by embracing and encouraging loyalty to the United States, middle-class self-improvement and religious and political toleration.

Five Confederate generals were Irishmen during the American civil war. However, there was more Irish support for the Union, with forty-eight Union regiments having the word 'Irish' in their names. At least 144,221 Irish-born

15 Doyle, 'Irish in North America,' in Vaughan (ed.), *Union I, 1801–70*, p. 683. **16** Bielenberg, 'British empire,' in Bielenberg (ed.), *Irish diaspora*, pp 215–34. **17** Kenny, *American Irish*, p. 62. **18** Ibid., p. 70. **19** Kenny, *Molly Maguires*.

men served in the Union army, and it helped Irish integration into American society. After the civil war, many ex-soldiers joined the new Fenian organization whose object was to achieve Irish independence by armed force if necessary. American Fenianism was marked by internecine organizational conflict. Eventually in the 1870s the Clan na Gael organization became pre-eminent among Irish nationalist organizations in the United States.

Most other destinations for Irish emigrants were part of the British empire. Argentina was an exception: 30,000 Irish people went there, nearly half of them from Westmeath.[20] The British army provided career opportunities abroad for Irishmen. Consistently throughout the nineteenth century the proportion of Irishmen in the British army was a third higher than the Irish proportion of the United Kingdom population. A small Irish community grew up in the British colonies in southern Africa.[21] The adjacent Boer republics were viewed by some Irish nationalists with great sympathy. There was a more significant Irish presence in India, some of whose top colonial and imperial officials were Irish peers. The Irish formed one fifth of the metropolitan countries' population there. Most of them were professionals and colonial administrators, though there were a few missionaries. Irish religious personnel generally followed Irish emigrants to America, Britain and British settler colonies. Missionary work among non-European populations was generally a twentieth-century phenomenon.[22]

There was significant Irish emigration to New Zealand, initially from Munster but then from Ulster, though in 1886 the Irish component in the New Zealand population only amounted to 8.9 per cent.[23] In Australia, however, the Irish were a founding people and formed the basis for a significant proportion of the population.[24] Between 1791 and 1850, 40,000 Irish convicts were transported to Australia from Ireland and a further 8,000 from Britain. In the 1800s some of them were political prisoners, exiled after the 1798 rebellion, and in March 1804 there was a United Irishmen uprising in New South Wales. In 1823 the population of the colony was 40,000, of whom 10,000 were Catholics. Of these latter, 2,000 were of colonial birth and 8,000 were Irish-born. One third of the Irish-born were convicts. The rest were mostly emancipated convicts. Only five hundred had arrived in Australia free.

Subsequent Irish immigration gravitated towards rural areas rather than the cities, and in the 1850s and 60s assimilation into Australian society took place through working in the goldmines. In 1861, 15.6 per cent of the New South

20 McKenna, 'Argentina,' in O'Sullivan (ed.), *Patterns of migration*, pp 63–83. **21** Akenson, *Primer*, p. 143; McCracken, 'South African experience,' in Bielenberg, *Irish diaspora*, pp 251–71. **22** Bielenberg, 'British empire,' p. 223; Holmes, 'Irish in India,' in Bielenberg, *Irish diaspora*, pp 235–50. **23** Bielenberg, 'British empire,' p. 222. **24** O'Farrell, 'Australia and New Zealand, 1791–1870,' in Vaughan (ed.), *Union I, 1801–70*, pp 660–81; O'Farrell, 'The Irish in Australia and New Zealand, 1870–1990,' in Vaughan (ed.), *Union II, 1870–1921*, pp 703–24.

Wales population was Irish but one third of those convicted of crime were Irish. Most immigrants were from Munster, though Leinster became more prominent from the 1880s. By the early twentieth century one quarter of the populations of Queenland, Victoria and New South Wales was Irish. The Orange Order took root in the Protestant immigrant community, but so did the Catholic Church among Irish Catholics. Two thousand priests went to Australia in the nineteenth century, from places such as All Hallows Missionary College Dublin. Catholics did well in Australia, and the erstwhile Young Irelander, Charles Gavan Duffy, became premier of Victoria and was eventually knighted.

Because Australian culture was relatively conducive to Irish Catholic immigration, no religious-ethnic Irish politics emerged and the Irish Australians were less anti-British than their American counterparts. Catholic ecclesiastics such as Cardinal Moran, a nephew of Paul Cullen, encouraged integration. However, Irish nationalist politicians who toured Australia in search of funds in the late nineteenth century, such as the Redmond brothers in 1883 and John Dillon in 1889, were generally well received.

Of all the British possessions, however, it was of course Great Britain itself which was the principal destination for Irish emigration.[25] In 1841 there were over 400,000 Irish in Britain, constituting 1.82 per cent of the English and 4.82 per cent of the Scots populations. By 1871 it was over three quarters of a million, making up 2.49 per cent and 6.18 per cent of the English and Scots populations respectively. Emigrants to Scotland tended to come from Ulster, to southern England from Munster and Leinster and to northern England from Connaught. English poor law unions provided some minimal relief to Irish people fleeing to Britain during the famine, though British authorities retained and often exercised the right to deport paupers back to Ireland.

Liverpool, Manchester, Glasgow and London were early destinations for large numbers of immigrants. There was a tendency for the Irish to congregate in new, poorly constructed suburbs and in inner city areas, sometimes called 'Little Irelands', though they were not ghettos as such. By mid-century one in five of the populations of Liverpool, Glasgow and Dundee was Irish-born, and one in ten of Manchester, Salford, Stockton, St Helen's, Newport, Paisley and Kilmarnock. However, Irish people were also spreading more generally throughout Britain.[26]

The politics of the Irish in Britain was greatly influenced by that in Ireland, though to a more muted degree. There were only proportionately one third as many Fenians in Britain as in Ireland, for example. In 1890 out of 300,000 Irish-

25 Fitzpatrick, 'The Irish in Britain, 1801–70', in Vaughan (ed.), *Union I, 1801–70*, pp 623–60; Fitzpatrick, 'The Irish in Britain, 1871–1921,' in Vaughan (ed.), *Union II, 1870–1921*, pp 653–702. **26** Davis, 'Irish in Britain,' in Bielenberg, *Irish diaspora*, pp 19–36.

born males in Britain, only 41,000 belonged to the National League of Great Britain, the principal moderate nationalist organization of the time. Contributions from the Irish in Britain to Irish nationalist movements during the land war and home rule years amounted to one third of that given by the Irish in Australia and to one twenty-fifth of that given by Irish Americans. The Irish never became a significantly organized political lobby in England. They supported the Liberals and the Labour party in turn, though T.P. O'Connor served as a nationalist MP for the Scotland division of Liverpool for forty-four years.

The Catholic Church encouraged Irish assimilation to British society. Ecclesiastics discouraged Irish nationalism, and the idea of Catholic schools gained some acceptance in official circles because they strove to create a loyal Irish working class.[27]

There was a narrow range of work open to unskilled Irish men. It was mostly in factories and docks, though theories that the Irish injured the British working class by holding down wages are now less strongly held.[28] Irish navvies were a relatively esteemed group. The Irish were certainly over represented in prisons, something forming five times their proportion in the population, though this was in part due to over-zealous policing of working-class areas.[29] There were middle-class Irish people in Britain as well. Those who were most visible tended to be journalists in a line that led from William Maginn to Justin McCarthy and beyond.[30]

Overall, the theory of the Irish as the outcasts of Victorian Britain, from British capitalism, politics, religion and Anglo-Saxon racial identity, has come to be modified recently.[31] The Irish in Britain were not necessarily the emigrants of despair rather than the emigrants of hope who went to America, though conditions in Britain were often harsh and there was hostility and prejudice against the immigrant community. There was Orange opposition to Irish Catholic emigrants, and anti-Irish disturbances such as the Stockport riots of 1852 and the Murphy riots of 1867. However, in a good number of British cities, such as Dundee, Hull and Bristol the Irish lived in relative peace, often thanks to Irish leadership, such as that of the Hull newspaper editor E.F. Collins, who championed good housing and religious toleration.

Patterns of Irish immigration varied greatly in different countries. Institutions such as the Orange Order did flourish around the world and often functioned as one response by wary host Protestant countries to the presence of Irish Catholic immigrants. However, Irish Protestant immigrants tended to integrate into their new societies as individuals without the need to be part of a

27 Hickman, *Education of the Irish in Britain*. **28** Swift, 'Outcast Irish,' *Irish Historical Studies* 25:99 (1987), p. 264. **29** Ibid., p. 268. **30** Foster, *Paddy and Mr Punch*, p. 290. **31** Swift and Gilley (eds), *Victorian city*; Swift, 'Outcast Irish,' p. 274; Swift and Gilley (eds), *Irish in Britain*; Swift and Gilley (eds), *Victorian Britain*; Davis, 'Irish in Britain,' pp 23, 27, 28.

pronouncedly Irish ethnic community. Irish Catholics tended to bond into ethnic groups centred around Catholicism, and to integrate into society precisely through a Catholic Church anxious to be part of those new societies. Ironically, it was in the United States, the one significant country of destination not under British rule, that the most pronouncedly Irish Catholic nationalist community grew up. Within twenty years of the famine, the American Irish community, with its defined Anglophobia, would begin to have a significant political impact on Ireland itself, not least through the Fenian movement.

CHAPTER 10

Origin of Fenian species, 1850–78

If titles are important, then Ireland has mostly been rather inefficient at producing resounding titles whose imagery is both formative as well as expressive of outlook, culture, commitment and identity. The two notable exceptions are the Orangemen and the Fenians, and it is instructive that the name 'Fenian', with its martial Gaelic connotations, which originated in an American organization, came to be applied to its Irish associate, whose official title was the Irish Republican Brotherhood.

The Fenians stood in marked contrast to the United Irishmen. The latter posed a formidable military challenge to Britain but, when suppressed, faded into oblivion, leaving little in the way of an organic political legacy, though much later generations would claim links with them. The former were militarily inept but, in defeat, their influence expanded from a relatively confined section of nationalist society to the mainstream and contributed in the 1870s to a social and political shift away from deference to the state and its institutions and towards a more assertive and confident nationalism.[1] This change has received relatively little attention, but it was this that enabled the political assertion of the home rule and land war years of the 1880s and the revolution in high and popular culture of the 1890s and beyond.

The Fenians were in some ways more a symptom than a catalyst for this deep change, which was nothing less than that revolution in Irish polity which many had feared and others hoped for as a result of Catholic emancipation. For, in spite of all that had happened since then, nationalist Ireland remained relatively compliant and deferential, even in the 1860s. Thus when a pro-Fenian mayor of Cork made anti-royal remarks, in what he imagined was the safety of a private function, in 1869, and these remarks were subsequently published, he was forced to resign in the face of almost universal condemnation and a bill in parliament to remove him from office. Sixteen years later, however, the prince and princess of Wales were forced to curtain a visit to the same city because of the unrestrained public hostility of its nationalist population.[2]

From the famine until the end of the 1860s, that sharp enough distinction between constitutional and 'physical force' nationalism which was the legacy of O'Connellism remained intact. Constitutional movements did not make much progress but demonstrated at least two interesting and ultimately contradicto-

1 Foster, *Paddy and Mr Punch*, p. 272; Jackson, *Ireland*, p. 95. **2** Murphy, *Abject loyalty*, pp 176–80, 230–40.

ry features which were subsequently to be lost. These were the desire for a political alliance with the Protestant population of Ulster and an explicitly Catholic clerical input into politics.[3]

The former took the form of the Irish Tenant League, founded in 1850 to press through political lobbying and not mass agitation for land reform. Its leaders included Charles Gavan Duffy and James McKnight of Belfast and they were allied with the Co. Down landowner and Rochdale radical MP William Sharman Crawford (1781–1861). At the same time Britain was undergoing one of its last outbreaks of anti-Catholic paranoia which resulted in the Ecclesiastical Titles Act (1851), a singularly ineffective piece of legislation designed to prevent Catholic bishops from using territorial titles, following a bumptious statement by the English Cardinal Wiseman. A group of Irish MPs, called the 'Irish Brigade', formed in the Commons to oppose the measure. In September 1852 the Irish Brigade and the Tenant League formed the Independent Irish Party. Over forty MPs pledged to support it, though it effectively collapsed when two prominent members, John Sadlier (1815–56) and William Keogh (1817–78), took office in the Aberdeen government and the movement ran up against the opposition of Archbishop Cullen.

A variety of individuals aspiring to parliamentary leadership enjoyed passing prominence in the next decade and a half. They included The O'Donoghue of the Glens (1833–89), Sir John Gray (1816–75), A.M. Sullivan (1830–84) and John Blake Dillon, the former Young Irelander who served a brief but impressive term in the Commons just before his early death.[4] That there was a significant line of demarcation between them and revolutionary groups is attested to by the bitterness evinced by the Fenians towards A.M. Sullivan, who was perhaps the most radical, or at least vociferous, of these constitutional leaders *manqués*. The Fenians were intent on frustrating the formation of a constitutional political party and were not above breaking up political meetings. They need not have worried much, however, as the constitutional politicians were subject to internecine conflict. The essentially backward-looking nature of their agendas can be evidenced in labels such as neo-O'Connellite Liberal and neo-Young Irelander sometimes applied to them.

It was often difficult for Irish politicians to promote a serious political agenda, as they were in permanent political opposition in the United Kingdom. The tendency of rising politicians to claim the mantles of revered dead predecessors as a substitute can be seen in the energy invested in disputes in the 1860s over public statues in Dublin, whose corporation acted as a forum for nationalist fac-

3 Comerford, 'Churchmen, tenants,' in Vaughan (ed.), *Union I, 1801–70*, pp 396–414. 4 Comerford, 'Conspiring brotherhoods,' and 'Gladstone's enterprise,' in Vaughan (ed.), *Union I, 1801–70*, pp 415–50.

tions.[5] Sir John Gray entered the field with his sponsorship of a statue of his old mentor O'Connell. William Smith O'Brien emerged from his retirement long enough to suggest that the statue be placed in the Dublin slums. Sullivan was cannier than to oppose the O'Connell statue directly but found another route to strike at Gray, when the latter backed moves for a monument to the late Prince Albert at College Green. As the site faced the formed Irish parliament, Sullivan was able to mount a successful campaign for the site it to be reserved for a statue to Henry Grattan. Prince Albert was duly relegated to Leinster Lawn, and Sullivan gained the advantage over Gray in a conflict whose outcome left Dublin with a legacy of outstanding statuary by Irish sculptors of international renown such as J.H. Foley (1818–74), whose services were retained by all political sides. His work was preceded and succeeded by that of John Hogan (1800– 58), John Hughes (1865–1941) and others. The statue controversies also illustrated a lively interaction between politics and the arts, in contradiction to the notion, itself based on false literary premises, that Ireland was subject to a cultural vacuum between the 1840s and 1890s.

Eventually, Archbishop Cullen stepped in to sponsor the National Association of Ireland in 1864. Cullen, essentially a Catholic Whig, anxious for Catholics to occupy positions of influence in the existing power structures, had disapproved of too close a link between the Catholic Church and a nationalist party. The new movement did not flourish, but its political agenda, especially disestablishment, was taken up by Gladstone, the coming Liberal leader, under the banner of 'justice for Ireland'. He was anxious to counter Fenianism by concessions to more moderate groups and to build up a coalition of minorities behind his brand of Liberalism. It began a new sort of alliance between nationalism and Liberalism that lasted initially until a dispute over university education in 1873. The experiment was also to lay the foundation for the more enduring alliance between Irish nationalism and the Liberals which was to last essentially from the 1880s to the first world war.

Priests had widespread influence in the political process, but a directly clerical politics was never to emerge. One of the reasons for this can be traced to the Church's hostility to the Fenians, a secret, oath-bound society. In part that hostility was due to a clerical predilection for larger tenant farmers rather than for the groups from which the Fenians themselves sprang, in contrast to its support for the Land League in the 1880s which did advance the interests of larger farmers.[6] As a result, when the Fenians themselves became a component of the political mainstream in the 1870s, the culture of political nationalism developed a certain clerical wariness, though not an open anti-clericalism.[7]

5 Murphy, *Abject loyalty*, pp 133–45. 6 Newsinger, 'Fenianism revisited:' *Saothar* 17 (1992), pp 46–52 7 Rafferty, *Fenian threat*, p. 142.

Another group with widespread political influence in the 1850s and 60s was the landlords.[8] Between 1832 and 1859, 81.2 per cent of Tory and 65.1 per cent of other Irish MPs were landowners. Between 1859 and 1885, it was 63 per cent and 45.1 per cent respectively.[9] Overall, nearly two thirds of MPs were landed until 1885. Voting was in public until the 1872 Ballot Act and was often accompanied by unruly scenes. In the towns, shopkeepers were prone to financial pressure both from landlords and peasants. Nearly three quarters of borough (urban) elections were contested, but only just over one third of county (rural) elections.[10] The low contestation rate in rural areas was due to landlord power, but from the 1860s the countryside was once more open to politicization based on national rather than local issues.[11] The franchise act of 1850 had given the vote to all £12 rateable occupiers.[12] But the electorate remained unchanged until 1884, in spite of the 1868 reform act. Thus in 1869, whereas one third of British men had the vote only one sixth of Irishmen had it. It was all the more remarkable then that home rule made such electoral progress from the 1870s, an indication of social and political change.

It was thus in mid-century and especially under the direction of a local star, Lord Naas, that Irish Tories underwent something of a revival, actually winning a majority of seats in 1859 with nearly half of them outside Ulster. Even among non-Tories, Protestant influence was strong. As late as 1880, almost one third of non-Tory Irish MPs were Protestants. It was only in 1886 that the proportion was greatly reduced with ten Protestants joining nearly seventy-five Catholics in the non-Tory camp.[13]

James Stephens (1824–1901) founded a revolutionary organization in Dublin in 1858 which was eventually to be known as the Irish Republican Brotherhood – its American, supposedly-subordinate, counterpart, the Fenian Brotherhood, being founded at the same time in New York by John O'Mahony (1815–77).[14] The IRB incorporated the Skibbereen Phoneix Literary and Debating Society and spread in the south and west. Alert at an early stage to the existence of the new organization the authorities moved to arrest members at the end of 1858 and early in 1859. The massive funeral of the former Young Irelander, Terence Bellew MacManus (1823–60) in 1861, the organization of which was effectively taken over by the IRB, was both an occasion for political radicalization and a boost to the standing of the Fenians. In 1863 Stephens founded the newspaper, the *Irish People*, providing a secret organization with a rather public face. However, hopes for help from America for an insurrection were delayed by the American civil war. Its end, though,

8 Hoppen, *Elections*. **9** Ibid., p. 336. **10** Hoppen, 'Landlords, society,' in Philpin (ed.), *Nationalism and popular protest*, p. 291 **11** Hoppen, 'Nationalist politics,' in Cosgrove and McCartney (eds), *Studies in Irish history*, pp 190–227 **12** Hoppen, 'Landlords, society,' p. 306. **13** Hoppen, *Elections*, p. 264. **14** Comerford, *Fenians*; Newsinger, *Fenianism*.

released numerous, willing Irish American ex-soldiers for potential service in Ireland.

The year 1865 was the optimum time for a Fenian rising in Ireland, with 6,000 firearms in readiness, 50,000 men willing to take part and even some support among Irish soldiers in the British army.[15] In September, though, the *Irish People* was raided and prominent Fenians such as Thomas Clarke Luby (1822–1901), John O'Leary (1830–1907) and Jeremiah O'Donovan Rossa (1831–1915) were arrested. Stephens was also captured but escaped. February 1866 saw further widespread arrests with the suspension of habeas corpus. Disarray in Ireland was matched by disunion in America, ostensibly over proposals for a Fenian attack on Canada, which was actually attempted on several occasions, though without success. O'Mahony was edged aside in the leadership by Col. W.E. Roberts of the 'Senate' wing of the Fenians. Meanwhile, in December 1866 Stephens who had promised an insurrection that year found himself deposed on a visit to New York. He was replaced by Col. Thomas J. Kelly, who set off for Britain and Ireland to organize what turned into a fiasco of an insurrection in early 1867. It consisted of futile operations in Co. Kerry, the Dublin mountains and elsewhere and an abortive raid on Chester Castle in Britain.[16]

The Fenians of the 1860s were strongest in Leinster and Munster. Many Fenians were young urban men, and during the years 1851–71 the proportion of the population living in towns rose from 17 per cent to 22 per cent. One quarter of Fenians were shopkeepers and shop assistants and one third artisans, such as shoemakers and tailors.[17] On the one hand, these young men were relatively prosperous. On the other, artisans in particular were a declining group as farmers prospered. Opportunities for self-expression and social mobility were limited.[18] It was a scenario for social discontent finding expression in nationalist commitment that would be repeated frequently over the next seventy years.[19]

In spite of its undoubted political dimension, the social aspect to Fenianism was of great importance. It provided an opportunity for young men to meet and enjoy outings and activities, including drilling, together. An interest in politics could arise out of a social engagement. This again was part of a pattern that has already been identified in the Confederate Clubs of the 1840s. It explains, too, why the IRB was to take such an interest in the Gaelic Athletic Association in the 1880s.

The year 1867 may have been a disaster for the Fenians militarily, but it was also to open the door for them to a new and more influential future. In May

15 Comerford, 'Gladstone's enterprise.' **16** Takagami, 'Fenian rising,' *Irish Historical Studies* 29:115 (1995), pp 340–62. **17** Hoppen, *Elections*, p. 361. **18** Townshend, *Political violence*, p. 30. **19** Garvin, *Nationalist revolutionaries*.

1867 there was widespread protest at the impending execution of a Fenian called Thomas Burke. He was reprieved. Then on 11 September two Fenians, including Col. Kelly, were arrested in Manchester. A week later an attempt to release them from a police van by a group of thirty armed Fenians ended in the death of an unarmed policeman. On 1 November five men, none of whom was actually thought to have fired the fatal shot, were sentenced to death. Two of them were reprieved, but on 23 November three were executed.[20] It produced an enormous turn around in Irish public opinion, with outrage at the executions and a new sympathy for Fenianism, which survived the horrific Fenian explosion at Clerkenwell Jail on 3 December in which twelve people died.

'God Save Ireland', the cry from the dock by one of the two subsequently reprieved, was turned into an unofficial national anthem by T.D. Sullivan (1827–1914), whose brother A.M. Sullivan had been so execrated by the Fenians. Mock funerals were held in Ireland, often at night with torch-lit processions. Those executed were presented as Christian martyrs and depicted as well-groomed men in illustrations. Seventeen monuments were erected to them over the next forty years, and thirty years after the executions twenty-six annual commemorations were still being held throughout the country, one of them lasting until the 1990s.[21]

The popular momentum generated by the Manchester executions soon found a new outlet in the Amnesty Association, which campaigned for four years from 1868 for the release of Fenian prisoners, who were held in harsh conditions in British prisons, and, indeed, many prominent Fenians were released in January 1871. The Amnesty Association's president was Isaac Butt, who went on to found the Home Government Association in 1870 and the Home Rule League in 1873. Meanwhile, the IRB itself was now under the control of a new committee called the Supreme Council. In 1873 it adopted a constitution which signalled a halt to any further military action until a mandate had been gained from the Irish people. In 1875 it formed links with Clan na Gael, which under John Devoy (1842–1928) had gained ascendancy in America.

Fenianism had now become a significant element in Irish politics, beyond the control of any organization. Nonetheless, in the 1870s the IRB was riven with conflicts over how far to engage with the political mainstream. Charles J. Kickham and O'Leary were strongly opposed to any dallying with constitutionalism, and the Supreme Council ordered members to withdraw from the Home Rule League, provoking a series of resignations and expulsions. In the late 1870s the new nationalist leader C.S. Parnell managed to convince Devoy and a section of Fenianism to support an alliance between themselves, land agitators and Irish parliamentarians in the so-called 'new departure'.

20 Murphy, *Abject loyalty*, pp 153–9. **21** Owens, 'Manchester executions,' in McBride (ed.), *Irish nationalist imagination*, pp 18–36

Not all Irish republicans agreed with the new trend. Some of those who did not resorted to terrorism. The breakaway Irish National Invincibles were responsible for the murders of Lord Frederick Cavendish and T.H. Burke, chief and under secretaries respectively in the Irish government, in May 1882. They were drawn from a Dublin lower middle-class and artisan background. The 'dynamite war' affected Britain between 1880 and 1887 with property as the target for the most part. Most explosions took place in London, Liverpool and Glasgow. It was sponsored by two Irish American groups; one was a faction of Clan na Gael, and the other reliant on O'Donovan Rossa.[22]

By the 1870s the composition of rank-and-file Fenianism had changed. In the early 1870s it had attracted some journalists and businessmen. By the later 1870s the growth areas for the organization had spread to north Connaught and south Ulster, to the territory once held by 'Ribbonism'.[23] Fenians came to represent the agrarian aspirations of small farmers. When land agitation began at the end of the decade, many Fenians found themselves easily absorbed into the political alliance between the Land League and Irish Parliamentary Party, effectively abandoning Fenianism. Official Fenianism wrongly believed that land reform would not be granted and that the land war would pave the way for revolutionary politics. Many of the new Irish MPs had had Fenian backgrounds, twenty-one according to police reports,[24] and brought a radical assertiveness and new independence to constitutional agitation. Parnellism, that great alliance of so many interest groups in Irish life, had brought Fenianism in from the margins to the political centre,[25] albeit into a new political establishment whose purpose, whatever the backgrounds of its political agitators, was to safeguard the interests of bourgeois Catholic nationalism. The line of demarcation between constitutional and physical force nationalism had been blurred, but to the advantage of constitutional politics. The 1880s were years that enabled the consolidation of constitutional nationalism rather than the stoking up of a new revolutionary impetus.[26]

Nonetheless, Fenianism continued to exist, though now more as an ideological rather than as a military force, and would prove influential again in future decades. In the 1880s Fenians were active in Dublin intellectual circles whose activities presaged and influenced the Irish revival of the 1890s. The Fenians took over one group called the Young Ireland Society, and it eventually became a vehicle for John O'Leary. Establishing himself in Dublin intellectual and literary circles, he was able to influence rising thinkers and writers such as W.B. Yeats.[27] Of greater importance, though, was the IRB takeover of the

22 Short, *Dynamite war*. **23** Comerford, *Fenians*, p. 213; Newsinger, *Fenianism*, p. 76. **24** Bew, *Land*, pp 226, 229. **25** Comerford, *Fenians*, p. 218. **26** Jackson, *Ireland*, p. 104; Newsinger, *Fenianism*, p. 78. **27** Brown, *Yeats*, pp 28–9; Kelly, 'Dublin Fenians,' *Historical Journal* 4:3 (2000): pp 729–50.

Gaelic Athletic Association, which had been founded in 1884.[28] The later nineteenth century was a period when sport was being organized for the first time on a large scale because better transportation, notably the bicycle, enabled travel and competition between teams. Michael Cusack (1847–1907) founded the GAA because other sporting organizations were not interested in Irish games and because of the exclusion of labourers and artisans from sporting organizations. C.S. Parnell, Michael Davitt, the land agitator, and Archbishop Croke were named as patrons of the GAA, but in 1886 John O'Leary, by then president of the Supreme Council, was added. By that time the IRB had come to dominate the organization, and Cusack had withdrawn from it. The next year policemen were banned from taking part in GAA events. Though the level of its power within the GAA fluctuated the IRB was to maintain a keen interest in the organization, remembering how male homosocial recreation in the 1860s had been an important element in its own initial success.

The Fenian input into Irish social and political life in the mid-nineteenth century ought not to be exaggerated. But it was significant. It was yet another factor in the mutual political and social alienation of Ireland from Britain, though of course as communications increased Irish culture was also increasingly seeming like a variant of British culture. Irish novelists were ever keen to shore up positive British perceptions of Ireland by explaining away Fenian violence, though often in highly improbable ways. The hero of *A fair Saxon* (1873), a novel by the future Irish nationalist parliamentarian Justin McCarthy (1830–1912), is an Irish nationalist member of parliament who does everything he can to undermine the Fenians but discovers that they are helped at almost every turn by English people.[29]

Hostile British attitudes to Ireland drew heavily, it has been argued, both on a racism that was derived from the Celtic-Anglo-Saxon debate going on in intellectual circles and from a parody of Darwinism. On the other hand, Roy Foster has argued that class and religion rather than race were the operative factors in the British dislike of Ireland. Perhaps, though, racial dislike came to function as an unpleasant shorthand for prejudices derived from religion and class.[30]

Cartoons of Irish people in magazines, such as *Punch*, have come in for special attention by scholars such as Perry Curtis.[31] The images that were developed in these publications drew on a variety of traditions that saw the Irish as apes and as white Negroes. Dr John Beddoe (1826–1911) had written an *Index of nigrescence* in which he placed Celts closer to Negroes than to Anglo-Saxons. Cartoons were also influenced by physiognomy that equated physical with

28 Mandle, *The Gaelic Athletic Association*. **29** Murphy, *Catholic fiction*, p. 20; Murphy, 'Between drawing-room and barricade.' **30** Foster, *Paddy and Mr Punch*, p 193; Gilley, 'English attitudes,' in Holmes (ed.), *Immigrants*, p. 93. **31** Cullen, *Visual politics*, pp 81–115; Curtis, *Anglo-Saxons and Celts*; Curtis, *Apes and angels*.

mental traits, phrenology that linked skull capacity with mental ability, and criminal anthropology. Key texts in these latter pseudo-sciences included Sir Charles Bell's *Essays on the antatomy of expression in painting* (1806) and the work of Pieter Camper (1722–89). Camper had put great store by facial angle with abnormal 'prognathism', in which the mouth and jaw project outward, being contrasted with normal 'orthognathism', in which there is a vertical line from forehead to mouth.

The process of change in caricatures of the Irish took place between 1840 and 1890, with the 1860s, the decade during which the Fenians loomed largest in the British public mind, the key period. Whereas in the work of early illustrators such as James Gillray (1756–1815) and George Cruickshank (1792–1878), there had been a tendency to increase the prognathism of the still-human images of 'Paddy', John Tenniel (1820–1914) in *Punch* pushed the process into a fully simian direction, with Paddy now looking like a gorilla. In 1860 Charles Kingsley described the people of Sligo as being like 'white chimpanzees'.[32] Not all British publications were so hostile, a notable example of the latter being the *Illustrated London News*, thanks to the work of Aloysius O'Kelly (1851–1926). Meanwhile home rule cartoonists in Ireland, such as John Fergus O'Hea (1850–1912), reversed the stereotyping. Similar tensions can be seen in the depiction of the allegorical 'Hibernia', especially in the cartoons of the 1880s. Whereas British cartoons depicted her as a virginal maid protected by a martial Britannia, Irish cartoons saw her variant 'Erin' as dark-skinned and stately.[33]

None of this was good for British imperialism in Ireland, however, because it is easier to rule if one can love happy but feckless natives rather than having to loath simian monsters.[34] Indeed, rather than the hated and feared African, the Irish had since the sixteenth century sometimes been classified in British colonial typology alongside the native American, for whom paternalistic affection might safely be felt. And Victorian society did have a cultural forum ideally suited (because of its need to entertain, amuse and move to tears) for the generation of those necessary, positive stereotypes of the Irish. It was the theatre.[35]

Apart from a period in the eighteenth century, there was no autonomous Irish theatre until shortly before the Irish revival at the end of the nineteenth century. There were Irish playwrights, Irish characters, Irish themes and Irish plays, but the latter were largely written for British, and later American, audiences, though they were also performed in Ireland.[36] London success led to an Irish production. Dublin's Theatre Royal, founded in 1821, the most important theatre in the city, was indistinguishable from a London theatre. It was not until

32 Gibbons, 'Racial discourse,' *Oxford Literary Review* 13 (1991), p 96. **33** Innes, *Woman and nation*, pp 13, 17. **34** Gibbons, 'Racial discourse,' pp 95–117. **35** Nelson, 'Boucicault's Myles,' *Éire-Ireland* 13:3 (1978), pp 79–105. **36** Kosok, 'Nineteenth-century drama,' in Genet and Cave (eds), *Irish drama*, pp 50–67.

James Whitbread (1847–1916) came from England to rescue the Queen's Theatre, founded in 1844, where he was appointed manager in 1884, that there was any real interest in Ireland in Irish plays.[37]

Irish characters had appeared in English plays since the seventeenth century, being portrayed as treacherous and, later in the next century, as comic. Stock characters were principally the Elizabethan kern or soldier and the Jacobean cowardly 'Tague'. Their successors in the eighteenth century were the Irish solider of fortune and the Irish servant and, in the nineenth century, the fugitive vagrant and the tradesman or tenant.[38] In the later eighteenth century, Irish characters have Gaelic surnames and Ascendancy characteristics and are thus social hybrids, betraying a distance from the economic, political and religious realities of Ireland.[39]

There were many prominent Irish playwrights in the early nineteenth century, among them James Sheridan Knowles (1784–1862), author of *Brian Boroimhe* (1811), and Richard Lalor Shiel (1791–1851), author of *Adelaide* (1814). But it was John Buckstone (1802–75), an English actor-manager and playwright, who had the most lasting affect in shifting the Irish theatrical stereotype in a more positive direction. At a time when political cartoonists where beginning to depict the Irish in ape-like ways, the influence of Buckstone and others ensured that the Irish appeared as less other and more Anglicized in appearance on stage. National character was now to be portrayed as more subtle and psychological rather than physical. As Paddy replaced Teague on stage, positive sides to the Irish national character came to the fore, with the Irish being seen by Buckstone as eloquent and sociable, superstitious and amorous.

The process was taken a stage further by Dion Boucicault (1820–1890).[40] He made his name as an actor-manager and playwright on the London stage in the 1840s, extending his work to America later on. He was married three times and often led a precarious financial existence. Many of his dozens of plays were Regency comedies, spectacular melodramas or pseudo art plays. He wrote nine Irish plays, three of which *The colleen bawn* (1860), based on *The collegians*, *Arrah-na-pogue* (1864) and *The shaughraun* (1875) left a last impression. Boucicault took the already quite positive theatrical stereotype of the Irish and refined it.[41] That he did not reject it outright and create something new ensured that his reputation would not last the generation of those who did precisely that, Yeats, Synge and Lady Gregory.

Boucicault deserves more serious consideration, however, as he was the first person to inject a positive appraisal of Irish nationalism into the theatre, albeit

37 Morash, *Irish theatre*; Watt, 'Boucicault and Whitbread,' *Éire-Ireland* 18:3 (1983), pp 23–53. **38** Truninger, *Stage Irishman*. **39** Leerssen, *Mere Irish*, pp 77–150. **40** Clarke, *Irish peasant play*, pp 65–96; Hogan, *Boucicault*. **41** Nelson, 'Boucicault's Myles,' p. 103. **42** Grene, *Irish drama*, pp 6–17; Harrington, 'Boucicault, dramatic tradition,' *Éire-Ireland* 30:2 (1995), pp 89–103.

rendered innocuous by the conventions within which he was writing.[42] *Arrah-na-pogue* is set in 1798 but *The shaughraun*, which was first performed in New York in 1874, is set in the near-contemporary Fenian period of the late 1860s. When it opened in London in 1875 Boucicault published an open letter to Disraeli, then prime minister, about releasing Fenian prisoners, and it was said that the London audience regularly cheered at the mention of amnesty in the play. However, the play is a romance set against the background of politics. It is about internal betrayal and does not present a compelling political analysis. Its reassuring picture of the possibility of reconciliation between landlords and tenants assuaged rather than challenged its English audience. At the same time it fed into the nostalgia of Irish Americans and the pride of Irish audiences.[43] Boucicault's radicalism was played out within a theatrical context whose whole ideological tenor was to reassure rather than rile Britain about its interaction with Ireland. And if theatrical conventions were breached, legal coercion lay at hand. When Boucicault included 'The Wearing of the Green' in *Arrah-na-pogue* he found it banned in productions within the British dominions. Ironically, relations between landlords and tenants in Ireland were just about set to worsen considerable as agricultural distress provoked a new form of rural agitation in what would become known as the 'land war'.

43 Grene, *Irish drama*, p. 17.

CHAPTER 11

Loved land, lost leader, loyal legion, 1879–91

One of the principal effects of the famine was the reduction in the diversity of the structure of Irish rural society and the emerging dominance and coherence of the farming class which was now in a better position to use collective action if necessary. Farmers rose as a proportion of the rural workforce from 28 to 40 per cent and labourers declined from 61 to 38 per cent between 1841 and 1881.[1] Labourers' wages in fact increased after the famine because of their relative scarcity, and they still constituted a potentially powerful enough group for the Land League not to want to alienate them in the 1880s. However, their relative decline meant that now, if it came to it, they could be ignored. In any event, labourers found it hard to organize for political or agrarian causes. They could be evicted from their cottages with little notice. They did not have a vote until 1884, and emigration, which was to have such a sedative effect on social change, increasingly siphoned off those discontented with their lot.[2]

Most of Ireland's half a million tenant farmers in 1861 had yearly tenancies, though one in five had leases. Yearly tenancies, though, continued from year to year unless the landlord decided otherwise. Tenants could be evicted if the rent fell into one year's arrears or after six months' notice to quit approved by a court, though after eviction many farmers were readmitted as tenants or caretakers. In the third quarter of the century, between 700 and 800 families were evicted annually, though this amounted to only around one fifth of 1 per cent of the total number of farmers per year.[3] Evictions were a matter for the civil rather than criminal law and were overseen by the local sub-sheriff and bailiffs.

Fishing as a means of employment went into a steep decline with 63,000 men employed in 1850 and 24,500 in 1880. The linen industry underwent semi-continuous growth in the third but depression in the fourth quarter of the century.[4] Agriculture experienced the most dramatic changes with cereal production halving. The numbers of cattle trebled to four million, with sheep and pig numbers roughly doubling.

From 1879 to 1882 there was an agricultural slump, followed by a depression until 1896. Before that, the picture had been very different.[5] From the increased demand caused by the Crimean war in the early 1850s until the late

1 Clark and Donnelly (eds), *Irish peasants*, p. 277; Fitzpatrick, 'Irish agricultural labourer,' *Irish Economic and Social History* 7 (1980), pp 66–92; Hoppen, 'Landlords, society,' in Philpin (ed.), *Nationalism and popular protest*, p. 286. **2** Vaughan (ed.), *Mid-Victorian Ireland*, p. 11. **3** Ibid., pp 20–6. **4** Gribbon, 'Economic and social history,' in Vaughan (ed), *Union II, 1870–1921*, pp 260–356.

1870s, there had been agricultural prosperity, punctuated by periods of downturn only in the years 1859–64 and in 1867.

Agitation on behalf of farmers usually took the form of the demand for 'tenant right', also known as the 'Ulster custom' because it existed mostly in Ulster. This was a nebulous concept. It was often stated in terms of the 'three Fs' – fair rent, free sale and fixity of tenure. Central to it was the notion that departing tenants might sell their 'interest' in their farms. This interest included not only a price for improvements made to the farm, such as drainage, but the difference between a real, market rent and the lower actual rent paid. Incoming farmers sometimes had to pay as much as twenty times this difference.

This practice had two important implications. The first was the landlord's ownership of the land was not as absolute in Ireland as elsewhere. Mid-century legislation such as Caldwell's and Deasy's acts had attempted to replace this tendency towards dual ownership with a notion of contract which might safeguard landlord ownership.[6] Gladstone's 1870 land act attempted to legalize and regularize tenant right but was a failure.

The second implication, though it has been disputed,[7] was that the actual rents were low compared with putative market rents. During the post-famine and pre-land war era, rents rose by 20 per cent but output rose by 70 per cent, a situation greatly favouring the tenants. The traditional explanation for the outbreak of the land war in 1879 put it down to three factors – agricultural distress, the readiness of a nationalist-agrarian leadership and the actions of bad Irish landlords. But how well do they now stand up?

Landlords have been reviled in the nationalist recollection. Unlike the anonymous corporations of modern capitalism that can make large numbers of urban workers redundant with impunity by merely citing market forces, Irish landlords in the late nineteenth century were highly visible, living in mansions and sometimes holding territorial titles. They were no longer a true aristocracy, having no control over the police, the Catholic clergy and, from 1872, the electorate. Their influence as magistrates in the courts' system was limited at various levels by the presence of stipendiary, resident magistrates and presiding, assistant barristers. Yet they were too immersed in Irish country life to seek the anonymity of modern capitalism and become proper rentiers, concealed behind corporations and trusts.

Absenteeism continued to be descried as a great evil. However, some of the best-managed estates, such as those of the Devonshires in Cork and Waterford, were owned by absentees. And in reality absenteeism was a relatively minor phenomenon, with roughly one half of estates having a resident landlord, a

5 Vaughan, *Mid-Victorian Ireland*. **6** Dowling, *Tenant right*; Winstanley, *Ireland*. **7** Turner, *After the famine*.

quarter having a landlord resident elsewhere in Ireland and only a quarter being owned by public institutions and true absentees. Of 8,412 Irish landlords in 1861, 8,159 had been born in the country.

Landlords were far from the uniform group that is remembered. Remarkably, only 48 per cent belonged to the Church of Ireland; 7 per cent were Presbyterian; and an astonishing 43 per cent were Catholics, though most of the latter were among the smaller landlords. Protestant landlords tended to be Tory in political inclination, and Catholics Liberal. The size of estates varied greatly. One third of the land was owned by 302 proprietors and 50 per cent held by just 750 families. However, at the other end of the scale, 80.5 per cent of landowners held just 19.3 per cent of the land.[8]

Undoubtedly, there were bad landlords such as Lord Leitrim, assassinated in 1878, and John George Adair of Donegal, who cleared his estate of tenants.[9] Because of debts and entailed estates that might pass to distant relatives, Irish landlords did not invest properly in improvements. If around 10 per cent of annual rents had been spent on drainage, one fifth of the land in the country might have been upgraded. Another 10 per cent would have provided 40 per cent of tenants with better housing. Improved housing and land might have been a better way to control tenants than confrontation. W.E. Vaughan has argued that landlords might have avoided their class demise had they used the thirty years before the land war in a more rational, if more ruthless, way by raising rents, becoming true rentiers and creating a class of entrepreneurial farmers.[10] However, as it turned out, the Tory analysis that the problem with Ireland was that there were still too many people on the land lost out to a new Liberal analysis. This was influenced both by Irish nationalism[11] and by a questioning of land ownership in British radical circles in the 1870s.[12] It held that it was the landlord-tenant relationship that was at fault. From this it was an easy step for Gladstone to accept the nationalist analysis about home rule.

If the landlords were not necessarily more villainous than most people with power over others' lives, the two other traditional explanations for the land war – agricultural distress and a ready leadership – were valid, though not sufficient. Isaac Butt's Home Government Association was founded in 1870, initially as a movement opposed to the Gladstonian-Irish-Catholic coalition.[13] It was hoped that it might attract disillusioned Tories, keen to have an Irish legislature whose House of Lords might be able to block measures such as disestablishment.[14] And it was an idea compatible with what would become a growing movement over the next few decades for imperial federation, as a means to

8 Winstanley, *Ireland*, p. 11. **9** Ó Gráda, *Economic history*, p. 256. **10** Vaughan, *Mid-Victorian Ireland*, p. 221. **11** O'Callaghan, *British high politics*, p. 6. **12** Comerford, *Fenians*, p. 236. **13** Comerford, 'Isaac Butt ,' in Vaughan (ed.), *Union II, 1870–1921*, pp 1–25. **14** Jackson, *Ireland*, p. 110.

strengthen and assure the continuance of the British empire for the future. Ironically, the notion of a federal empire, with local and imperial levels of government, was never adopted, largely because Britain's trade was for the most part not with its own Empire.

Having hoped to attract Tories, Butt's movement, which became the Home Rule League in 1873, actually began to attract Irish Catholics, whose alliance with the Liberals was then foundering, and to adopt a more nationalist agenda. In 1874, 60 home rulers were elected to parliament, along with 33 Tories and 10 Liberals. Within a few years MPs with IRB links such as Joseph Biggar were beginning to make their presence felt in parliament by adopting a policy of obstructing Commons business with long speeches and the use of procedural devices. Butt opposed it but lost ground to Charles Stewart Parnell (1846–91), who was eventually to gain control over the Irish Parliamentary Party and to build an extraordinary political coalition of farmers, shopkeepers, clergy and neo-Fenians. On the question of the land, for example, a variety of views were held together even within the political leadership with Michael Davitt (1846–1906) favouring land nationalization and T.M. Healy (1855–1931) favouring the consolidation of the rural bourgeoisie.[15] Parnell, of Ascendancy and American ancestry, was a tactical political genius who attracted an enormous personal following, though he lacked the political substance of his predecessor as uncrowned king of Ireland, Daniel O'Connell. Ironically for an age which put paid to the old ruling class, part of Parnell's appeal was his aristocratic demeanour, accepting a gift of £37,000 from the Irish people in 1883 to rescue his own estate with notable disdain.

Parnell mostly lived in England but had a retinue of vigorous, if turbulent, lieutenants in Ireland. By the middle of the 1880s, almost all prominent IPP members were around forty years of age or younger. Many worked as journalists in England and had radical instincts. They recognized, however, that their position depended on supporting the interests of the Catholic nationalist farming classes.[16]

With agricultural depression setting in in 1879, both official and voluntary relief measures were quickly put in place.[17] In 1880 half a million people were granted outdoor relief, and between 1880 and 1882 government relief grants amounted to £99,000 and loans to £2,070,000. Rival relief committees were established in Dublin. That of the duchess of Marlborough, wife of the lord lieutenant, raised £135,000. The Mansion House Committee, a nationalist grouping, raised £180,000. Irish American groups sent relief that came to £830,000. In 1880 the potato crop was good. A famine was not in prospect, but

15 Ibid., p. 119. **16** Comerford, *Fenians*, p. 218; O'Day, *Irish nationalism*, p. 22. **17** Comerford, 'The land war,' in Vaughan (ed.), *Union II, 1870–1921*, pp 26–52.

financial difficulty for farmers and their creditors certainly was. Landlords began to turn their minds to recovering the arrears into which many tenants had fallen during the crisis.

Organized land agitation began in Co. Mayo, where the Land League of Mayo was founded by Michael Davitt on 16 August 1879 with Parnell's support. It paved the way for the establishment of the Irish National Land League on 21 October 1879. At the 1880 election, 63 home rule MPs were elected with Parnell as chairman of the IPP, though he could really only command the loyalty of 27 members and would have to wait for some time before having total domination over the party.

The new Liberal government under the emerged-from-retirement Gladstone attempted to remedy the Irish situation with a Compensation for Disturbance Bill, but it was thrown out by the House of Lords. Rural disturbances began to increase exponentially in the Irish countryside. There were 2,585, 4,439 and 3,433 outrages respectively in 1880, 1881 and 1882, three times the normal level, though the vast majority of incidents consisted of acts of intimidation, such as sending threatening letters, rather than actual acts of violence.[18] On average there were seventeen murders of landlords and their associates per year during the land war, as well as acts of violence such as cattle maiming redolent of the agrarian agitation of the early nineteenth century. These attracted much attention in the British media, making the highlighting of apparent miscarriages of justice on the state's side, such as the execution of Myles Joyce on 15 December 1882 for the Maamtrasna murders, a necessity for nationalist propagandists.

However, much of the success of the agitation came not from a resort to outrages but from the strategies of disciplined, legal action organized by the Land League. The response was thus less communal and more associational in character, reflecting a new form of mass organization. On the question of the payment of rent, which the League claimed to be excessive in a time of recession, tactics varied from the payment of no rent, to an affordable rent, a rent based on Griffith's valuation or a rent reduced between 20 and 25 per cent. When threatened with eviction tenants adopted a variety of responses, from resisting the process serving, by which notice of eviction was given, to challenging landlords in court, passive resistance until the point of eviction and then paying the rent, and allowing eviction to take place followed by resuming occupancy or camping near the property to deter new tenants.

The most celebrated and novel strategy was the ostracism that Parnell advocated from September 1880 and which was known as boycotting from its most famous victim, Captain Boycott. Boycott was a land agent. However, most victims of boycotting were would be successor tenants after evictions. Parnell's

18 Townshend, *Violence*, p. 151.

support for boycotting has been seen as advocating a constitutional alternative to widespread violence. However, boycotting, though highly successful, was accompanied by increased rather than reduced violence.[19] Of the 1,893 families evicted in 1880, only 152 were evicted in the last quarter. However, of the 2,590 outrages, 1,696 were committed in the same period.[20] Parnell and others were charged with conspiracy but their trial collapsed in January 1881.

Early in 1881 the government, much to its distaste, introduced coercion but followed it up with a concessionary land act. Its principal theoretical legacy was the introduction of what turned out to be the unstable notion of dual ownership of the land by landlords and tenants. In practice its chief effect was the setting up of land courts which reduced rents and eroded the basis for agitation. In the autumn the government detained the leadership of the Irish nationalist and land agitation under the coercion legislation and banned the Land League. Calls for increased agitation through the 'No Rent Manifesto' failed. By May 1882 Parnell had reached an agreement with the government in the so-called Kilmainham Treaty. He agreed to end the land war and co-operate with the government in return for the release of the leadership, the easing of coercion and the bringing of tenants in arrears and lease holders within the ambit of the 1881 act. Thus ended the first phase of the land war.

The campaign had been a stunning phenomenon, though perhaps not the total defeat for landlordism which some maintained, for 11,215 evictions took place during it.[21] Indeed, it has been argued that it was more damaging to tenants than to landlords as it put an end to landlord investment and distracted tenants from the business of farming.[22] The deeper reasons as to why and how it took place remain hotly debated. One view is that the vehemence of the tenant action was the result of the frustration of rising expectations,[23] and certainly living standards had risen between the famine and the land war,[24] only to be imperilled by the agricultural slump.

Frustrated rising expectations, however, may not have been as important for the perennially poorer farmers of the west as they were for the better off farmers of the east. Another important issue therefore relates to the degree to which the farmers who supported the land war were part of a unified and assertive collectivity or a coalition of different classes which was subject to internal division and within which the interests of larger farmers were to dominate.[25] In support of the former position is the remarkable politicization that led to the Land League and the determination with which the land war was pursued.[26] In evidence of the latter opinion is the assessment that the withholding of rent as a

19 Jackson, *Ireland*, p. 120. **20** Moody, *Davitt*, p. 567. **21** Vaughan, *Landlords*, p. 31. **22** Ó Gráda, *Economic history*, p. 255. **23** Donnelly, *Land and people*. **24** Ó Gráda, *Economic history*, p. 250. **25** Bew, *Land and the national question*, p. 190; Clark, 'Agrarian classes,' in Drudy (ed.), *Ireland, land, politics and people*, pp 31. **26** Clark, *Irish land war*, p. 352.

land-war strategy may have been suitable for midlands and eastern farmers but not for western farmers, who could not bear the legal costs.[27] Large and middling farmers were in search of rent reduction for the most part. The agenda of the small-holders of the west was for the redistribution of land, and the labourers of the south wanted a general strike for better wages but both these groups were less successful in achieving their aims during the course of the conflict than were the stronger farmers.[28]

The rhetoric of the Land League, no doubt sincerely held, was that of poor farmers struggling against rich landlords. Advocates of the united struggle view argue that this was the result of the wider farming community having embraced the concerns and anxieties of its more insecure sections[29] rather than any exercise in political presentation for mere propaganda effect.

Of additional significance concerning the land war is the degree to which the local leadership of the Land League was provided by urban dwellers, journalists, publicans and, especially shopkeepers. There were 125 local papers in operation in 1880 in Ireland, one fifth of them having recently changed political allegiance and come out in favour of nationalism.[30] Part of the motivation of the shopkeepers may have been that the farmers, whose cause they were espousing, owed them money. It is possible therefore to see the land war as a struggle between two groups of creditors, the shopkeepers trying to have their bills paid, and the landlords trying to recover arrears. Each group sought to recover debts caused by the agricultural slump, though social and family ties enabled a farmer-shopkeeper alliance against the landlords.[31] There was no moral economy between landlords and tenants that have united them against the commercial class, though writers such as Lever in *Lord Kilgobbin* (1872) had imagined it as a possibility and depicted the commercial class as the enemy.

The land war was unusual inasmuch as it began in Co. Mayo. The most significant and distinctive regions in nineteenth-century Ireland were Ulster and the south Leinster-north Munster Catholic core. Connaught, the apparently least developed and most Gaelic area, became an area of key symbolic importance from the 1890s for those elements of the Irish revival intent on identifying a Gaelic essence to be recovered and made the core of a new Irish identity. This was in the future in 1879, however, when the Land League of Mayo paved the way for the rest of nationalist Ireland. Perhaps here at last was a case of the subaltern speaking and not yet another example of a more prosperous and bourgeois group conveniently assuming the mantle of national grievance and destitute suffering: apparently not.

Some of the poorest parts of the west of Ireland had maintained a pre-famine

27 O'Callaghan, 'Irish history,' *Historical Journal* 29:2 (1986), pp 481–95. **28** Bew, *Land and the national question*, p. 223. **29** Clark, *Irish land war*, p. 365. **30** Legg, *Newspapers and nationalism*, pp 125, 128. **31** Vaughan, *Landlords*, p. 32.

pattern of economic and social activity until the 1880s. Seasonal migration and the use of wasteland had facilitated this in part.[32] Holdings had not been amalgamated to the extent of the rest of the country. The marriage age was still low, and there was the least shift from tillage to pasture of any region. Mayo, however, had a very particular economic structure, with a central lowland based on large-scale livestock farming and a periphery with potato growing and small-scale grazing. The prosperous core farmers only accounted for 5 per cent of the total, whereas 54 per cent of farms were on fifteen acres or less. Nonetheless, the smaller farmers were economically dependent on the larger ones as they supplied them with calves. Economic led to political dependence and to support for the new Land League and for the land agitation whose roots were in the more prosperous centre of the county.[33]

Released from prison in 1882, Parnell set about reasserting his authority by side-lining figures such as Davitt and John Dillion (1851–1927) and demeaning the work of the remarkable Ladies Land League. It had been founded in Ireland and New York by Parnell's own sisters, having 400 branches at its height and spending £70,000 in aid of tenants over an eight-month period.[34] A new organization, the Irish National League, was founded in October 1882 whose explicit predilection for larger farmers marked a significant move to the right. A year later an alliance was formed with the Catholic bishops over the question of education. Meanwhile, the Liberal government, whose governing ideology for Ireland had been undermined by the land war, was casting around for some solution that might command the consent of Irish nationalists. Parnell, while not quite announcing it as his Repeal Year, increased the political pressure in 1885 and the IPP was to turn the visit of the prince and princess of Wales that year to Ireland into a rout of the royal couple. The previous popularity of royal visits to Ireland had always enabled British governments to conjure up before their own minds a deeper and more loyal Irish public opinion than that represented by Irish nationalist politicians. They were thus able to dismiss the latter as having distracted the gullible Irish people from their own deeper loyalty.[35]

Various limited 'central board' schemes for Ireland, the most restricted form of local administration, were considered by the Gladstone government before it fell in June 1885. The brief successor Tory government made overtures to Parnell that impressed him to the extent that he called for Irish voters in Britain to support it at the subsequent general election. After that election, Gladstone

32 Cousens, 'Population change,' *Economic History Review* 17 (1964), pp 319; Davis, 'Irish famine,' in O'Sullivan, *Meaning of the famine*, p. 23. **33** Jordan, *Land and popular politics*; Jordan, 'The famine,' in Morash and Hayes (eds), *'Fearful realities,'* pp 35–48. **34** Te Brake, 'Irish peasant women,' *Irish Historical Studies* 28:109 (1992), pp 63–80; O'Sullivan, 'Visual representation of women,' in Foley and Ryder (eds), *Ideology in Ireland*, pp 181–96; Walsh, *Ireland's independence*, pp 12–14. **35** Murphy, *Abject loyalty*, p. 197.

made it clear that he now favoured home rule and introduced a bill to that effect in the spring of 1886 when he returned to power. The proposal forced Irish nationalists at last to come off the fence of the unreal demand for a return to the eighteenth-century Irish parliament and tied the IPP for the rest of its existence into an acceptance of home rule within the United Kingdom as a satisfaction of the demand for national self-determination. When a significant section of Gladstone's party defected over the issue, the bill was defeated and at a subsequent general election the Tories were returned to power.

A second land war prompted by reduced cattle and dairy product prices took place between 1886 and 1891, resulting from a manifesto entitled 'The plan of campaign'. A landlord's refusal to reduce rent would result in all the tenants on the estate going on a rent strike. The plan of campaign was not supported by Parnell, who feared it might damage his Liberal alliance, and it was condemned by the Holy See to the chagrin of many Irish bishops who did approve of it. In all, 203 estates were affected, two-thirds of them in Munster and Connaught.[36] Financially weakened landlords were often targeted by the hard-nosed organizers of the campaign in order to bankrupt them and enable their estates to be sold off cheaply to their tenants.

The government under Chief Secretary A.J. Balfour (1848–1930) responded with a strong measure of coercion, though tensions were heightened when the police fired on a crowd at Mitchelstown on 9 September 1887, killing three. The government also encouraged landlords to combine together to resist the plan. The organizer of those who did so, A.H. Smith Barry, had his own estate targeted. The plan of campaign phase of the land war petered out with the internecine strife of the IPP in 1891.

The Tory government was to remain in power until 1905 with a brief Liberal interlude during which Gladstone made a second, unsuccessful attempt to introduce home rule. A.J. Balfour posed as the restorer of order to Ireland, having suppressed a degree of criminality that his own measures had helped to create.[37] One of his last acts as chief secretary, however, was to establish the Congested Districts Board in 1891 to provide economic infrastructure for the poorer parts of the country. It presaged the constructive unionism which was to be pursued in Ireland by his brother Gerald (1853–1945), as chief secretary from 1895, in an attempt to win the good will of nationalists.

From early on in their two decades in power beginning in 1885, the Tories determined to solve the Irish land question. Realizing that what they regarded as the Liberals' disastrous dual-ownership concession of 1881 could not be withdrawn, they took the logical course of encouraging landlords to sell their estates to their tenants. A series of land acts, whose high points were the

36 Geary, *Plan of campaign*; see also Ambrose Macaulay, *The Holy See, British policy and the plan of campaign*. **37** Crossman, *Politics, law and order*, p. 179.

Ashbourne (1885) and Wyndham (1903) Acts, provided the loan funds for this to take place, though as late as 1902 only 15 per cent of farmers were actually owners.[38] Eventually almost all farmers came to own their own land, reinforcing the economically and socially conservative tone of twentieth-century Irish rural society; but this was not the outcome which most had imagined from the land war, whose principal issue had been rent reduction rather than land ownership.

Part of the Tories' success in putting home rule on the back burner until just before the first world war was their recasting of the Irish problem in terms of the defeat of crime. In 1887 a series of articles appeared in the London *Times* on the topic of 'Parnellism and crime' which linked Parnell with the Phoenix Park murders of 1882. A Special Commission investigated the matter, and Parnell's reputation was spectacularly restored (perhaps more so than it deserved), when the letters on which the articles were based were revealed as forgeries. However, even by having to prove that they were not criminals Irish nationalists were playing the Tory game.

Parnell died in 1891 after a traumatic year in which his being named in a divorce case lost him control over most of his party. His refusal to resign as leader following his denunciation, firstly, by English nonconformism (an all-important element in the Gladstonian coalition) and then by the Irish Catholic Church, revealed the handicapping dimension to a quality which had previously helped him, his aristocratic disdain. Had he resigned, he might have been able to return. Instead he chose to defy the *realpolitik* of the situation with tragic personal consequences, though in his desperate attempts to win political support in Ireland in 1891 he began to articulate a new and radical agenda.[39]

Reflecting the move towards mass democracy, the 1880s had been the first decade in Irish political culture in which presentation had mattered so much. Propaganda images vied with each other of Irish tenants as destitute or violent, of the British government as cruel or fair, and of the Irish party as determined or criminal. Irish images of Parnell during his heyday had emphasized his aristocratic calm.[40] Now in 1891 his enemies in the majority section of the IPP that had rejected him, most notably T.M. Healy, denounced his regal manner as the aristocratic trick of 'Mr Landlord Parnell' and Parnell himself as a traitor and libertine.[41]

The fall of Parnell left two legacies. The first was a tested and now provenly sophisticated political culture in nationalist Ireland that was able to survive the fall of a leader who had generated such a cult of personality. The IPP was split into several factions but was reunited after a decade. The second legacy was

38 Clark and Donnelly (eds), *Irish peasants*, p. 272; O'Callaghan, *British high politics*, p. 103. **39** O'Callaghan, *British high politics*, p. 121. **40** McBride, 'Political illustrations,' in McBride (ed.), *Irish nationalist imagination*, pp 73–94. **41** Callanan, *Healy*, pp 321–33.

a psychological transition within Irish culture concerning the place of the Catholic Church. Though it clung to its self-image as the beleaguered defender of a downtrodden people it was now clearly a powerful establishment force within nationalist Ireland, able to exercise both an external control and an internal moral surveillance of people's lives, whether they liked it or not. Urban intellectuals would find this increasingly oppressive, intent as they were on an individual self-realization which would become the norm in most urban western societies but not in rural-dominated Ireland. Among them were novelists such as the former priest Gerald O'Donovan (1871–1942) and the journalist W.P. Ryan (1867–1942).[42] The trauma of the fall of Parnell, classically immortalized in the Christmas dinner scene in *A portrait of the artist as a young man* (1916) by James Joyce (1882–1941), a novel more typical of its times than is often realized, came to symbolize this perceived oppression. The Church's growing authoritarianism and advocacy of a cultural quarantine of Ireland reflected a continuing insecurity, born of memory and a fear of the potentially shattering effects on Catholic Ireland of an encounter with modernity.[43]

In terms of the development of Irish society, the land war was of crucial significance in consolidating the lower-middle-class structure of the rural community. The political struggle for home rule in the mid-1880s was to a large extent more an episode in British rather than in Irish history; but its legacy in Ireland was the political visibility, in the emergence of Ulster Unionist politics, of an enormous social and cultural change that had been brewing in Ulster for several decades.

The home rule crisis of the 1880s was marked by visits to Belfast by prominent British politicians opposed to home rule, such as Lord Randolph Churchill in February 1886, to rally support. Col. Edward Saunderson (1837–1906) formed the first Unionist political grouping in parliament in 1885. There were as many as a quarter of a million southern Unionists, mostly from the landed classes, though their significance would decline with the end of landlordism. The last Tory lord mayor of Dublin held office in 1881, presaging a future loss of political power. Ulster Unionism, on the other hand, was on its way to becoming a distinctive political identity and not simply as a response to the threat of home rule.[44] It subsumed almost all strands of society in Ulster, except of course the large Catholic minority, within a polity which included an alliance with British conservatism and a revitalized Orangeism.

The Orange Order had been almost dormant until the 1860s, crippled by the Party Processions Act which banned sectarian demonstrations and was not repealed until 1870, while Fenian demonstrations seemed to go unchecked. The law, and official Orange acquiescence in it, was challenged in 1867 by

42 Murphy, *Catholic fiction*. **43** Garvin, *Nationalist revolutionaries*, pp 56–77. **44** Gibbon, *Ulster Unionism*.

William Johnston (1829–1902) of Ballykilbeg who staged a parade at Newtownards which attracted 40,000 participants.[45] A spell in jail as a result turned him into a Protestant hero, able to defy an official patrician Conservative candidate and rely on working men's groups to get himself elected to parliament. Ulster Conservatives were to learn the lesson of the need to reorganize themselves to take greater account of differing class needs. Belfast Conservatives, relying on the British-orientated economic success of that city and the decline of Ulster's rural aristocracy, were eventually able to establish authority both over the urban working class and over rural tenant farmers.

Liberalism had been strong in Ulster, with the *Northern Whig* newspaper as its voice, both among Catholics and Presbyterians whose ancestors had been eighteenth-century radicals. The 1880s were a turbulent time with T.M. Healy's 1885 election in Monaghan sparking off talk of a new 'invasion' of Ulster and riots in several Ulster towns. Lord Rossmore lost his magistracy after he called on Orangemen to resist nationalists. The political events of 1886 saw persistent rioting in Belfast in which fifty people died. In the polarization of those years, Ulster Protestants of all denominations rallied to the Conservative Unionist cause, and Liberalism was squeezed out.

An Ulster Unionist identity, based largely on religion rather than ethnicity, was taking shape. Though it was too early to speak of partition (the solution eventually implemented thirty years later), there were signs as early as 1881 that northern Protestants and southern Catholics could no longer co-operate at a national level or, indeed, any longer image themselves as part of the same Irish nation. That year plans for a National Exhibition of Irish Manufactures in 1882, the next in a series which had begun in 1853, collapsed over a proposal to have the queen as patron of the exhibition. For the Belfast delegation, the inclusion of Queen Victoria would have marked out the exhibition as non-political. For the southern nationalists, it would have sent precisely the opposite signal. There could be no compromise, and when an exhibition did take place in Dublin in August 1882 it was a purely nationalist affair, centring on the unveiling of Foley's huge statue of O'Connell in Sackville Street.[46]

45 Patterson, *Belfast labour movement.* **46** Murphy, *Abject loyalty*, pp 213–15.

CHAPTER 12

Urban refinement and wretchedness, 1801–91

By the end of the nineteenth century there were 120 Irish towns with their own local government structure. But Ireland was an overwhelmingly rural country, and towns were heavily reliant economically on their surrounding country areas. Nonetheless, urban areas were important, providing the institutional settings for intellectual, scientific, architectural, artistic and musical life. There were three real cities, Dublin, Belfast and Cork, whose size enabled them to a degree to generate a culture that was independent from the countryside; but they also tended to be places of intense urban squalor, especially for poorer people.

In the forty years after 1851, Ireland's population decreased by over a fifth. Its decline was less in towns with over 10,000 people and there was an increase in Dublin, Belfast, Kingstown (Dunleary), Londonderry and Newry. Ireland was becoming a marginally more urban country. Over the same period, the proportion of the population working in agriculture declined from 48.4 to 41.1 per cent. On the other hand, the figures for manufacturing declined from 22.8 to 16 per cent. However, those involved in domestic service rose from 9.4 to 18 per cent and those in the professions and public service from 2.2 to 5 per cent. The latter figure reflected to a degree the expansion of the civil service, entrance to which was opened to competition in 1870. In 1885 there were 45,000 customers for gas lighting in Irish towns. The next decade saw the advent of municipal electricity supplies.[1]

Before the union, 249 peer and 300 MPs had resided in Dublin. By 1821 there were only thirty-four peers and five MPs.[2] Merchants and professionals now attended the functions of the vice regal court at Dublin castle, and by 1841 there were 700 doctors and 2,000 lawyers. In 1853 a group of professionals and merchants purchased the 700-year old patent for the Donnybrook fair, whose name had entered the English language as a byword for disorder, in order to close it down. The middle classes were leaving their mark on Dublin life.[3]

Dublin's population rose from 182,000 in 1800 to 260,350 in 1901. Though its port expanded with the growth of railways, it declined in importance relative to Belfast. Apart from the brewing and biscuit businesses, the city's economy did not prosper.[4] There was a slow decline in Protestant control over the higher occupations. Four fifths of the male workforce were Catholic towards the end

1 Gribbon, 'Economic and social history,' in Vaughan (ed.), *Union II, 1870–1921*, pp 260–356. 2 Hill, *Dublin civil politics*, p. 292. 3 Saris, 'Great exhibition ,' in Litvack and Hooper (eds), *Regional identity*, p. 83. 4 Daly, *Dublin*, pp 3, 10.

of the century. In 1871, 47 per cent of professionals and public servants were Protestants, the number declining to 44 per cent ten years later. Protestants also held one third of positions in the clerical, banking and insurance worlds. There were some Protestants in working-class occupations, though only 3 per cent of labourers were Protestants in 1871. Protestants congregated in greater numbers in Dublin's middle-class suburbs, though they were also present in the city itself. In 1891, 16 per cent of the city population was Protestant. In the suburbs of Blackrock, Kingstown, Pembroke and Rathmines the figures were 31, 30, 36 and 43 per cent respectively.[5]

One third of the male workforce was involved in manufacturing in 1841, though it was reduced to one fifth by 1911. Working-class Protestants were often involved in skilled trades which were in decline and which tended to exclude migrants into the city from the countryside. As a result, among unskilled workers those who were able to secure the better positions tended to be the very migrants who had been excluded from the trades, whereas casual labourers tended to be native Dubliners. All of this resulted in the paradox of a buoyant class of labourers of country backgrounds in a relatively depressed city.[6]

The Municipal Corporations Act (1840) replaced the guild freeman with an electorate based on property in elections for Dublin city's ruling corporation. However, by the 1890s advances in the wider electorate meant that there were only 8,000 municipal voters compared with 37,000 for parliamentary elections, ensuring a continuing and significant Protestant Tory presence in municipal politics. Larger merchants dominated the membership of the corporation in the period after reform, but the number of merchants and professionals halved and those of publicans and grocers quadrupled in the course of the last half of the century.[7] However, the city was ill served by its local government. Because Dublin Corporation was one of the most prestigious elected bodies within the United Kingdom, vying for precedence with that of Edinburgh corporation after the corporation of the city of London, it became in some senses a partial-parliament for Irish nationalists able to hold a majority within it.[8] Its members tended to be more interested in national politics rather than Dublin issues and were often from other parts of the country – from Daniel O'Connell (lord mayor 1841–2, from Co. Kerry, and MP for Co. Cork), to Thomas Sexton (lord mayor 1888–89, from Co. Waterford, and MP for Belfast).

For most people Dublin was a miserable and unhealthy city in which to live, racked by contagious disease, poor sanitation, overcrowding in tenement buildings and homelessness.[9] In spite of the Vartry scheme which increased the city's water supply in the 1860s, typhoid persisted until late in the century and,

5 Daly, 'Two cities,' in Cosgrove (ed.), *Dublin*, pp 119–20. 6 Daly, 'Dublin working class,' *Irish Historical Studies* 23:90 (1982), pp 121–33. 7 Daly, *Dublin*, p. 204. 8 Murphy, *Abject loyalty*, p. xxxi. 9 Prunty, *Dublin slums*.

indeed, killed the poet Gerard Manley Hopkins (1844–89), who was professor of Greek at University College Dublin. Cholera also raged periodically until the 1860s. There were slums in every part of the city. In mid century, in the South City ward, 62 per cent of all children were dead within the first ten years of life. In the 1830s the average age at death for merchants was 55–60 years, but 35–40 for tailors.[10] Annual death rates per 1,000 in that decade were 28.6, but 29.5 in the 1880s, much higher than London or Glasgow; there was no significant decline in Dublin until the twentieth century. The death rate per 1,000 for those in service was 34.71, but even for middle-class people it was 26.98. In 1900 Dublin had the fifth highest death rate in the world.[11]

Towards the end of the century, greater efforts were being made at improved sanitation, with 7,800 water and 17,200 dry closets in the city by 1879. Housing schemes were developed such as the Coombe and Plunkett Street.[12] In the early nineteenth century charity work was controlled by the Established Church and was largely funded by the state, the Catholic Church at the time being legally barred from endowing charities. By the end of the century, the state was funding Catholic religious orders to care for children, and nuns were being employed in workhouse hospitals. As has been noted earlier, the mid-century saw denominational tensions in charity work between institutions financed by the Irish Church Missions, on the one hand, and Catholic charities, such as St Brigid's outdoor orphanage for girls and boys, on the other.[13]

Ireland's two other principal cities presented very different profiles, with one in decline and the other in exponential growth. Cork experienced some economic growth up until 1840 with shipbuilding, engineering, brewing, and other activities. However, most industries went into a decline thereafter, though flour milling and the woollen and brewing industries grew. One of the reasons for what happened was the decline in the city's economic hinterland. Cork city's population stood at 82,635 in 1851 and did not change much over the next fifty years. Over the next forty years, though, the county's population declined from 649,000 to 439,000.[14] Early nineteenth-century Cork had been a generator of literary and artistic talent from William Maginn to Daniel Maclise (1806–70), though much of it was forced to find an employment outlet in London. There was a core of 7,000 wealthy people in the city, though there was also a rapid turnover of Cork merchant families. Merchants dominated the Cork corporation after the 1840 reform. As in Dublin there was a two-thirds to one-third division between Catholics and Liberal Protestants on the one hand and Tories on the other.[15]

10 Daly, *Dublin*, pp 241–3. **11** Ibid., pp 270, 276. **12** Prunty, *Dublin slums*, pp 80, 122. **13** Ibid., p. 243. **14** Bielenberg, *Cork's industrial revolution*, pp 116–26. **15** D'Alton, *Politics in Cork*; Jupp and Doyle, 'Cork city elections,' *Irish Historical Studies* 29:13 (1994), pp 13–43; O'Brien, 'Society in Cork,' in O'Flanagan and Buttimer (eds), *Cork*, pp 699–720.

The population of Belfast surged from 19,000 in 1801 to 349,180 by 1901. The linen industry moved from the countryside to factories in the city, the number of flax and linen factories increasing in the city from 69 in 1850 to 129 in 1879. Shipbuilding flourished because of a combination of infrastructure, skilled labour and enterprise. The Harland and Wolff company benefited greatly from its links with the White Star Line. The partnership of Harland and Wolff had begun in 1862, though it only retained a workforce of 1,500 in that decade. Two decades later it was 5,000, though economic setbacks at the time forced its reduction to 3,000.[16]

Scientists and doctors had a significant profile in nineteenth-century Ireland. Robert Graves (1796–1853), William Stokes (1801–78), John Cheyne (1777–1836), Sir Dominic Corrigan (1802–80) and Sir William Wilde (1815–76) were leading members of the medical profession and doctors of international reputation.[17] Scientists included the astronomer Lord Rosse (1800–67), the chemist Sir Robert Kane (1809–90), the geologist Sir Richard Griffith (1784–1878), and the seismologist Robert Mallet (1810–81).[18] Lord Kelvin (1824–1907), one of the century's greatest scientists, was born in Belfast though he is more associated with Scotland.

Corrigan and Kane were Catholics. Though there were considerably fewer Catholics than Protestant scientists, this was because the pursuit of science generally required a social and economic position beyond the reach of most Catholics.[19] Contrary to what is sometimes held, Catholic schools encouraged science. It was the centrepiece of the curriculum at Castleknock College, for example.[20] The institutional setting for science had been an Ascendancy one in the Royal Irish Academy, Royal Dublin Society and Trinity College. As the century wore on, new institutions were set up, such as the Museum of Irish Industry, founded by Kane in 1846, from which the Royal College of Science developed in 1867. Later in the century the Department of Science and Art in South Kensington, London, took over several Irish scientific institutions.[21]

The British Association for the Advancement of Science held six meetings in Ireland during the century, three in Dublin, two in Belfast and one in Cork. The Irish Astronomer Royal, Sir William Rowan Hamilton (1805–65), an important mathematician, presided at the Dublin meeting in 1835, and Lord Rosse at the Cork meeting in 1843. At the former meeting, half the papers in physics, maths and chemistry were given by Irish scientists.[22]

16 Patterson, *Belfast labour movement*. **17** Fleetwood, *History of medicine*, p. 183. **18** Terry Eagleton, *Scholars and rebels*, p. 90. **19** Bennett, 'Science and social policy,' in Bowler and Whyte (eds), *Science and society*, pp 37–8; Foster, 'Natural history,' ibid., pp 119–23; Whyte, *Science, colonialism*, pp 6–7. **20** James H. Murphy (ed.), *Castleknock College*, pp 72–3. **21** Whyte, *Science, colonialism*, p. 89. **22** Johnston, 'Science and technology,' *Crane Bag* 7:2 (1983), p. 59.

The most significant meeting was in Belfast in 1874 at which its then president, John Tyndall, from Co. Carlow, advanced his own version of Darwinism, called atomic theory, leaving little room for religious explanations of life. Though it elicited a condemnation from the Irish Catholic bishops, Darwinism was just one more in a long list of modern liberal evils for Catholics, many of them remote from Irish experience. It had caused a traumatic debate in England, where Protestantism and modernity had not been automatic enemies. As a result the Tyndall address provoked its greatest response from Belfast Protestant ministers, such as John Scott Porter and William McIlwaine.[23]

Socialism, albeit of an elite variety, flourished briefly in pockets in Ireland in the 1820s and 30s. William Thompson (1785–1833) of Clonkeen, Roscarberry, Co. Cork, published books on the redistribution of wealth in 1824 and 1830 and was seen by Robert Owen as something of a rival. He failed, however, to have a utopian commune established, an achievement realized by Edward Thomas Craig, together with the Owenite landlord John Scott Vandeleur at Ralahine, Co. Clare, in 1831.[24]

Trade unions were decriminalized in 1824.[25] Cork was one of the earlier areas for trade union activity among craft workers.[26] The Cork Trades Association was founded in 1832, and by 1845 there were nineteen craft unions in Cork. Five years later there were forty-five unions in Dublin. From 1846–48 the Dublin Regular Trades Association acted as a forum for Dublin unions. Prior to that, another pan-union organization, the National Trades Political Union, had found itself taken over by supporters of O'Connell.[27] The relationship between trade unionism and politics was always difficult for the former in Ireland. Sharing the nationalist consensus that the free trade of the United Kingdom was damaging the Irish economy many workers tended to throw in their lot with nationalism.

The Irish Democratic Association, 1849–50, tried to combine socialism with nationalism in a manner which did not lead merely to the absorption of the former by the latter. At the end of 1851 the *Christian Social Economist* was briefly in publication under the editorship of a priest, Thaddeus O'Malley.[28] In October 1862 the Dublin United Trades Association was founded and lasted for several years as an association of skilled workers' unions.[29] In Dublin unions tended to be small, whereas in Belfast the larger engineering and building unions flour-

23 Brooke, 'Religion and secular thought,' in Beckett et al., *Belfast*, pp 111–28; Foster, 'Tyndall, Darwin,' in Stewart (ed.), *Hearts and minds*, pp 40–70; Livingstone, 'Darwin in Belfast,' in Foster and Chesney (eds), *Nature in Ireland*, pp 387–408. **24** Ellis, *Irish working class*. **25** O'Connor, *Labour history*, p. 200. **26** Cronin, 'Cork city and county,' in O'Flanagan and Buttimer (eds.), *Cork*, pp 721–58. **27** Boyle, *Irish labour movement*, pp 45–7. **28** Geoghegan, 'Irish socialism,' in Boyce, Eccleshall and Geoghegan (eds), *Political thought in Ireland*, pp 100–23. **29** Boyle, *Irish labour movement*, p. 54.

ished. In the 1860s British-based unions, such as the Amalgamated Society of Engineers, the United Operative Plumbers Association and the Amalgamated Society of Carpenters and Joiners arrived in Irish cities and towns. The trend throughout the latter half of the nineteenth century was for the absorption of Irish trade unionists into large British unions, though clashes between Irish and British unions could result as in the case of the tension between the Dublin Topographical Provident Society and English print unions in Ireland.[30]

After 1857 some Cork unions were founded under the influence of the IRB In 1873 the first branch of an agricultural labourers' union was established at Kanturk, Co. Cork.[31] The years after 1889 were ones of enormous growth for trade unionism and socialism in Ireland, with semi-skilled workers and labourers organized into general unions and the foundation of the Fabian Society in Dublin and the Belfast Independent Labour Party, both in 1892, the Irish Trade Union Congress in 1894, and the Irish Socialist Republican Party in 1896.[32] The 'new unionism' between 1889 and 1891 embraced transport, general employment, the Belfast shipyards, agriculture and textiles, with women linen workers in Belfast being unionized in 1890. In that year there were sixty-nine strikes. The seamen's strike in Dublin, Belfast, Cork and Derry of 1889 attracted the most attention. However, over a quarter of the disputes in 1891 resulted in the dismissal of all or some of the workers involved.[33] The new unionism began to ebb and it would be over fifteen years before trade unionism would become reinvigorated and find a more lasting Irish rather than British base under Jim Larkin (1876–1947).

Ireland had its fair share of Victorian intellectuals whose contributions tended to be disparaged in the subsequent years of the Irish revival. Men such as Edward Dowden (1843–1913), professor of English at Trinity College Dublin, who championed Walt Whitman, eschewed the Irish revival and was despised by W.B. Yeats. His greatest achievement, however, was to establish English literature as a liberal university discipline. By the time of his death, thirty of his students were established in chairs of English throughout the world.[34]

Doctors, lawyers, academics, popular historians, politicians, artists, clerics, journalists and literary figures formed the Irish intelligentsia. Many were 'traditional' conservatives rather than 'organic' progressives. Yet traditional intellectuals in such settings as the Ordnance Survey and the *Dublin University Magazine* had produced 'organic' results, assisting the very nationalist movement they had sought to resist.[35] This was the case of W.E.H. Lecky (1838–1903) who was the only Irishman to approach the category of the

30 Keogh, *Irish working class*, pp 21–5. **31** Cronin, 'Cork city and county,' p. 743; O'Connor, *Labour history*, p. 43. **32** Boyle, *Irish labour movement*, p. 183. **33** O'Connor, *Labour history*, pp 47–57. **34** Brown, 'Dowden,' in Brown, *Ireland's literature*, pp 29–48. **35** Eagleton, *Scholars and rebels*, pp 1–39.

Victorian sage, in the tradition of Carlyle, Ruskin and Arnold. His work was quoted by both unionists and nationalists alike.

Lecky was a political moralist who used history as the vehicle for his thought.[36] In works such as *The leaders of public opinion in Ireland* (1861) and *A history of Ireland in the eighteenth century* (1892) – extracted from his *History of England in the eighteenth century* (1878–90) – he valorized the Protestant Patriot tradition and tended to undermine the moral validity of the union. His work on the eighteenth century had been prompted by the analysis of J.A. Froude (1818–94), Carlyle's literary executor and author of *The English in Ireland in the eighteenth century* (1872). Froude's low opinion of the Irish capacity for self-government was matched by his castigation of the failure of Britain to be firm in Ireland and support the Ascendancy.[37]

Lecky's liberalism, however, underwent a revision in the 1880s when faced with what he saw as the betrayal of his dreams which in his case was marked by Parnellism, in the same way as it had been O'Connellism in the era of the Edgeworths and Morgans. Lecky retreated into conservatism and from any notion of home rule. He served as MP for Trinity College from 1895–1902 and in 1896 published his pessimistic *Democracy and liberty*.

Music and, to a large extent, the visual arts had their institutional bases in the cities. Architecture had an impact throughout the countryside. James Gandon (1743–1824) and Francis Johnston (1761–1829) were still alive in the early nineteenth century and some of the great Dublin buildings of the Georgian period were built in the early part of the century, notably the Four Courts (1802), Nelson's Pillar (1808–9) and the General Post Office (1815–17), the first by Gandon and the latter two by Johnston. However, nineteenth-century Ireland in architecture was not a period for great country houses, though some were built, or for Dublin public buildings, but of churches, several thousand of which were built during the period.

Church building style was highly ideological.[38] In the eighteenth and early nineteenth centuries Catholic and Presbyterian churches adopted the same architectural styles, the Grecian temple style in the towns and the t-plan style, which derived from a seventeenth-century Presbyterian tradition, in the countryside. This identity reflected the parity of the Catholic and Presbyterian Churches in their exclusion from full participation in civil society.

From the mid-nineteenth century, during the devotional revolution years, there was an enormous investment by the Catholic community in church building, and a determination, largely accomplished, that they ought to overtake

36 McCartney, *Lecky*. **37** Wyatt, 'Froude,' *Irish Historical Studies* 19:75 (1975), pp 261–85. **38** Rowan, 'Irish Victorian churches,' in Gillespie and Kennedy (eds), *Ireland: art into history*, pp 207–30.

Church of Ireland churches in quality and size. Roman basilica and baroque styles were associated on the continent (where many Irish priests were still being trained) with the counter-reformation, and Cardinal Cullen was known to be keen on them, insisting that the chapel of his new seminary at Clonliffe in Dublin be done in a Roman style. The Church of Ireland (and, indeed, the Anglican church worldwide) had adopted the Gothic revival style and remarkably the Irish Catholic Church was eventually to do the same thus two rival church architectural or 'ecclesiological' societies came into operation. One view is that the reason for the Catholic embrace of Gothic was part of staking a claim for pre-Reformation continuity and validity and denying it to the Church of Ireland and thus paralleled the debate on Christianity going on in contemporary Irish Celticism. Indeed, the Church of Ireland was for a time to embrace a Celtic revival architecture, partly in order to trump the Catholic choice of Gothic. Of more importance though was the personal predilection for Gothic of the leading British architect of the day, Augustus Welby Pugin (1813–52), who worked on the new Palace of Westminster and was a Catholic convert who believed that Gothic was the only appropriate style for churches. His religion made him much sought after in Ireland and his commissions included Killarney cathedral and St Aidan's cathedral, Enniscorthy, as well as Adare manor and Lismore castle. His son Edward Welby Pugin (1834–75), partner of G.C. Ashlin (1830–1921), continued his father's work but his most important Irish successor was J.J. McCarthy (1817–82), who built over sixty churches.[39]

In public and private buildings of substance, embracing museums, workhouses, country houses, banks and suburban villas, a wide variety of styles were employed from Hibernian monumental, neo-Gothic and neo-Renaissance to Ruskinian Venetian, Baronial and neo-Tudor.[40] The most important architectural partnership for secular building was that of Benjamin Woodward (1815–61) and Sir Thomas Deane (1792–1871). Together with the latter's son, Thomas Newenham Deane (1827–99), they had an enormous influence on Irish architecture in general in favour of Gothic.

Much traditional music was lost during the famine, especially singing, though folk instrumental music survived in the playing of instruments such as the fiddle, union pipes, tin whistle, flute, melodeon, concertina and accordion.[41] Country people played music in their homes in the winter and at the crossroads in the summer. Older dances had died out and the jig, reel and hornpipe taken over, the jig having some Irish roots and the reel and hornpipe being largely English and Scots.

39 Richardson, *Gothic revival*; Sheehy, *McCarthy*. **40** Barrett and Sheehy, 'Visual arts and society,' in Vaughan (ed.), *Union II, 1870–1921*, pp 436–99. **41** Fleishchmann, 'Music and society,' ibid., pp 500–22.

Though partisan ballads were a powerful force in Irish politics, Victorian middle-class musical life, which flourished in towns and especially cities, was part of the shared culture of Ireland and Britain. Twenty-two musical societies were active in Dublin between 1841 and 1867. The Antient Concerts Society, which had rooms in Great Brunswick Street, had five concerts per season. The exhibitions of 1853 and 1865 opened with performances of choir and orchestra of 1,000. Sir Charles Stanford (1852–1924) was the country's most prominent composer but there were other composers such as Michael Balfe (1808–70) and Vincent Wallace (1812–65), who wrote popular operas, and John Field (1782– 1837), who while working in Russia anticipated Chopin in developing the nocturne.

Musical life was slower to develop in Belfast, though things were helped with the opening of the Ulster Hall in 1862 which could accommodate as many as 3,000 people. In 1854 the Athenaeum, later rebuilt as the Opera House, opened in Cork with a capacity of 2,000. In Dublin the Theatre Royal, with a capacity of nearly 3,800, hosted Italian operas usually performed by the Covent Garden and Haymarket companies from London. The 'Swedish nightingale', Jenny Lind, toured Ireland in 1849.

The Irish Academy of Music was founded in 1848, becoming the Royal Irish Academy of Music in 1872. In 1875 Joseph Robinson began the Dublin Musical Society which arranged three concerts per season with choir and orchestra, for over twenty-five years. The Belfast Philharmonic Society was founded in 1874 and the Cork Musical Society in 1869. In 1871 the Gaiety Theatre opened in Dublin and hosted companies such as those of D'Oyly Carte and Carl Rosa. Towards the end of the century, the Cecilian Society, founded in 1878 and promoted by Heinrich Bewerunge (1862–1926), professor of Church chant and organ at Maynooth, sponsored a bourgeois Catholic art music, though it was overtaken by the Irish revival of the 1890s.[42]

Whereas literature became deeply involved with issues of politics and nation, the other arts in late nineteenth-century Ireland did not. This was especially paradoxical in the case of music, as it figures greatly in nationalist iconography and mythology, the harp indeed being a central symbol for Ireland.[43] Yet somehow it was the idea of music rather than music itself which was important. The Young Irelanders, for all their interest in ballads, were more concerned with lyrics than with melodies. Ironically, the enormous symbolic political weight that music was supposed to bear in practice crushed it and deterred composers from attempting to effect that bridge between ethnic and art traditions which Chopin had managed so brilliantly for Poland. Folk music became a substitute rather than a resource for an art tradition and prevented the creation of modern Irish modes of musical expression in the nineteenth century.

42 White, *Music and cultural history*, pp 74–93. **43** Ibid., pp 36–52, 151–60.

The story of the lack of a connection between the Irish visual arts and politics is even more complex. Both nationalism and unionism relied on images. Shamrocks, harps, Irish wolfhounds and round towers became the stock in trade of nationalism. Increasingly, also, the image of Hibernia, later Erin, was used to represent Ireland. It was pioneered by the sculptor John Hogan in his monument to Bishop Doyle in Carlow cathedral and in his 'Erin with a bust of Lord Cloncurry'.[44] Later, in the propaganda war of the 1880s, Erin appeared as a much more assertive figure in nationalist images than the dependent Hibernia, reliant on a strong Britannia, of British images.[45]

Paintings of Ireland were also produced by British artists but tended to play the same anaesthetic role for British culture concerning Ireland as the theatre, avoiding the reality of Irish poverty and presenting comforting images instead. Sir David Wilkie (1785–1841) visited Ireland in 1835 and produced pictures such as *The Peep O-Day Boy's cabin* (1836) and *The Irish whiskey still* (1840) which portrayed happy Irish peasant families in the pictorial tradition of the holy family.[46] Erskine Nicol (1825–1904) had a studio in Westmeath and produced genre vignettes of peasant life. His *An ejected family* (1853) depicts an eviction scene of well-fed people. Though later Victorian artists such as Ernest Waterlow (1850–1919) and W.H. Bartlett (1809–54) presented a less fanciful Ireland, their work failed to engage with Irish realities which might discomfort British sensibilities. There was one example of a painting that did, however. *Eviction* (1890) by Elizabeth Butler (1846–1933) was a starkly depicted scene and was much criticized in London where it was exhibited. Perhaps it disconcerted the deeply cynical prime minister Lord Salisbury more than he cared to admit, when he commented of it that the beauty of the scene made him almost wish he had been taking part in the eviction himself.[47]

London had been the destination of talented Irish artists since the eighteenth century.[48] Nathaniel Hone (1718–84) had been a thorn in the side of Sir Joshua Reynolds. *The education of Achilles* by James Barry (1741–1806) had promoted republican views. Beginning with Martin Archer Shee (1769–1850), however, Irish artists ceased to antagonize the London art establishment and longed to become insiders, especially within the Royal Academy. William Mulready (1786–1863) became an academician in 1816 and Daniel Maclise rose to fame in the Royal Academy in the 1830s.

Maclise moved in Tory journalistic and political circles in London, though his friendship with the young Disraeli ended in 1836 when it was revealed that they were both lovers of Lady Sykes, together with Lord Lyndhurst.[49] He

44 Loftus, *Mirror*; Sheehy, *Celtic revival*, pp 55–6. **45** Curtis, *Images of Erin*. **46** Cullen, *Visual politics*, pp 116–59. **47** Bhreathnach-Lynch, 'Victorian paintings,' *Journal of Victorian Culture* 2:2 (1997), pp 245–63. **48** Cullen, *Visual politics*, pp 14–49. **49** Turpin, 'Maclise, Disraeli,' *Éire-Ireland* 15:1 (1980): pp 46–63; Weston, *Maclise*.

worked closely with Maginn, whose 'Gallery of illustrious literary characters' he illustrated, and also with Mahony on illustrating *The reliques of Fr Prout*. His greatest professional success came with the commission to provide epic historical frescoes for the new palace of Westminster in the 1860s, depicting Wellington and Nelson.[50]

Maclise produced a number of large-scale paintings in his early career such as *Snap apple night, or All Hallows eve: Ireland* (1833) and *The installation of Captain Rock* (1834). Then later on came *The marriage of Strongbow and Eva* (1854). *Captain Rock* has been criticized as merely offering a collection of grotesque figures rather than a serious depiction of Irish life and the supposed pro-Irish tone of *Strongbow and Eve* has also been doubted.[51] However, one detail in *Captain Rock*, in which a youth is being encouraged to shoot directly towards the viewer of the picture, exposes the viewer as a hostile spectator of the scene and perhaps unmasks the aggressive imperial intent behind the refinement of art.[52] Carleton had encountered similar problems with the narrators of his fiction and had found a solution in having them straddle both peasants and readers' worlds.

As the nineteenth century advanced, Dublin and Cork provided the institutional setting for Irish art.[53] The Royal Hibernian Academy was founded in 1824 and its school of fine art was eventually to open itself to women such as Sarah Purser (1848–1943) and Rose Barton (1856–1929). The late 1850s, however, witnessed a destructive dispute within the RHA between its secretary, Michael Angelo Hayes (1820–77), a painter of military subjects, and that great cultural polymath, George Petrie, who was elected president in 1857.

The Dublin Society—'Royal' was added to the title in 1820—sponsored the teaching of modelling in the early part of the century, though the original momentum in sculptural teaching would be lost until it was revived by John Hughes towards the end of the century.[54] In mid-century the government sponsored the teaching of design, founding a school of design in Dublin, under the auspices of the RDS, which was later reconstituted as the Metropolitan School of Art and connected to the South Kensington Department of Science and Art.[55] Schools of design were also founded in Limerick, Belfast and Cork. The latter was to become the Crawford Municipal School of Art. In 1861 the Queen's Institute for the Training and Employment of Educated Women was founded in Dublin. It was a forerunner to the home industries movement which promoted lace making and embroidery and later wood and metal work. In 1894

50 Turpin, 'Maclise and his place,' in *Anglo-Irish studies* 1 (1975), pp 51–69. **51** Cullen, *Visual politics*, pp 44, 47. **52** Gibbons, 'Art and agrarian insurgency,' in Foley and Ryder (eds), *Ideology and Ireland*, pp 23–44. **53** Barrett and Sheehy, 'Visual arts and society.' **54** Turpin, 'Sculptural education,' *Éire-Ireland* 24:1 (1989), pp 40–58. **55** Turpin, 'Dublin Metropolitan School of Art,' *Dublin Historical Record*, 36:2 (1983), pp 42–64.

the Arts and Crafts Society of Ireland would take up the campaign and sponsor seven arts and crafts exhibitions between 1895 and 1925.[56]

The nineteenth century had been an era in Ireland of great exhibitions of arts and science on the model of the 1851 Crystal Palace Great Exhibition in London.[57] There were five exhibitions in Dublin (1853, 1861, 1865, 1872, 1882), two in Cork (1852, 1882), one in South Kensington (1888) and an 'Irish village', organized by Lady Aberdeen, at the Chicago World's Fair (1893). Each one had its own distinct ideological complexion. However, from the viewpoint of the institutions of Irish art the most important was that of 1853, as it led on to the creation of Ireland's national cultural institutions. It was also the most impressive with 455 sculptures and 1,023 paintings displayed and over half a million daily and one third of a million season tickets sold. It had been sponsored by the railway-builder William Dargan, and afterwards a committee was formed to memorialize his generosity. At the same time a group called the Irish Institution was formed which sponsored six exhibitions of old masters over the following years. Meanwhile, the government was persuaded to finance Irish museums. In 1857 a Natural History Museum was inaugurated with a lecture by Dr David Livingstone. In 1864, after many financial vicissitudes, the National Gallery of Ireland was opened on the Leinster Lawn site of the 1853 exhibition. It had been the idea of the Irish Institution, but the Dargan committee was persuaded to support it. It began with a collection of 105 paintings and remained open in the evenings, lit by gas and attracting 100,000 visitors annually for the first five years, though numbers subsequently dropped off. A National Library and National Museum were opened in 1890, completing the museum complex in the vicinity of Leinster House.

Ireland produced a large number of painters in a variety of genres, among the most notable of whom were Sir Frederick William Burton (1816–1900), Nathaniel Hone (1831–1917), John Butler Yeats (1839–1922), Sarah Purser (1848–1943), Sir John Lavery (1856–1941), Walter Osborne (1859–1903), Roderic O'Conor (1860–1940), William Orpen (1878–1931) and W.J. Leech (1881–1968). Yet if Dublin and other Irish cities provided one institutional setting which provided an alternative to London for the study and production of Irish art, many of the more important Irish artists found a more congenial setting on the continent. In France, in particular, they found themselves free from both nationalist and pro-union political agendas. O'Conor, for example, was a friend of Gaugin. He lived and worked at Pont-Aven and painted in Brittany. Nathaniel Hone, a relation of his eighteenth-century namesake, spent eighteen years in France before returning to Ireland. In the 1870s and 80s there was an

56 Paul Larmour, *The arts and crafts movement in Ireland* (Belfast: Friars Bush, 1992). **57** De Courcy, *National Gallery of Ireland*; Murphy, *Abject loyalty*, pp 112–20, 151–3, 191, 213–16.

Irish artists' colony at Antwerp, whose most important member was Walter Osborne.

Irish cities in the nineteenth century were places of grim living conditions for many but they also provided the setting for the high cultural activities of music and art, as well as literature. However, whereas literature was increasingly absorbed in the conflict between nationalism and unionism, music found itself stunted by the cultural pressures of Irish politics, while some forms of art flourished by escaping the pressure altogether and decamping to France.

CHAPTER 13

From plough to parlour, 1801–91

The study of gender in nineteenth-century Ireland has yielded some significant results in the case of women. There has also been a limited degree of attention to men, generally in connection with their participation in organizations such as the police and the Fenians.[1] Issues concerning women and gender identity include both their participation in the very public spheres of politics and writing, especially in campaigns for political rights for women, and their experience of sexuality, marriage, family, work, education and emigration. The latter were connected to the social conditions of the times and the various structures of constraint to which women were subject.

Though generally disenfranchized politically, women were sometimes actively involved in movements of political radicalism. There were women members of the United Irish movement, and Mary Ann McCracken in particular proved herself to be an influential figure in the movement, though subsequent histories tended to down play her own independent role and to portray her in terms of her devotion to her brother Henry Joy McCracken. As with most Irish political and cultural movements, the United Irishmen used female iconography to depict Ireland, though their version of Hibernia was seen in terms of strength and heroism rather than in the more usual terms of dependence.[2]

Later nineteenth-century British images of Hibernia continued to present her as dependent on a martial and protective Britannia. By contrast, Irish nationalist images of the now rival Erin were of a much more assertive figure.[3] Ironically, male nationalist politicians in the years of the land war regarded women's participation in public affairs as tolerable only in the exceptional circumstances of crisis. This is also reflected in Rosa Mulholland's novel *Marcella Grace* (1886), with its very different view of the land crisis from that of the Land League, whose heroine manages an estate and engages in a public campaign but only so long as her husband is in jail.[4]

In October 1880 the Ladies Land League was founded in New York by Fanny Parnell (1849–82) as a fund-raising body. It was set up in Ireland in January 1881 by Anna Parnell (1852–1911) as a force for land agitation, holding public meetings, resisting evictions, and housing evicted tenants.[5] By the

1 Griffin, 'The Irish police,' in Kelleher and Murphy (eds), *Gender perspectives*, pp 168–78; Joyce, 'The Fenians,' ibid., pp 70–80. **2** Thuente, 'United Irish images of women;' Gray, 'McCracken;' and Kinsella, 'Women of 1798' in Keogh and Furlong (eds), *Women of 1798*, pp 9–25, 47–63 and 187–99. **3** Innes, *Woman and nation*, pp 13, 17. **4** Murphy, 'Gender and nationalism,' in Kirkpatrick (ed.), *Irish women writers*, pp 58–78. **5** Luddy 'Women and politics,' in Valiulis and

end of that year it had 400 branches in Ireland with many women from farming backgrounds as members, though prominent middle-class women also joined. These included Katharine Tynan (1861–1931), Hannah Lynch (1862–1904) and Jennie Wyse Power (1858–1941). Some of them would go on to become political radicals in their subsequent careers. The Ladies Land League flourished after the wider Land League was suppressed and while Parnell and his lieutenants were in prison. On his release, the organization was sidelined, and this caused Anna Parnell's permanent estrangement from her brother.

In a second irony, active campaigning for women's political rights, especially for the right to vote, tended at least initially to come from the other end of the political spectrum. Anna Maria Haslam (1829–1922) and Isabella Tod (1836– 1896) were the leading activists for women's political rights.[6] Haslam was one of the founders of the Queen's Institute (1861) and of Alexandra College (1866) for the higher education of women, both in Dublin. Tod worked for women's education in Belfast with the founding of the Ladies Collegiate School (1859) and Ladies Institute (1867), eventually helping women to gain degrees at Queen's College, Belfast, in 1882. Tod was also involved with the National Association for the Promotion of Social Sciences which gave a platform to women activists. Haslam and Tod both campaigned for women's suffrage. Haslam founded a Dublin Women's Suffrage Association in 1874 and Tod one in Belfast in 1872. Both also campaigned against home rule through the Women's Liberal Unionist Association.

As Haslam and Tod's careers demonstrate, educational opportunities for women were opening up in the nineteenth century not only at primary level but, for those who could afford it, also at secondary and tertiary levels. Women could qualify as doctors from 1876 and were able to sit for degrees of the Royal University a few years later.

Better off and more leisured women could find an outlet for their energies in charity work, which was generally arranged along denominational lines. Such work could range from fund-raising and giving advice to visiting the homes of the poor and working in orphanages, prisons and workhouses.[7] In the Catholic community much of this work was already being done by nuns.[8] In the late eighteenth and early nineteenth centuries well-off Catholic women such as Nano Nagle (1718–84), Mary Aikenhead (1787–1858), Frances Ball (1794– 1861) and Catherine McAuley (1778–1841) began movements which led respectively to the founding of the Presentation, Irish Charity, Loreto and Mercy sisters. Other native religious congregations were also founded and were joined in mid-centu-

O'Dowd (eds), *Women and Irish history*, p. 98; Te Brake, 'Irish peasant women,' *Irish Historical Studies* 28:109 (1992), pp 63–80; Côté and Hearne, 'Anna Parnell,' in Cullen and Luddy (eds), *Women, power and consciousness*, pp 263–93. **6** Cullen, 'Haslam'; and Luddy, 'Tod'; ibid., pp 161–96, 197–230. **7** Luddy, *Women and philanthropy*, p. 214. **8** Clear, *Nuns*.

ry by continental congregations. The work of nuns began with projects for the poor. The education of middle-class girls was added in mid-century and towards the end of the century increasing links were forged between nuns and the state through work in state-financed institutions. In spite of their prodigious activity nuns have been criticized as social disciplinarians, retarders of social progress, maintainers of class divisions, monopolizers of social work and identifiers with patriarchal structures.[9]

Women could also embark on careers in painting and writing, though most of them needed to be quite affluent in order to do so. Sarah Purser and Rose Barton studied fine art at the Royal Hibernian Academy. The Dublin Queen's Institute for the Training and Employment of Educated Women led on to the founding of the arts and crafts movement in Ireland in which some women found employment.

Earlier in this work the careers of writers such as Charlotte Brooke, Maria Edgeworth, Lady Morgan, Mary Balfour, Mary Leadbeater, Selina Bunbury and Anna Maria Hall were noted. There was a significant group of women writers, most of them poets, associated with the *Nation*, as has also been observed.[10] Some of them managed the paper for a time in 1848, another example the pattern of women's empowerment at times of crisis. There were large numbers of women novelists and poets working towards the end of the century and several families of literary women, such as the Sweetmans and Furlongs, many of them from upper-middle-class Catholic as well as Protestant families.[11] The work of several of them, including Annie Keary, Margaret Brew, Charlotte Riddell, May Laffan, Letitia McClintock, Elizabeth Owens Blackburne, Fannie Gallaher, Rosa Mulholland, M.E. Francis, Katharine Tynan and Emily Lawless will be explored under a variety of headings in the next chapter.

Women writers who were from Ireland or who wrote about it worked mostly as individuals, defying easy generalizations. Lady Blessington (1789–1849) was a novelist and scandalous leader, with her lover Count D'Orsay, of a literary circle in London. Her near contemporary Charlotte Elizabeth Tonna (1790–1846) wrote thirty novels but was a fervent evangelical. Asenath Nicholson (*c.*1794–1855)[12] was an American visitor to Ireland whose accounts of the famine appeared to transcend the boundaries of religious polemic. Margaret Anne Cusack (1832–99), the 'nun of Kenmare', was an Irishwoman who changed religious denominations twice and spent some time living in America. She was a social activist, novelist, historian and polemicist whose autobiographies are accounts largely of her turbulent relationship with male ecclesiastical authority. Not all women writers, though, led lives of public fame. Attie O'Brien (1840–83)

9 Ibid., pp 157, 160, 162, 165. **10** Anton, 'Women and the *Nation*,' *History Ireland* 1:3 (1993), pp 34–8. **11** Colman, *Irish women poets*. **12** Kelleher, *Feminization of famine*, pp 74–86; Murphy, 'Vincentian parish missions,' pp 162–3.

was an invalid from asthma and only one of her four novels was published during her lifetime. Her *Through the dark night* (1897), set in the 1860s, perceptively explores the connection between perceptions of social inferiority and an Anglophobic nationalism.[13]

For the vast majority of women life was often much grimmer and for some it amounted to a continuing struggle for existence. Female images, especially those of mothers unable to feed their children, were used to convey the horror of the famine in the 1840s. The nineteenth century, however, saw a remarkable change in patterns of women's economic activity, both in paid positions in agriculture and in manufacturing and in unpaid work on the home farm. It was a change moreover that accompanied and advanced a very significant social adjustment.

At the beginning of the nineteenth century, large numbers of women were employed in the domestic textile industry. Thus in 1821 half a million women were involved in spinning. But by 1861 in Connaught, for example, the number of spinners had fallen from 100,000 to a mere 13,000, with the concentration of the textile industry in factories.[14] In that year, 846,000 women were in employment in Ireland. The number fell to 550,000 by 1901, though the real decline occurred after 1881.[15] Even in 1891 over a quarter of women were in paid employment, many of them in domestic service and teaching. Increasingly, clerking and shop assisting were opening to women as sources of employment.[16] Efforts to encourage needlework and lace making met with limited success. They had been pioneered in the 1850s[17] and later encouraged by the Irish Industries Development Association,[18] founded in 1887, and by Lady Aberdeen, whose contribution to Irish life on many levels was later discounted because she was the wife of a lord lieutenant. Poultry rearing and dairy work were encouraged by the co-operative movement from the 1890s, though ironically the result tended to be the entrusting of the decision-making of such enterprises to men.[19] On the other hand, the *Irish Homestead*, the journal of the movement, may have had some impact in contributing to the politicization of women.[20]

Perhaps surprisingly this reduction in women's participation in the public sphere of work which was accompanied by their almost exclusive presence in the domestic sphere of the home has not been seen simply as a victory of patriarchy. The change has been ascribed to the embourgeoisement of Irish society.[21] The days when women took part in faction fights were now long gone.

13 Murphy, *Catholic fiction*, pp 26–8, 41–3. **14** Daly, *Women and work*, pp 16, 25. **15** Bourke, 'Economic power of women,' *Irish Economic and Social History* 18 (1991), p. 36. **16** Luddy, 'Women and work,' in Whelan (ed.), *Women and paid work*, p. 52. **17** Cronin, 'Female industrial movement,' in Whelan (ed.), *Women and paid work*, pp 69–85. **18** Bourke, *Husbandry to housewifery*, p. 112. **19** Luddy, 'Women and work,' p. 49. **20** McPherson, 'Women, Irish national identity,' in *Éire-Ireland* 36:3 & 4 (2001), pp 131–52. **21** Hollander, 'Depictions of Irish female

Increased prosperity for those left in the country meant greater work in the home for women. This was because families could for the first time afford quite a large selection of household goods. These, however, had to be made from raw materials. Enjoying a greater affluence was thus labour intensive. It made more sense for women to devote their energies to household work rather than farm or paid work, according to this line of thought.[22] And, as society became more middle-class, so women's educative and moral authority within it was strengthened.

Reference to the home raises another question, the extent to which marriage was normative for intimate relationships. Same-sex relationships and sexual activity have been under-explored, and most of what information there is relates to people towards the top of the social scale. Male, homosexual activity, when it became public, was always inscribed within a discourse of scandal. This was the case when in 1822 an Established Church bishop, Percy Jocelyn, a member of the Roden family, was found having sex with a soldier.[23] Ironically, until the 1890s, the increasing public disapproval of homosexual activity made it less possible to make use of scandals for political purposes. Thus the Maamtrasna murder case of 1882 provided the Irish Parliamentary Party with valuable political ammunition against a government intent on highlighting Irish outrages during the land war. However, nationalists were less able to make use of the 1884 trials of Dublin Castle officials for homosexual crimes because such things could no longer be easily spoken of. The Ladies of Llangollen, Lady Eleanor Butler (1739–1829) and Sarah Ponsonby (1750–1831), were the most famous female same-sex partnership of the century. They were Irish Ascendancy women living together in Wales, whose simultaneous openness about their partnership and denial of it created a conceptual gap in the public imagination, enabling them to live together both happily and famously.[24]

As for heterosexual relationships, one way of determining the extent to which marriage was normative is to extrapolate from the figures for children born outside of marriage. There was undoubtedly a stigma attached to a non-marital child, and the future of such children was bleak. In the thirty years up to 1826, the Dublin Foundling Hospital received 52,000 children, one quarter of whom died as infants. Indeed, only around a quarter survived until discharge at the age of fourteen.[25]

It is agreed that towards the end of the nineteenth century the numbers of non-marital children as a percentage of births were low. In the 1890s at 2.6 per cent it was extremely low internationally when compared with England and Wales at 4 per cent and Portugal at 12.1 per cent.[26] It is less certain now that

types,' in McBride (ed.), *Irish nationalist imagination*, p. 54. **22** Bourke, *Husbandry to housewifery*, p. 235. **23** Bardon, *Ulster*, p 250. **24** Castle, *Apparitional lesbian*, p 241; Lanser, 'Female intimacies,' *Eighteenth-century Studies* 32:2 (1998–9), pp 179–98; Mavor, *Ladies of Llangollen*. **25** Connell, *Peasant society*, p. 71. **26** Ibid., pp 51–86; Connolly, *Priests and people*, p. 214.

the rate was equally low before the famine and thus before the development of such a strong puritan sexual ethic within the religious denominations. It may indeed have been around 6 per cent in both Catholic and Protestant communities. Moreover, as only half of pregnancies came to term and as one in ten women married pregnant it can be concluded that one fifth of women became pregnant while unmarried and presumably that an even higher proportion of unmarried women were sexually active with sexually active men.[27] During the famine itself, non-marital birth rates rose in some areas and declined in others, for which no explanatory pattern has yet been discerned.[28] Overall, it is certainly possible to conclude that sexual activity was more confined to marriage at the end of the nineteenth century than it was before the famine.

Prostitution was a common phenomenon, especially in Dublin. There were 2,849 arrests for prostitution in the city in 1838. The figure rose to 4,293 in 1849, at the end of the famine, and diminished to 1,102 by 1879, though there were ninety-six brothels in the city in that decade. There were also Magdalen asylums for prostitutes hoping to change their situation, some of which seemed to have offered open rather than coercive assistance, albeit under the moralistic rubric of penitence.[29] The large numbers of soldiers in garrison towns throughout the country provided one of the settings for prostitution. Government concern that venereal disease might enfeeble valuable soldiers resulted in the 1846 Prevention of Contagious Diseases at Certain Naval and Military Stations Act. Irish bases such as the Curragh, Cork and Queenstown (Cobh) came within the ambit of the law where women suspected of carrying disease could be detained for treatment. Public disquiet at the treatment of women under it, in which Haslam and Tod played a prominent role, eventually led to its repeal in 1886.[30]

After the famine, the structure of the family changed. The previous pattern had been, in broad terms, that of the nuclear family, with marriage in the mid-twenties, high fertility and the subdivision of land among several heirs. After the famine, the stem family became typical, with marriage at a higher age, inheritance of the family farm by one principal heir and continuing high fertility, accompanied by high emigration and overall population decline.[31] This changed pattern was a reality though perhaps not as totally as has sometimes been stated. One of the effects of the stem family system was that non-heirs who did not emigrate were forced to remain celibate. Before the famine, one in ten persons aged fifty was unmarried; by the First World War, it was a quarter.[32]

27 Akenson, *Small differences*, p 35. **28** Kennedy, 'Bastardy and the great famine,' in King (ed.), *Famine, land and culture*, pp 6–28. **29** Blair, 'The Salvation Army rescue network,' in Kelleher and Murphy (eds), *Gender perspectives*, pp 179–92; Luddy, 'Prostitution,' in Luddy and Murphy (eds), *Women surviving*, pp 52–5; Prunty, *Dublin slums*, pp 264–70. **30** Malcolm, 'Diseased women,' *Irish Economic and Social History* 26 (1999), pp 1–14. **31** Akenson, *Primer*, p. 25. **32** Fitzpatrick, 'Marriage,' in Cosgrove (ed.), *Marriage in Ireland*, pp 116–31.

As the discussion (above) concerning patterns of sexual behaviour indicates, the unmarried state after the famine was mostly accompanied by a genuine celibacy. This was bolstered, though, by a religiously sanctioned, sexual repression which could occasionally result in psychiatric illness.[33] The shift to impartible inheritance, however, may not have disadvantaged those who did not inherit the farm as much as is sometimes thought. Ensuing that non-heirs emigrated in advantageous circumstances may have been seen as a proper form of settlement on children.[34]

Unmarried women had more difficult lives than unmarried men, who could enjoy bachelor society and especially alcohol.[35] Older spinsters were often now distant relatives of the owner of the farm and were sometimes consigned to the workhouse. As a result, the numbers of women emigrating eventually overtook those of men, and girls were kept on later at school to equip them with educational skills for life in a new country. Abroad, young Irishwomen enjoyed more independence and had a greater chance to marry than they did at home. To balance this bleak view of life at home, however, it should be remembered that by 1911 around one in eight Irish farmers was actually a woman.[36]

Marriages were often arranged and dowries paid by the bride's father, though a farmer might be able to afford a dowry for only one of his daughters. By contrast with spinsters, married women had quite a high social status as producers of heirs and bringers of dowries.[37] The dowry was used to compensate those on the farm, such as mothers and sisters, who had been deprived of power by the arrival of the farmer or heir's new wife.

Structures of control over women's lives were both social and institutional. In the realm of the non-Christian supernatural, as has been seen, the changeling accusation was a means of disciplining a woman while apparently believing that the changeling and not the woman herself was being punished. The violence sometimes associated with it could become extreme, as in the case of Bridget Cleary. Domestic violence without any associations with the supernatural was widespread and was often reported in the newspapers. There was no public outcry against it, however, because it militated against the positive self-image of Irish nationalism.[38]

As the century wore on, new methods of patriarchal control asserted themselves. The pressure of Victorian respectability and the new strength of institutional religion could be coercive. It is difficult today, however, to appreciate the degree to which the norms of social and sexual behaviour were also embraced because of an internal assent. Outright refusal to comply with such norms, how-

33 Scheper-Hughes, *Mental illness*. **34** Guinnane, *Households, migration*, p. 164. **35** Fitzpatrick, 'Irish Female,' in O'Flanagan, Ferguson, Whelan (eds), *Rural Ireland*, pp 162–80; Rhodes, *Women and the family*, pp 332, 249. **36** Ibid., p. 193. **37** Ibid., p. 331. **38** Steiner-Scott, 'Domestic violence,' in Valiulis and O'Dowd (eds), *Women and Irish history*, pp 125–43.

ever, represented a problem for families within Ireland's increasingly disciplined Victorian social structure. The new institutions of the state came to provide a way out. One solution was thus to confine undisciplined members of the family, both male and female, to an asylum. Having a relative in an asylum was never to be the social stigma which having someone in the poorhouse was.[39] In both sorts of institutions, however, women actually tended to do better than men in terms of resources and discharge. The ultimate state sanction was, of course, prison. In 1870 there were 16,154 female committals to prison in Ireland and 29,935 male committals. Twenty years later the figure for men had dropped slightly to 29,173 while that for women had risen slightly to 17,236.[40] Institutions such as prisons of course also provided opportunities for employment. Delia Theresa Lidwill (1811–89), for example, was the first matron of Mountjoy Female Prison, a post she held for many years.

It can be argued that there were compensations for the general removal of women from the plough and confinement to the parlour occurred in nineteenth-century Ireland. And, indeed, it was a process that was far from confined to Ireland. Nonetheless, it also represented a narrowing of choice and as such is an example of a phenomenon characteristic of nineteenth-century Ireland by which apparent advance brought new limitation.

39 Malcolm, 'The asylum, the family,' in Malcolm and Jones (eds), *Medicine, disease and the state*, pp 177–91. **40** Luddy, *Women and philanthropy*, p. 151.

CHAPTER 14

Curious canon, 1801–91

It is commonly assumed that Irish literature in the nineteenth century was somehow a failure and that fiction in particular was unable to reach that condition known as 'realism' which was so characteristic of the best of English, Russian and, indeed, French fiction of the period. In general the reason for this has been put down to the condition – the colonial condition – of Ireland itself. Ireland was, to use Seamus Deane's phrase, a strange country.[1] It was unable to sustain the conditions of realism, that struggle for the ethical integration of the individual into society through work and relationships.

In the past, political instability and the supposed smallness of the middle class were proffered as the deeper reasons for the assumed failure of realism. More recently, Terry Eagleton has been argued that as the goal of realism is totality and social integration, it was just not possible to achieve this in Ireland because of the gulf between landlords and tenants.[2] David Lloyd sees instability as an ingredient in the formation of realism in the novel but argues for a specific crisis of representation in Ireland in the 1830s, as evidenced by agrarian and tithe agitation.[3] Such activity was threatened by a localism unsusceptible either to pro-union or nationalist political views and was therefore corrosive of realism and of the novel's project, in the age of Morgan and Edgeworth, to bring about the reconciliation of landlord and tenant in a union context. It was of course true that both Morgan and Edgeworth ceased writing Irish fiction around this time, the latter famously commenting that it was now impossible to write fiction as realities had become too strong and party passions too violent. O'Connellism, however, rather than agrarianism was the context.

While many of these positions have something to commend them, they work on the false assumption that after Edgeworth, Morgan, Griffin, the Banims and Carleton, Irish fiction somehow died out or became worthless. The reverse is the case in fact at least in terms of production. Vast numbers of novels were written, avidly read and, indeed, copiously indexed as long ago as

1 'It is obvious that the ease or difficulty encountered by a community in verbally representing itself has an effect on the ease or difficulty it has in being politically represented. That is clearly a problem that Irish works of fiction engaged with throughout the nineteenth century; it is part of the explanation for "strangeness" and the aspiration to overcome it so that it might be appropriately represented as it is, in its own normality, rather than misrepresented as an oddity for which there is no available language.' Deane, *Strange country*, p. 150. 2 Eagleton, *Heathcliff*, pp 147–52. 3 Lloyd, *Anomalous states*, pp 134–55. 4 Brown, *Ireland in fiction*. 5 Denvir, 'Language and literature,' *New Hibernia Review* 1:1 (1997), pp 44–68. 6 Herbison, 'Ulster-Scots poetry,' in Erskine and

1916.[4] They have also been studiously or even blithely ignored by most critics who have tended to work out of the categories of what became known as Anglo-Irish literature. This was a canonical conceptualization of Irish writing in which, as it applied to the nineteenth century, the list of novelists mentioned above, together with a dash of Protestant Gothic, was matched by a short list of poets which included Ferguson, Davis and Mangan and perhaps Moore. Significantly, the political differences between these writers were, for the most part, forgotten. It is instructive, however, to ponder on the history and assumptions of the canon of Anglo-Irish literature and to consider whether a broader basis for analysing the literature of the nineteenth century might not be desirable.

Those writers who figure in the canon were of course important. They have featured prominently in this present work because of their importance but also because their canonical status has made them the focus of scholarship. It is, however, worth noting some of the hitherto neglected figures, movements and issues. The literature of Gaelic speakers, for example, is accessible not only through the works of such as Mícheál Óg Ó Longáin (1766–1837) and Antoine Raifteraí (1779–1835) but is available from sermons, letters and other documents.[5] The Ulster Protestant literary tradition was strong, though its radical rather than conservative tendency has received what little attention there has been. William Drennan (1754–1821) was a prominent United Irishman and poet, influenced by Locke, Molyneux, Paine, Thomas Gray and the Scottish Enlightenment. He was also a doctor and later editor of the progressive *Belfast Monthly Magazine* (1803–13). His poems included 'The wake of William Orr' and 'Glendalloch', but by the time many of them were published his political, religious and poetic views were running against the tide.

James Orr of Ballycarry (1770–1816), James Campbell (1758–1818) of Ballynure, Samuel Thomson of Carngranny (1766–1816) and Thomas Beggs (1789–1847) of Ballyclare were among the leading members of the rhyming weaver poets.[6] They too belonged to the radical tradition of Presbyterianism and wrote in English and Ulster Scots. With the move of the textile industry to the factories and the turn of Presbyterianism towards conservatism their position was marginalized.

Presbyterian radicalism survived into mid-century in figures such as Francis Davis, 'The Belfastman' (1810–85), and to an extent the more conservative William McComb (1793–1873), who was known as the 'laureate of Presbyterianism'.[7] Dr John Swanwick Drennan (1809–93), son of William Drennan, however, wrote poetry against home rule,[8] and, indeed, there is a significant, if

Lucy (eds), *Cultural traditions*, pp 129–45. **7** Vance, *Irish literature*, pp 132–5. **8** Hewitt, 'Northern Athens,' in Beckett et al., *Belfast*, pp 71–82.

neglected, tradition of Ulster unionist literature. Thus, for example, William Johnston (1829–1902) of Ballykilbeg, who radicalized the Orange Order in the1860s, was the author of political and historical novels, such as *Nightshade* (1857) and *Under which king?* (1872).

In broadly national and nationalist poetry, a number of significant writers have been discarded from the canonical memory. At the same time, Ferguson, a unionist, whose poetry was not very successful in its own day,[9] was included. Indeed, he was declared to be a nationalist whether he liked it or not, undoubtedly because of his Anglo-Irish Celticism.[10] Among the forgotten are Thomas Caulfield Irwin (1823–92), an Irish Tennysonian; Denis Florence MacCarthy (1817–82), who was a journalist and translator as well as a poet; and John Francis O'Donnell (1837–74), who was editor of the Fenian *Irish People*.[11] Thomas D'Arcy McGee (1825–68), Young Irelander, 'father' of Canada and victim of Fenian assassination was a poet, historian and biographer. His popular historical work is evidence that the canonical perspective of Irish literature has been defective in *genre* as well as in region and politics.[12] Popular history was a central *genre* in Irish nationalism. Mitchel's writings of the recent past had an extraordinary impact. Important, too, was the historical work of A.M. Sullivan, especially his *Story of Ireland* (1870) and *New Ireland* (1877) which ran counter to Mitchel's thought both in its praise of constitutional politics and rejection of the genocidal theory of the famine.[13]

Recovering lost figures from obscurity, as Norman Vance has done, has been a most welcome development. Recently new approaches have gone even further, broadening the entire perspective on nineteenth-century literature in a way which bypasses rather than augments the old canon. At their heart is a thematic or topical approach, the two most important being the famine and feminism, though social class and the land war have also featured. Many other topics from rebellion to religion would repay equal attention. Between the famine and the end of the century, some fourteen novels and a hundred poems were written about the famine in English.[14] Three approaches can be discerned which see the famine in terms of apocalyptic, of progress and of claiming the dead. De Vere's 'Ireland in 1851' is an example of the first. Trollope's *Castle Richmond* (1860), *Castle Daly* (1875) by Annie Keary (1825–79) and Margaret Brew's *The chronicles of Castle Cloyne* (1884) are instances of the second. John Mitchel's writings illustrate the third. There is also a rich literature in Gaelic.[15]

9 O'Driscoll, 'Ferguson,' *Éire-Ireland* 6:1 (1971), pp 91–2. **10** Yeats, 'Ferguson,' in Frayne (ed.), *Prose of W.B. Yeats*, vol. 1, pp 87–104. **11** Schirmer, *Irish poetry*, pp 123–4, 130–1. **12** Vance, *Irish literature*, pp 153–64. **13** Leerssen, *Remembrance and imagination*, pp 151–5. **14** Kelleher, *Feminization of famine*; Morash (ed.), *Poetry of the Irish famine*; Morash, *Writing the Irish famine*; Morash, 'Literature of the Irish famine,' in O'Sullivan (ed.), *Meaning of the famine*, pp 40–55. **15** MacLachlainn, 'Famine in Gaelic tradition,' *Irish Review* 17–18 (1995), pp 90–108.

Peatsaí Ó Callanán (1791–1865) wrote 'Na fataí bána' (the white potatoes), a thirty-three verse lament on the state of Ireland in 1846. 'Ceol na mbacah' (the song of the beggars) by Aodh MacDhomhnaill (1802–67) is filled with a sense of outrage and led to several other polemical and satirical poems on the famine.

The second thematic approach is that of feminism which has yielded important results for canonical writers such as Morgan and Edgeworth as well as new writers. The women writers associated with the *Nation* have already been noted. The oppositional nature of their work makes them attractive to critics.[16] However, hundreds of novels were written by women in nineteenth-century Ireland, reflecting a spectrum of political positions and evoking and confirming a variety of audiences that remain to be explored. Thus Charlotte Riddell (1832–1906) wrote nearly fifty books, among them *Struggle for fame* (1883), an autobiographical novel about a women writer's professional life in London.[17] The novels of May Laffan (1849–1916) patrol the borders of class and religion. A Catholic uncomfortable with her religion's Irish social position, her work lacerates Catholic middle class *arrivistes* and fits within an exploration of class as well as gender.[18]

Of course, the focus of all of this interest is social and cultural and not directly literary in an aesthetic sense. But then this was always true of nineteenth-century Irish literature, where politics and history lie so close to the surface of the ostensibly artistic. And, indeed, cultural and historical interests largely continue to drive the study of that literature, not least because, with a few exceptions, it lacks a modern non-academic readership. The reason for this lack of appeal lies in its discontinuity from modern experience and goes back to that gap between the lives of the Anglican landed Ascendancy, on the one hand, and those of the largely Catholic tenantry on the other, which is the central theme of nineteenth-century Irish fiction. The contemporary reader can still relate to the world of Jane Austen, for example, because the internal and external struggle of the individual to negotiate the social and economic mores of society and to forge a subjectivity in the process seems as relevant today as it was in Austen's otherwise very different society, whose specific circumstances can be ignored. The contemporary reader, however, cannot so easily relate to a world where the central conflict, that between landlords and tenants, is an almost purely external one and best understood in terms of a particular set of historical circumstances. Landlords and tenants lacked a moral economy. They were sealed off from each other socially and neither had that sort of internal ideological or moral purchase on the other, the resolution of which might allow today's readers still to find an echo of their own struggles. The reader is thus not able to consume nineteenth-

16 Kelleher, '"Factual fictions".' **17** Kelleher, 'Charlotte Riddell's *A struggle for fame*,' *Colby Quarterly* 34:2 (2000), pp 116–31. **18** Murphy, *Catholic fiction*, pp 29, 65–6.

century Irish literature so that it confirms a belief in a universal human experience. By contrast, twentieth-century Irish fiction, as inaugurated by James Joyce and others, is able to communicate with contemporary readers, precisely because its central conflict, that between the individual and Catholicism, does have an internal dimension in the experience and identity of the individual in revolt. It is a conflict, moreover, which is able to find a resonance with readers' own conflicts, even in non-religious registers of experience.

The term 'Anglo-Irish literature' came into usage only in the 1890s, eventually creating a selection from the varied literatures of eighteenth and nineteenth-century Ireland, for then current ideological purposes. There were two stages in the development of the canon. The second phase was largely the work of W.B. Yeats, but he built on the first or metropolitan phase, a canon of nineteenth-century Irish literature created by English critics, readers and political circumstances.

As has been noted, the market for Irish fiction in the early nineteenth century was an English one. By the end of the century there were numerous publishers for Irish fiction not only in Britain and America but also in Ireland.[19] When Carleton first began publishing fiction, however, there was no publisher of novels in Dublin.[20] Publishers as well as audience were thus essentially British at the beginning of the century. Indeed, until the mid-1840s there was a good deal of interest in the British reading public for Irish fiction. This interest was caused both by internal factors to British reading tastes, such as the popularity at one stage of national tales, and, especially in the early period, by an apparently genuine interest in understanding Ireland which was now in union with Britain. Reviews of Irish fiction featured in journals and magazines from the *Quarterly Review* and *Edinburgh Review*, through *Blackwood's Magazine*, *Fraser's Magazine*, the *Athenaeum* and the *Gentleman's Magazine*, to the *London Literary Gazette*.[21]

By the 1850s the British market had tired of Irish fiction and was not really to return to it until perhaps the 1880s. Carleton found the market much reduced in the latter part of his career.[22] Serious and even humorous analysis was banished. Ireland no longer seemed a candidate for assimilation into a British polity and culture and the Irish were best depicted as the apes of *Punch* or the hapless fools of the theatre. Lever who had once been compared with Dickens and Scott was almost a forgotten figure in the 1860s. He was excluded from the Yeatsian canon on account of his humorous early novels, perhaps because Yeats had not read his later,[23] more interesting, work. If this is true, it illustrates how the Yeatsian built on the metropolitan canon.

19 Reilly, 'Cover art,' in McBride (ed.), *Irish nationalist imagination*, pp 95–112. **20** Hayley, 'British critical receptions,' in Zach and Kosok (eds), *Reception and translation*, p. 39. **21** Hayley, 'British critical receptions,' p. 44. **22** Wolff, *Carleton*, pp 122. **23** Jeffares, *Irish writing*, p. 158.

Perhaps the best example of the closing of the metropolitan canon of Anglo-Irish literature in the 1840s and 1850s is to be found in the experience of the English novelist Anthony Trollope (1812–82), who had spent the 1840s working for the post office in Ireland in counties Offaly and Tipperary.[24] Ireland fascinated Trollope and he wrote five novels about it, including his first, *The Macdermots of Ballycloran* (1847) and last *The Landleaguers* (1883). However, he was told after *The Macdermots of Ballycloran* and especially after the failure of *The Kellys and the O'Kellys* (1848) that the English market for Irish fiction had dried up.[25]

The closing of the metropolitan canon was one thing, but it did not mean that Irish writing had also automatically gone into a total decline with the passing of the Banim and Morgan generations and that there was something necessarily and deleteriously inward-looking about Irish novelists who now wrote for the growing domestic market for fiction.[26] Of course, Irish fiction was also still read in Britain, especially in the 1880s and 1890s. These decades produced a substantial body of land war fiction. Though it has not received the critical attention it deserves, it was part of that great propaganda war, previously adverted to, within British politics and for the heart of Liberalism. That Trollope returned to an Irish story at the end of his life is an indication of the reawakened interest of the British reading public of the 1880s. Significantly there is no large body of novels dealing with the home rule crisis, perhaps confirming its status as an episode in British rather than Irish political history. Land war novels included *A boycotted household* (1881) by Letitia McClintock, *The heart of Erin* (1882) by Elizabeth Owens Blackburne and *Thy name is truth* (1884) by Fannie Gallaher.[27] *Doreen* was a novel of reconciliation between Britain and Ireland written by an English author, Edna Lyall.[28] The most significant land war novel was *Marcella Grace* (1886) by Rosa Mulholland (1847–1921), a novel which advocated as a solution to Ireland's land troubles the replacement of the Protestant Ascendancy by a Catholic gentry. Because of a congruence of religion the latter would be able to establish a new moral economy with the tenantry.[29] It is embodied in the novel's heroine who represents a fusion both of classes and of urban-rural divides. She has grown up in poverty in Dublin with her father, an experience that prepares her for the role of landlord when she inherits an estate through the family of her dead Catholic gentry mother. Though Yeats included a story by Mulholland in *Representative Irish tales* (1891) the Victorian respectability of her work did not endear her to him in the longer

24 McCaw, 'Victorian fiction,' in Geary (ed.), *Rebellion and remembrance*, pp 159–74; Morash, 'Novels of Charles Lever,' in Rauchbauer (ed.), *Ancestral voices*, pp 61–76; Pollard, *Anthony Trollope*. **25** Bareham, 'Irish Lever,' in Bareham (ed.), *Charles Lever*, pp 1–17. **26** Hayley, 'British critical receptions,' p. 48; Mercier, *Literature*, pp 35–63. **27** Kelleher, ' "Factual fictions." ' **28** Murphy, *Catholic fiction*, p. 43. **29** Ibid., pp 20–1, 35, 44–7, 49, 53; Murphy (ed.), Mulholland, *Marcella Grace*.

run. An instructive instance of the ways in which twentieth-century critics accentuated the choices of the Anglo-Irish literature canon was the selection of *Priests and people, a no rent romance* (1891) for inclusion in the Garland series of reprints of nineteenth century Irish novels in the 1970s. *Marcella Grace*, against which it seems likely to have been written, was not included, however.[30]

The Anglo-Irish literary revival gathered pace in the 1890s.[31] Its leading figures were from the Ascendancy or Protestant middle class. They prized heroism, aristocracy and Celticism and envisioned a Celtic past, whose values they hoped to resuscitate in the present, as a world of pagan peasants and aristocrats, a world conducive to their own leadership role and to the occlusion of Catholicism. It was in some senses a final, and very powerful, version of the Ascendancy bid for cultural dominance in Ireland, albeit one which was now broadly nationalist, was no longer evangelical, and was critical of many aspects of the Ascendancy past.

In the 1880s it was common in English papers to publish lists of the best books. The fashion caught on in Ireland in the 1890s. Yeats's lists of books and republishing projects helped to form the notion of Anglo-Irish literature in the essential form it held thereafter.[32] Nationalism and Celticism were implicit criteria, the latter being more important than the former. It made it possible to embrace not only Ferguson but also the Tory popularizer of Celtic legend Standish James O'Grady (1846–1928) to be embraced.[33] Indeed, one remarkable feature of the canon is its capacity to elide the political differences that separated authors such as Carleton and the Banims and to weld them into a harmonious whole.

Yeats's final criterion was his dislike of bourgeois values. He was in revolt against Victorian progress and respectability. This was represented not only by the Dublin, middle-class Protestant establishment of his father's generation but also by the Catholic middle classes. There was even a Catholic proto-literary establishment in Dublin, centred around the *Irish Monthly* magazine, edited by the Jesuit Matthew Russell, which had been founded in the 1870s and published poetry, fiction and articles on social and literary issues.[34] Its agenda was the vindication of Irish respectability within Victorian discourse. Thus Russell provided a preface for *Knocknagow* (1873), the immensely popular saga of rural Irish life by the diehard Fenian Charles J. Kickham (1828–82), which refocused it in acceptably respectable Catholic terms. The novel also manages to present rural Irish society as simultaneously riven with conflict and oppression and blessed with unity and harmony – thereby providing a pleasing self-image to the rural

30 Murphy, *Catholic fiction*, 46–7. **31** Brown, *Yeats*; McCormack, *Ascendancy and tradition*, p. 294. **32** Foster, *Mage*, p. 98; Frayne, *Yeats*, pp 382–87; Jeffares, *Irish writing*, pp 164–78; Kelly (ed.), *Yeats*, pp 440–5. **33** Cairns and Richards, *Writing Ireland*, pp 52–6; McAteer, *Standish O'Grady*; Marcus, *Standish O'Grady*. **34** Murphy, *Catholic fiction*, pp 15–63.

society which was to emerge from the land war. That society still liked to think of itself as downtrodden while enjoying the benefits of a new security.[35]

Among those others who wrote for the *Irish Monthly* were Mulholland, M.E. Francis (1859–1930), a member of the Sweetman family, and Katharine Tynan (1858–1931), whose anthology of Irish writing offered a much broader range of work than Yeats.[36] *A drama in muslin* (1886), an early Irish novel by George Moore (1852–1933), deals with both the land war and the strictures of Catholicism in an upper middle-class context which in some ways is best seen as a counter to the work of the *Irish Monthly* group. Tynan was a friend of Yeats and as a young writer in the 1880s Yeats had had valuable links with the better-known writers of the day. Indeed, both he and Oscar Wilde published some of their first work in the *Irish Monthly*.

Nonetheless, the Yeatsian canon of Anglo-Irish literature as set out in various articles in the 1890s tended to prize other values than those bourgeois ideals displayed in the *Irish Monthly* and elsewhere. Yeats praised the Banims and Carleton with their open and ribald explorations of peasant life to the dismay of the *Irish Monthly* which condemned him for it in July 1891.[37] About the only novelist whose reputation endured from the period was Emily Lawless (1845–1913), author of *Hurrish* (1886), a land war novel praised by Gladstone, and *Grania* (1892), a novel of a woman's experience on the Aran Islands. Perhaps Lawless retained enough of an Ascendancy perspective to irritate respectable Catholic nationalists and thus to survive. She was accused of having 'a sense of the inevitableness of Irish failure'. Thus in *Hurrish* a magistrate becomes very popular when he acquits the hero, whom the people in fact think is guilty.[38]

The *Irish Monthly* writers were eclipsed not only by the Anglo-Irish literary revival but by the coming of peasant ownership at the end of the land war which swept away their hopes for an upper middle-class leadership in Catholic Ireland. The consolidation of the new, rural, lower middle-class establishment which was to dominate Ireland in the twentieth-century elicited a new urban Catholic intelligentsia antagonistic to the narrowness of social and personal mores. As has been noted it was composed of figures such as W.P. Ryan (1867–1942), author of *The plough and the cross* (1910), and Gerald O'Donovan (1871–1942), author of *Father Ralph* (1913), and was also the context for the work of James Joyce (1882–1941).[39] Yet the 1880s were a distinct decade both in poetry and realist fiction by writers, many of them women, from Protestant as well as upper middle-class Catholic backgrounds. The Catholic writers were part of a larger Catholic cultural energy which included the Cecilian movement

35 Ibid., pp 79–88. **36** Read and Hinkson (eds), *Irish literature*. **37** Foster, *Mage*, p. 98. **38** Belanger, 'Irish identity in *Grania*,' in Litvack and Hooper (eds), *Regional identity*, pp 95–107; Cahalan, 'Emily Lawless,' in Kirkpatrick (ed.), *Border crossings*, pp 38–57; Murphy, *Catholic fiction*, pp 34, 43, 52. **39** Murphy, *Catholic fiction*, pp 89–152.

in music. It eschewed the militant religiousness of a minority of writers such as R.B. O'Brien (1809–85)[40] and had it survived might have fostered a different tone in post-independence Ireland. As it was, both the Anglo-Irish literary revivalists and the Catholic urban intellectuals, in spite of their assertiveness and enormous creativity, were defeated in the cultural battle with that lower middle-class Catholic society that was emerging. The literature of the 1880s, of the land war and of a proto-Catholic literature, was in the greater scheme of things a minor matter. But the fact that it still remains a largely forgotten literature is testimony to the continuing regrettable dominance of Anglo-Irish literature as a canonical construct. One of the purposes of this book has been to highlight and encourage the new ways in which scholarship sees the interaction of nineteenth-century literature and culture so that new perspectives can continue to emerge.

40 Ibid., pp 55–8.

Conclusion

In 1848 Mrs Cecil Frances Humphreys Alexander (1818-95), wife of a rising Established Church clergyman, published *Hymns for little children*. The third stanza of her 'All things bright and beautiful' is often quoted as a paean to a vision of Victorian, hierarchical stability:

> The rich man in his castle,
> The poor man at his gate,
> He made them high and lowly
> And ordered their estate.

The hymn, however, was composed at Markree Castle, Co. Sligo. In the late 1840s poor men and women were starving and some of the supposedly rich would soon have to be rescued by the Encumbered Estates Acts. It was in fact a time of rapid and traumatic change.

Change occurred in political culture and the sense of national identity in nineteenth-century Ireland. It occurred in the structure of land distribution and ownership and in the organization of both urban and rural life. It happened, too, in law and policing, in religion, in education and in the institutions of intellectual and artistic life. Communications changed not only within the country but, through emigration, with the wider world. Gender relations were also transformed.

Among the greatest changes were the eventual ruin of the landed classes and the eradication of the landless classes. The famine and subsequent emigration formed a new, less diverse but potentially more united and politically powerful farming community. By the 1880s, the farming classes, nationalist political elites and the Catholic Church had come into alignment with each other in nationalist Ireland. Importantly, each group was now more internally united than hitherto. A new political culture was born for this essentially petty-bourgeois, farming society and proved more long significant than the politicization of both the 1790s and the O'Connellite era. Ironically, from the 1890s it would look to the past, to the Irish language and Celtic mythology, and to the remnants of the past in the Irish-speaking areas of the west of Ireland for a self-image for the new Ireland. Meanwhile another version of Irishness was strengthening in Protestant Ulster – one favouring the continuing union with Britain.

The change that swept nineteenth-century Ireland can be thought of in terms of the now contested categories of modernization and progress. Surprisingly, its effect was to narrow options and to bring about convergence. The culture of convergence which helped to create the new Ireland was in many ways an enormous achievement though, after partition and independence in the twentieth century, it led to social, cultural and economic stagnation for many decades. If the narrower base for Irish society at the end of the nineteenth century seemed empowering, it was to prove enervating for most of the twentieth.

Bibliography

KEY

CELTICISM

Adams, G.B. 'Language in Ulster, 1820–50.' *Ulster Folklife*. 19 (1973). Pp 50–5.

Arnold, Matthew. *On the study of Celtic literature*. 1867. London: Dent, 1910.

Barrow, George Lennox. *The round towers of Ireland.* Dublin: Academy, 1979.

Blaney, Roger. *Presbyterianism and the Irish language*. Belfast: Ulster Historical Foundation, 1991.

Breathnach, R.A. 'Two eighteenth-century Irish scholars: Joseph Cooper Walker and Charlotte Brooke.' *Studia Hibernica*. 5 (1965). Pp 88–97.

Bromwich, Rachel. *Matthew Arnold and Celtic literature: a retrospect, 1865–1965*. Oxford: Clarendon, 1965.

Brown, Terence, ed. *Celticism*. Amsterdam: Rodopi, 1996.

Chapman, Malcolm. *The Gaelic vision in Scottish culture*. London: Croom Helm, 1978.

———. *The Celts: The construction of a myth*. Bastingstoke: Macmillan, 1992.

Cronin, Michael. *Translating Ireland: translations, languages, cultures*. Cork: Cork University Press, 1996.

Crowley, Tony. *The politics of language in Ireland, 1366–1922*. London: Routledge, 1999.

Denvir, Gearóid. 'Decolonizing the mind: language and literature in Ireland.' *New Hibernia Review*. 1:1 (1997). Pp 44–68.

Dunne, Tom. ' "Tá gaedhil bhocht cráidhte:" memory, tradition and the politics of the poor: Gaelic poetry and song.' In Geary, ed. *Rebellion and remembrance*. Pp 93–111.

Durkacz, V.E. *The decline of the Celtic language: a study of linguistic and cultural conflict in Scotland, Wales and Ireland from the Reformation to the twentieth century*. Edinburgh: Donald, 1983.

Gibbons, Luke. 'Race against time: racial discourse and Irish history.' *Oxford Literary Review*. 13 (1991). Pp 95–117.

Hardiman, James, ed./tr. *Irish minstrelsy, or Bardic remains of Ireland: with English poetical translations*. 2 vols. London: 1831.

Hindley, Reg. *The death of the Irish language: a qualified obituary*. London: Routledge, 1990.

Kelleher, John V. 'Matthew Arnold and the Celtic revival.' In Harry Levin, ed. *Perspectives of criticism*. Cambridge, MA: Harvard University Press, 1950. Pp 197–221.

Lloyd, David. 'Arnold, Ferguson, Schiller.' *Cultural Critique*. 1 (1985). Pp 137–69.

MacCana, Prionsias. *Celtic mythology*. New York: Peter Bedrick, 1983.

Murray, Damien. *Romanticism, nationalism and Irish antiquarian societies, 1840–80*. Maynooth: NUI Department of Old and Middle Irish, 2000.

Ó Bresláin, Diarmuid, and Padaí Dwyer. *A short history of the Irish language*. Béal Feirste: Glór na nGael Bhéal Feirste Thiar, 1995.

Ó Buachalla Séamus. 'Educational policy and the role of the Irish language from 1831 to 1981.' *European Journal of Education*. 19:1 (1984). Pp 75–92.

Ó Catháin, Diarmuid. 'An Irish scholar aborad: Bishop John O'Brien of Cloyne and the Macpherson controversy.' In O'Flanagan and Buttimer, eds. *Cork*. Pp 499–533.

Ó Ciosáin, Niall. 'Round towers and square holes: exoticism in Irish culture.' *Irish Historical Studies*. 31:122 (1998). Pp 259–73.

Ó Cúiv, Brian, ed. *A view of the Irish language*. Dublin: Stationery Office, 1969.

O'Halloran, Clare. 'Irish recreation of the Gaelic past: the challenge of MacPherson's Ossian.' *Past and Present*. 124 (1989). Pp 69–95.

O'Leary, Philip. *The prose literature of the Gaelic revival 1881–1921: ideology and innovation*. University Park: Pennsylvania State University Press, 1994.

Orr, Leonard. 'The mid-nineteenth-century Irish contexts of Arnold's essay on Celtic literature.' In Clinton Machann and Forrest D. Burt, eds. *Matthew Arnold in his time and ours: centenary essays*. Charlotteville: University Press of Virginia, 1988. Pp 135–56.

Pecora, Vincent P. 'Arnoldian ethnology.' *Victorian Studies*. 41:3 (1998). Pp 355–79.

Rowse, A.L. *Matthew Arnold: poet and prophet*. London: Thames and Hudson, 1976.

Sheehy, Jeanne. *The rediscovery of Ireland's past: the Celtic revival 1830–1930*. London: Thames and Hudson, 1980.

Snyder, Edward. *The Celtic revival in English literature, 1760–1800*. Harvard: Harvard University Press, 1923.

DIASPORA & EMIGRATION

General

Akenson, Donald H. *Small differences: Irish Catholics and Irish Protestants, 1815–1921: an international perspective*. 1988. Dublin: Gill and Macmillan, 1990.

———. *The Irish diaspora: a primer.* Belfast: Institute of Irish Studies, 1993.

Bielenberg, Andy, ed. *The Irish diaspora.* London: Longman/Pearson Education, 2000.

Crawford, E. Margaret, ed. *The hungry stream: essays on emigration and famine.* Belfast: Institute for Irish Studies, 1997.

Fitzpatrick, David. 'Irish emigration in the later nineteenth century.' *Irish Historical Studies.* 22:86 (1980). Pp 126–43.

———. *Irish emigration, 1801–1921.* Dublin: Economic and Social History Society of Ireland, 1984.

———. 'Emigration, 1801–70.' In Vaughan, ed. *Union I, 1801–70.* Pp 562–622.

———. 'Emigration, 1871–1921.' In Vaughan, ed. *Union II, 1870–1921.* Pp 606–702.

Fortner, Robert S. 'The culture of hope and the culture of despair: the print media and nineteenth-century Irish emigration.' *Éire-Ireland.* 13:3 (1978). Pp 32–48.

Guinnane, Timothy W. *The vanishing Irish: households, migration and the rural economy of Ireland, 1850–1914.* Princeton: Princeton University Press, 1997.

Harris, Ruth Ann. *The nearest place that wasn't Ireland: early nineteenth-century Irish labour migration.* Ames: Iowa State University Press, 1994.

Kennedy, Robert E. *The Irish: emigration, marraige and fertility.* Berkeley, CA: University of California Press, 1973.

McKenna, Patrick. 'Irish migration to Argentina.' In O'Sullivan, ed. *Patterns of migration.* Pp 63–83.

MacLaughlin, Jim. *Ireland: the emigrant nursery and the world economy.* Cork: Cork University Press, 1994.

Nolan, Janet. *Ourselves alone: women's emigration from Ireland, 1885–1920.* Lexington, KY: University Press of Kentucky, 1989.

Silverman, Marilyn, and P.H. Gulliver, eds. *Approaching the past: historical anthropology through Irish case studies.* New York: Columbia Unviersity Press, 1992.

O'Sullivan, Patrick, ed. *Patterns of migration. The Irish world wide, history, heritage, identity.* Vol. 1. Leicester: Leicester University Press, 1992.

———. *The Irish in the new communities. The Irish world wide, history, heritage, identity.* Vol. 2. Leicester: Leicester University Press, 1992.

———. *The creative migrant. The Irish world wide, history, heritage, identity.* Vol. 3. Leicester: Leicester University Press, 1994.

———. *Irish women and Irish migration. The Irish world wide, history, heritage, identity.* Vol. 4. Leicester: Leicester University Press, 1995.

———. *Religion and identity. The Irish world wide, history, heritage, identity.* Vol. 5. Leicester: Leicester University Press, 1996.

———. *The meaning of the famine. The Irish world wide, history, heritage, identity.* Vol. 6. Leicester: Leicester University Press, 1997.

America and Canada

Adams, W.F. *Ireland and the Irish emigration to the new world from 1815 to the famine.* 1932; Baltimore: Genealogical, 1980.

Akenson, Donald H. *The United States and Ireland.* Cambridge, MA: Harvard University Press, 1973.

———. *The Irish in Ontario: a study in rural history.* Kingston and Montreal, McGill-Queen's University Press, 1984.

———. *Being had: historians, evidence and the Irish in North America.* Port Credit, Ont: Meany, 1985.

———. 'The Irish in North America.' *Éire-Ireland.* 21:1 (1986). Pp 122–9.

Broehl, Wayne G. *The Molly Maguires.* Cambridge, MA: Harvard University Press, 1965.

Diner, Hasia. *Erin's daughters in America: Irish immigrant women in the nineteenth century.* Baltimore, MD: Johns Hopkins University, 1983.

Doyle, D.N. *Ireland, Irishmen and revolutionary America, 1769–1820.* Dublin: Mercier, 1981.

———. 'The Irish in North America, 1776–1845.' In Vaughan, ed. *Union I, 1801–70.* Pp 682–725.

———. 'The Remaking of Irish America, 1845–80.' In Vaughan, ed. *Union II, 1870–1921.* Pp 725–63.

Doyle, D.N. and O.D. Edwards. *America and Ireland, 1776–1976.* Westport, CT: Greenwood, 1980.

Drudy, P.J., ed. *The Irish in America: emigration, assimilation and impact.* Irish studies 4. Cambridge: Cambridge University Press, 1985.

Houston, Cecil J. and William J. Smyth. *The sash Canada wore: a historical geography of the Orange Order in Canada.* Toronto: University of Toronto Press, 1980.

———. *Irish emigration and Canadian settlement: patterns, links and letters.* Toronto: University of Toronto Press, 1990.

Kenny, Kevin. *Making sense of the Molly Maguires.* Oxford: Oxford University Press, 1998.

———. *The American Irish: a history.* Harlow: Longman, 2000.

Miller, Kerby A. *Emigrants and exiles: Ireland and the Irish exodus to North America.* New York: Oxford University Press, 1985.

Miller, Kerby A. with Bruce Boling and D.N. Doyle. 'Emigrants and exiles: Irish cultures and Irish emigration in North America, 1790–1922.' *Irish Historical Studies.* 22:86 (1980). Pp 97–125.

Miller, Kerby A., D.N. Doyle and Patricia Kelleher. ' "For love and liberty:" Irish women, migration and domesticity in Ireland and America, 1815–1920.' In O'Sullivan, ed. *Irish women and Irish migration.* Pp 41–65.

Miller, Kerby A. and Paul Wagner. *Out of Ireland: the story of Irish emigration to America.* London: Aurum, 1994.

Moran, Gerard. ' "In search of the promised land:" the Connemara colonization scheme to Minnesota, 1880.' *Éire-Ireland.* 31:3 and 4. (1996). Pp 130–49.

Neidhart, W.S. *Fenianism in north America.* London: Pennsylvania State University Press, 1975.

Schrier, Arnold. *Ireland and the American emigration, 1850–1900.* Chester Springs, PA: Dufour, 1997.

Senior, Hereward. *The Fenians and Canada.* Toronto: Macmillan, 1978.

Wilson, Catherine Anne. *New lease of life: landlords, tenants and immigrants in Ireland and Canada.* Montreal and Kingston: McGill-Queen's University Press, 1994.

Australia, New Zealand & British empire

Akenson, Donald H. *Half the world from home: perspectives on the Irish in New Zealand, 1860–1950.* Wellington, NZ: Victoria University Press, 1990.

———. *Occasional papers on the Irish in South Africa.* Grahamstown: Rhodes University, 1991.

Bielenberg, Andy. 'Irish emigration to the British empire.' In Bielenberg, ed. *Irish Diaspora.* Pp 215–34.

Fitzpatrick, David. *Oceans of consolation: personal accounts of Irish migration to Australia.* Cork: Cork University Press, 1994.

Fraser, Lyndon, ed. *Irish migration and New Zealand settlement.* Dunedin: University of Otago Press, 2000.

Holmes, Michael. 'The Irish in India: imperialism, nationalism and internationalism.' In Bielenberg, ed. *Irish diaspora.* Pp 235–50.

McCracken, Donal P. ' "Odd Man Out:" The South African experience.' In Bielenberg, ed. *Irish diaspora.* Pp 251–71.

MacDonagh, Oliver and W.F. Mandle, eds. *Ireland and Irish Australia.* London: Croom Helm, 1986.

O'Brien, John and Pauric Travers, eds. *The Irish emigration experience in Australia.* Dublin: Poolbeg, 1991.

O'Farrell, Patrick. *The Irish in Australia.* Kensington, NSW: New South Wales University Press, 1986.

———. 'The Irish in Australia and New Zealand, 1791–1870.' In Vaughan, ed. *Union I, 1801–70.* Pp 661–81.

———. *Vanished kingdoms. The Irish in Australia and New Zealand: a personal excursion.* Kensington: NSW, New South Wales University Press, 1990.

———. 'The Irish in Australia and New Zealand, 1870–1990.' In Vaughan, ed. *Union II, 1870–1921.* Pp 703–24.

Richards, Eric. 'Irish life and progress in colonial South Australia.' *Irish Historical Studies.* 27:107 (1991). Pp 216–36.

Rudé, George. *Protest and punishment: the story of the social and political protesters transported to Australia, 1788–1868.* Oxford: Clarendon, 1978.

Shaw, A.G.L. *Convicts and colonies: a study of penal transportation from Great Britain and Ireland to Australia and other parts of the British empire.* London: Faber, 1966.

Smith, F.B. *Ireland, England and Australia: essays in honour of Oliver MacDonagh.* Cork: Cork University Press, 1990.

Britain

Belchem, John. 'English working class radicalism and the Irish, 1815–50.' *Éire-Ireland.* 19:4 (1984). Pp 78–93.

Davis, Graham. *The Irish in Britain, 1815–1914.* Dublin: Gill and Macmillan, 1991.

———. 'The Irish in Britain, 1815–1939.' In Bielenberg, ed. *Irish diaspora.* Pp 19–36.

Devine, T.M., ed. *Irish immigrants and Scottish society in the nineteenth and twentieth centuries.* Edinburgh: John Donald, 1991.

Edwards, Owen Dudley and P.J. Storey. 'The Irish press in Victorian Britain.' In Swift and Gilley, eds., *Victorian city.* Pp 158–78.

Fielding, Steven. *Class and ethnicity: Irish Catholics in England, 1880–1939.* Buckingham: Open University Press, 1993.

Fitzpatrick, David. ' "A peculiar tramping people:" the Irish in Britain, 1801–70.' In Vaughan, ed. *Union I, 1801–70.* Pp 623–60.

———. 'The Irish in Britain, 1871–1921.' In Vaughan, ed. *Union II, 1870–1921*. Pp 653–702.

Gilley, Sheridan. 'English attitudes to the Irish in England, 1789–1900.' In Colin Holmes, ed. *Immigrants and minorities in British Society*. London: George Allen and Unwin, 1978. Pp 81–110.

Hickman, Mary. *Religion, class and identity: the state, the Catholic Church and the education of the Irish in Britain*. Aldershot: Avebury: 1995.

Jeffery, Keith, ed. *An Irish empire? Aspects of Ireland and the British empire*. Manchester: Manchester University Press, 1996.

Lowe, W.J. *The Irish in mid-Victorian Lancashire*. New York: Peter Lang, 1989.

McFarland, Elaine. *'Protestants first': Orangeism in nineteenth-century Scotland*. Edinburgh: Edinburgh University Press, 1990.

MacRaild, Donald. *Culture, conflict and migration: the Irish in Victorian Cumbria*. Liverpool: Liverpool University Press, 1998.

———. *Irish migrants in modern Britain, 1750–1922*. London: Macmillan, 1999.

——— ed. *The great famine and beyond: Irish migrants in Britain in the nineteenth and twentieth centuries*. Dublin: Irish Academic Press, 1999.

Newsinger, John. 'Old Chartists, Fenians and new Socialists.' *Éire-Ireland*. 17:2 (1982). Pp 19–45.

O'Connell, Bernard. 'Irish nationalism in Liverpool, 1883–1923.' *Éire-Ireland*. 10:1 (1975). Pp 24–37.

O'Dowd, Anne. *Spalpeens and tattie hokers*. Dublin: Irish Academic Press, 1991.

Swift, Roger. 'The outcast Irish in the British Victorian city: problems and perspectives.' *Irish Historical Studies*. 25:99 (1987). Pp 264–76.

——— ed. *Irish migrants in Britain, 1815–1914: a documentary history*. Cork: Cork University Press, 2002.

Swift, Roger and Sheridan Gilley, eds. *The Irish in the Victorian city*. London: Croom Helm, 1985.

———. *The Irish in Britain, 1815–1939*. London: Pinter, 1989.

———. *The Irish in Victorian Britain, the local dimension*. Dublin: Four Courts, 1999.

ECONOMICS

Bolger, Patrick. *The Irish cooperative movement: its history and development*. Dublin: Institute of Public Adminstration, 1977.

Boylan, Thomas A. and Timothy P. Foley. *Political economy and colonial Ireland: the propagation and ideological function of economic discourse in the nineteenth century*. London: Routledge, 1992.

Casserley, H.C. *Outline of Irish railway history*. Newton Abbot: David and Charles, 1974.

Coe, W.E. *The engineering industry of the north of Ireland*. Newton Abbot: David and Charles, 1969.

Collins, Brenda. 'Proto-industrialization and pre-famine emigration.' *Social History*. 7:2 (1982). Pp 127–46.

Collison Black, R.D. *Economic thought and the Irish question, 1817–1870*. Cambridge: Cambridge University Press, 1960.

Cousens, S.H. 'Regional variations in population change in Ireland, 1861–1881.' *Economic History Review.* 17 (1964). Pp 301–21.

Cullen, L.M. *Life in Ireland.* London: Batsford,1968.

———. *An economic history of Ireland since 1660.* London: Batsford,1972.

Daly, M.E. *A social and economic history of Ireland since 1800.* Dublin: Educational Co., 1981.

Delany, V.T.H. and D.R. Delany, *The canals of the south of Ireland.* Newton Abbot: David and Charles, 1966.

Doyle, Oliver, and Stephen Hirsch. *Railways in Ireland, 1834–1984.* Dublin: Signal, 1983.

Flanagan, Patrick. *Transport in Ireland, 1880–1910.* Dublin: Transport Research Association, 1969.

Goldstrom, J.M. and L.A. Clarkson, eds. *Irish population, economy and society.* Oxford: Clarendon, 1981.

Gribbon, H.D. 'Economic and social history.' In Vaughan, ed. *Union II, 1870–1921.* Pp 260–356.

Kennedy, Liam, and David S. Johnson. 'The union of Ireland and Britain, 1801–9121.' In Boyce and O'Day, eds. *Revisionist controversy.* Pp 34–70.

Lebow, R.N. *John Stuart Mill on Ireland.* Philadelphia: Insitute for the Study of Human Issues, 1979.

McCutcheon, W.A. *The canals of the north of Ireland.* London: David and Charles, 1965.

McDonnell, M.A. 'Malthus and George on the Irish question: the single tax, empiricism, and other positions shared by the nineteenth-century economists.' *American Journal of Economics and Sociology.* 36 (1977). Pp 401–16.

Mokyr, Joel. 'Malthusian models and Irish history.' *Journal of Economic History.* 40:1 (1980). Pp 159–66.

Murphy, A.E., ed. *Economics and the Irish economy from the eighteenth century to the present day.* Dublin: 1984.

Ó Gráda, Cormac. *Ireland before and after the famine.* Manchester: Manchester University Press, 1988.

———. 'Poverty, population and agriculture, 1801–45.' Pp 108–33. 'Industry and communications, 1801–45.' Pp 137–57. ' In Vaughan, ed. *Union I, 1801–70.*

———. *Ireland: a new economic history, 1780–1939.* Oxford: Oxford University Press, 1994.

O'Keeffe, P.J. *The development of Ireland's road network.* Dublin: Foras Forbatha, 1973.

O'Malley, Eoin. 'The decline of Irish industry in the nineteenth century.' *Economic and Social Review.* 13:1 (1981). Pp 21–42.

O'Neill, Kevin. *Family and farm in pre-famine Ireland.* Madison, WI: University of Wisconsin Press, 1984.

Slater, Eamonn and Terrence McDonough. 'Bulwark of landlordism and capitalism: the dynamics of feudalism in nineteenth-century Ireland.' *Research in Political Economy.* 14 (1994). Pp 63–118.

Strauss, Eric. *Irish nationalism and British democracy.* Westport, CT: Greenwood, 1975.

Turner, Michael. *After the famine: Irish agriculture, 1850–1914.* Cambridge: Cambridge University Press, 1996.

Whelan, Kevin. 'Settlement and society in eighteenth-century Ireland.' In G. Dawe and J.W. Foster, eds. *The poet's place: Ulster literature and society.* Belfast: Institute of Irish Studies, 1991. Pp 45–67.

EDUCATION, SCIENCE AND PRINT

Adams, J.R.R. *The printed word and the common man: popular culture in Ulster 1700–1900.* Belfast: Institute for Irish Studies: 1987.

———. 'Swine-tax and Eat-Him-All-Magee: the hedge schools and popular education in Ireland.' In Donnelly and Miller, eds. *Irish popular culture.* Pp 97–117.

Akenson, Donald H. *The Irish education experiment: the national system of education in the nineteenth century.* London: Routledge and Kegan Paul, 1970.

———. 'Pre-university education, 1782–1870.' In Vaughan, ed. *Union I, 1801–70.* Pp 523–37.

———. 'Pre-university education, 1870–1921.' In Vaughan, ed. *Union II, 1870–1921.* Pp 523–38.

Aspinall, Arthur. *Politics and the press, 1780–1850.* London: Home and Van Thal, 1949.

Bennett, James. 'Science and social policy in Ireland in the mid-nineteenth century.' In Bowler and Whyte, eds. *Science and society*. Pp 37–47.

Benson, Charles. 'Printers and booksellers in Dublin, 1800–50.' In Robin Myers and Michael Harris, eds. *Spreading the word: the distribution networks of print, 1550–1850.* Winchester: St Paul's Bibliographies, 1990. Pp 2–11.

Bowen, B.P. 'Dublin humorous periodicals of the nineteenth century.' *Dublin Historical Record.* 13:1 (1952). Pp 2–11.

Bowler, Peter R. and Nicholas Whyte, eds. *Science and society in Ireland.* Belfast: Institute of Irish Studies, 1997.

Coolahan, John. *Irish education: its history and structure.* Dublin: Institute of Public Administration, 1981.

Corish, Patrick J. *Maynooth College, 1795–1995.* Dublin: Gill and Macmillan, 1995.

Cullen, L. M. *Eason and Sons: a history.* Dublin: Eason, 1989.

Daly, Mary and David Dickson, eds. *The origins of popular literacy in Ireland: language change and educational development 1700–1920.* Dublin: Departments of Modern History, TCD & UCD, 1990.

Edwards, O.D. and P.J. Storey. 'The Irish press in Victorian Britain.' In Swift and Gilley, eds. *Victorian city.* Pp 158–78.

Foster, J.W. 'Natural history in modern Irish culture.' In Bowler and Whyte, eds. *Science and society*. Pp 119–33.

———. 'Changes of address: Tyndall, Darwin and the Ulster Presbyterians.' In Stewart, ed. *Hearts and minds*. Pp 40–70.

Foster, J.W. and H.C.G. Chesney, eds. *Nature in Ireland: a scientific and cultural history.* Dublin: Lilliput, 1997.

Johnston, Roy. 'Science and technology in Irish national culture.' *Crane Bag*. 7:2 (1983). Pp 58–76.

Livingstone, David N. 'Darwin in Belfast: the evolution debate.' In Foster and Chesney, eds. *Nature in Ireland.* Pp 387–408.

Lysaght, Sean. *Robert Lloyd Praeger and the culture of science in Ireland, 1865–1953.* Dublin: Four Courts, 1998.

McClelland, Aiken. 'The Ulster press in the eighteenth and nineteenth centuries.' *Ulster Folklife*. 20 (1974). Pp 89–99.

McDowell, R.B. and D.A. Webb, eds. *Trinity College Dublin, 1592–1952*. Cambridge: Cambridge University Press, 1982.

McLaughlin, P. J. 'Dr Russell and the *Dublin Review*.' *Studies*. 41 (1952). Pp 175–88.

McManus, Antonia. *The Irish hedge school and its books, 1695–1831*. Dublin: Four Courts, 2002.

Murphy, James H., ed. *Nos autem: Castleknock College and its contribution*. Dublin: Gill and Macmillan, 1996.

Ó Cíosáin, Niall. *Print and popular culture in Ireland, 1750–1850*. London: Macmillan, 1997.

Parkes, Susan M. 'Higher education, 1793–1908.' In Vaughan, ed. *Union II, 1870–1921*. Pp 539–70.

Pollard, Mary M. *Dublin's trade in books, 1550–1800*. Oxford: Clarendon, 1989.

Whyte, Nicholas. *Science, colonialism and Ireland*. Cork: Cork University Press, 1999.

FAMINE

Bourke, Austin. *The visitation of God? The potato and the great Irish famine*. Dublin: Lilliput, 1993.

Boylan, Thomas A., and Timothy P. Foley. ' "A nation perishing from political economy"?' In Morash and Hayes, eds. *'Fearful realities.'* Pp 138–50.

Connolly, S.J. "Revision revised? New work on the Irish famine." *Victorian Studies*. 39:2 (1996). Pp 205–16.

Crawford, E. Margaret, ed. *The hungry stream: essays on emigration and famine*. Belfast: Institute of Irish Studies: 1997.

Daly, M.E. *The famine in Ireland*. Dublin: Dublin Historical Association, 1986.

Davis, Graham. 'The historiography of the Irish famine.' In O'Sullivan, ed. *Meaning of the famine*. Pp 15–39.

Donnelly Jr., James S. 'The great famine: its interpreters old and new.' *History Ireland*. 1:3 (1993). Pp 27–33.

———. 'The construction of the memory of the famine in Ireland, 1850–1900.' *Éire-Ireland*. 31:1 and 2 (1996). Pp 26–61.

———. *The great Irish potato famine*. Stroud: Sutton, 2001.

Gray, Peter. 'Potatoes and providence: British government responses to the great famine.' *Bullán* 1:1. (1994). Pp 75–90.

———. *Famine, land and politics: British government and Irish society, 1843–50*. Dublin: Irish Academic Press, 1999.

Kelleher, Margaret. *The feminization of famine: expressions of the inexpressible?* Cork: Cork University Press, 1997.

———. ' "Philosophick views?" Maria Edgeworth and the great famine.' *Éire-Ireland*. 32:1 (1997). Pp 41–62.

Kennedy, Liam, Paul S. Ell, E.M. Crawford, L.A. Clarkson, eds. *Mapping the great Irish famine: an atlas of the famine years*. Dublin: Four Courts, 2000.

———. 'Bastardy and the great famine in Ireland, 1845–50.' In King, ed. *Famine, land and culture*. Pp 6–28.

Killen, John, ed. *The famine decade: contemporary accounts, 1841–51*. Belfast: Blackstaff, 1995.

Kinealy, Christine. *This great calamity: the Irish famine, 1845–52*. Dublin: Gill and Macmillan, 1994.

———. *A death-dealing famine: The great hunger in Ireland.* London: Pluto, 1997.

———. *The great Irish famine: impact, ideology and rebellion.* New York: Palgrave, 2001.

Kinealy, Christine and Trevor Parkhill, eds. *The famine in Ulster: the regional impact.* Belfast: Ulster Historical Foundation, 1997.

King, Carla, ed. *Famine, land and culture in Ireland.* Dublin: University College Dublin Press, 2000.

Lysaght, Patricia. 'Perspectives on women during the great famine from the oral tradition.' *Béaloideas.* 64–5 (1996–7). Pp 63–130.

MacAtasney, Gerard. *'This dreadful visitation:' the famine in Lurgan/Portadown.* Belfast: Beyond the Pale, 1997.

MacLachlainn, Antain. 'The famine in Gaelic tradition.' *Irish Review.* 17–18 (1995). Pp 90–108.

Miller, David W. 'Irish Presbyterians and the great famine.' In Hill and Lennon, eds. *Luxury and austerity.* Pp 165–81.

Mokyr, Joel. *Why Ireland starved? A quantitative and analytical history of the Irish economy 1800–50.* London: George Allen, Unwin, 1983.

Morash, Chris, ed. *The hungry voice: the poetry of the Irish famine.* Dublin: Irish Academic Press, 1989.

———. *Writing the Irish famine.* Oxford: Oxford University Press, 1995.

———. 'Making memories: the literature of the Irish famine.' In O'Sullivan, ed. *Meaning of the famine.* Pp 40–55.

Morash, Christopher and Richard Hayes, eds. *'Fearful realities:' new perspectives on the famine.* Dublin: Irish Academic Press, 1996.

Murphy, Ignatius. *Before the famine struck: life in West Clare, 1834–45.* Dublin: Irish Academic Press, 1996.

———. *A people starved: life and death in West Clare, 1845–51.* Dublin: Irish Academic Press, 1996.

Neal, Frank, *Black '47: Britain and the famine Irish.* London: Macmillan, 1998.

O'Farrell, Patrick. 'Whose reality? The Irish famine in history and literature.' *Historical Studies* (Melbourne). 20 (1982). Pp 1–13.

Ó Gráda, Cormac. 'Seasonal migration and demographic adjustment in post-famine Ireland.' *Studia Hibernica* 13 (1973). Pp 48–76.

———. *Famine 150: commemorative lecture series.* Dublin: Teagasc/UCD, 1997.

———. *Black '47 and beyond: the great Irish famine: history, economy and memory.* Princeton NJ: Princeton University Press, 1998.

O'Neill, Timothy P. 'Famine evictions.' In King (ed.), *Famine, land and culture.* Pp 29–70.

Póirtéir, Cathal, ed. *The great Irish famine.* Dublin: Mercier, 1995.

Ryder, Sean. 'Reading lessons: the famine and the *Nation,* 1845–9.' In Morash and Hayes, eds. *'Fearful realities.'* Pp 151–63.

GENDER

Blair, Gráinne M. ' "Equal sinners:" Irish women utilising the Salvation Army Rescue Netword for Britain and Ireland in the nineteenth century.' In Kelleher and Murphy, eds. *Gender perspectives.* Pp 179–92.

Bourke, Angela. *The burning of Bridget Cleary*. London: Pimlico. 1999.

Bourke, Joanna. ' "The best of all Home Rulers:" the economic power of women in Ireland, 1880–1914.' *Irish Economic and Social History*. 18 (1991). Pp 24–37.

———. *Husbandry to housewifery: women, economic change, and housework in Ireland, 1890–1914*. Oxford: Oxford University Press, 1993.

Bradley, Anthony and Maryann Gialanella Valiulis, eds. *Gender and sexuality in modern Ireland*. Amherst: University of Massachusetts Press, 1997.

Burgess, Miranda J. 'Violent translations: allegory, gender and cultural nationalism in Ireland, 1796–1806.' *Modern language Quarterly*. 59:1 (1998). Pp 33–70.

Castle, Terry. *The apparitional Lesbian*. New York: Columbia University Press, 1993.

Côté, Jane and Dana Hearne. 'Anna Parnell (1852–1911).' In Cullen and Luddy, eds. *Women, power and consciousness*. Pp 263–93.

Coulter, Carol. *The hidden tradition: feminism, women and nationalism in Ireland*. Cork: Cork University Press, 1993.

Cronin, Maura. 'The female industrial movement, 1845–52.' In Whelan (ed.), *Women and paid work*. Pp 69–85.

Cullen, Mary. *Girls don't do honours: Irish women's education in the nineteenth and twentieth centuries*. Dublin: Women's Education Bureau, 1987.

———. 'Anna Maria Haslam (1829–1922).' In Cullen and Luddy, eds. *Women, power and consciousness*. Pp 161–96.

Cullen, Mary, and Maria Luddy, eds. *Women, power and consciousness in nineteenth-century Ireland*. Dublin: Attic, 1995.

Daly, M.E. *Women and work in Ireland*. Dublin: Economic and Social History Society of Ireland, 1997.

Daly, Miriam. 'Women in Ulster.' In Eiléan Ní Chuilleanáin, ed. *Irish women: image and achievement: women in Irish culture from the earliest times*. Dublin: Arlen House, 1985. Pp 51–60.

Dunphy, Richard. 'Gender and sexuality in Ireland.' *Irish Historical Studies*. 31:124 (1999). Pp 549–57.

Fitzpatrick, David. 'The modernization of the Irish female.' In O'Flanagan, Ferguson and Whelan, eds. *Rural Ireland*. Pp 162–80.

———. 'Women, gender and the writing of Irish history.' *Irish Historical Studies*. 27:107 (1991). Pp 267–73.

———. 'Women and the great famine.' In Kelleher and Murphy, eds. *Gender perspectives*. Pp 50–69.

Foley, Timothy P. 'Public sphere and domestic circle: gender and political economy in nineteenth-century Ireland.' In Kelleher and Murphy, eds. *Gender perspectives*. Pp 21–35.

Griffin, Brian. 'The Irish police: love, sex and marriage in the nineteenth and early twentieth century.' In Kelleher and Murphy, eds. *Gender perspectives*. Pp 168–78.

Holmes, Janice and Diane Urquart, eds. *Coming into the light: the work, politics and religion of women in Ulster, 1840–1940*. Belfast: Institute of Irish Studies, 1994.

Innes, C.L. *Woman and nation in Irish literature and society, 1880–1935*. London: Harvester Wheatsheaf, 1993.

Joyce, Toby. ' "Ireland's trained and marshalled manhood:" the Fenians in the mid-1860s.' In Kelleher and Murphy, eds. *Gender perspectives*. Pp 70–80.

Kelleher, Margaret and James H. Murphy, eds. *Gender perspectives in nineteenth century Ireland: public and private spheres.* Dublin: Irish Academic Press, 1997.

Lanser, Susan. 'Befriending the body: female intimacies as class acts.' *Eighteenth-century Studies.* 32:2 (1998–99). Pp 179–98.

Luddy, Maria. 'Prostitution and rescue work in nineteenth-century Ireland.' In Luddy and Murphy, eds. *Women surviving*. Pp 51–84.

———. 'An agenda for women's history in Ireland, 1500–1900. Part two, 1800–1900.' *Irish Historical Studies.* 28:109 (1992). Pp 19–37.

———. *Women and philanthropy in nineteenth-century Ireland.* Cambridge: Cambridge University Press, 1995.

———. 'Isabella M.S. Tod (1836–1880).' In Cullen and Luddy, eds. *Women, power and consciousness*. Pp 197–230.

———. 'Women and politics in nineteenth-century Ireland.' In Valiulis and O'Dowd, eds. *Women and Irish history*. Pp 89–108.

——— ed. *Irish women's writing, 1839–88.* London: Routlege, 2000.

———. 'Women and work in nineteenth and early twentieth-century Ireland: an overview.' In Whelan, ed. *Women and paid work*. Pp 44–56.

Luddy, Maria and Cliona Murphy, eds. *Women surviving: studies in Irish women's history in the nineteenth and twentieth centuries.* Dublin: Poolbeg, 1990.

McLoughlin, Dympna. *Women, subsistence and emigration, 1840–70.* Dublin: Irish Academic Press, 2000.

McPherson, James. ' "Ireland begins in the home:" women, Irish national identity, and the domestic sphere in the *Irish Homestead*, 1896–1912.' *Éire-Ireland* 36:3 & 4 (2001). Pp 131–52.

Mavor, Elizabeth. *The ladies of Llangollen.* London: Penguin, 1971.

Murphy, Maureen. 'Asenath Nicholason and the famine in Ireland.' In Valiulis and O'Dowd, eds. *Women and Irish history*. Pp 109–24.

Owens, Rosemary Cullen. *Smashing times: a history of the Irish women's suffrage movement, 1889–1922*. Dublin: Attic, 1984.

Rhodes, Rita M. *Women and the family in post-famine Ireland: status and opportunity in a patriarchal society.* New York: Garland, 1992.

Sailer, Susan Shaw, ed. *Representing Ireland: gender, class, nationality.* Gainesville: University Press of Florida, 1997.

Steiner-Scott, Elizabeth. ' "To bounce a boot off her now and then:" domestic violence in post-famine Ireland.' In Valiulis and O'Dowd, eds. *Women and Irish history*. Pp 125–43.

Te Brake, Janet K. 'Irish peasant women in revolt: the Land League years.' *Irish Historical Studies.* 28:109 (1992). Pp 63–80.

Valiulis, Maryann Gialanella, and Mary O'Dowd, eds. *Women and Irish history: essays in honour of Margaret MacCurtain.* Dublin: Wolfhound, 1997.

Whelan, Bernadette, ed. *Women and paid work in Ireland, 1500–1930.* Dublin: Four Courts, 2000.

Walsh, Oonagh. ' "A lightness of mind:" gender and insanity in nineteenth-century Ireland.' In Kelleher and Murphy, eds. *Gender perspectives*. Pp 159–67.

GEOGRAPHY, CITIES AND COUNTIES

Aalen, F.H.A. and Kevin Whelan, eds. *Dublin city and county from prehistory to the present: studies in honour of J.H. Andrews.* Dublin: Geography Publications, 1992.

Beckett, J.C. and R.E. Glasscock. *Belfast: the origins of an industrial city.* London: BBC, 1967.

Beckett, J.C. et al. *Belfast: the making of a city, 1800–1914.* Belfast: Appletree, 1983.

Bielenberg, Andy. *Cork's industrial revolution, 1780–1880: development or decline?* Cork: Cork University Press, 1991.

Cosgrove, Art, ed. *Dublin through the ages.* Dublin: College, 1988.

Craig, Maurice. *Dublin, 1660–1860.* Dublin: Figgis, 1969.

Cronin, Maura. 'Work and workers: Cork city and county, 1800–1900.' In O'Flanagan and Buttimer, eds. *Cork.* Pp 721–58.

———. *Country, class or craft? The politicization of the skilled artisans in nineteenth-century Cork.* Cork: Cork University Press, 1994.

D'Alton, Ian. *Protestant society and politics in Cork, 1812–44.* Cork: Cork University Press, 1980.

Daly, M.E. 'The social structure of the Dublin working class, 1871–1911.' *Irish Historical Studies.* 23: 90. (1982). Pp 121–33.

———. *Dublin: the deposed capital: a social and economic history, 1860–1914.* Cork: Cork University Press, 1984.

———. 'A tale of two cities: 1860–1920.' In Cosgrove, ed. *Dublin.* Pp 113–32.

Dickson, David, ed. *Dublin: the gorgeous mask, 1700–1850.* Dublin. Trinity College Workshop, 1987.

Donnelly Jr, James S. *The land and people of nineteenth-century Cork.* London: Routledge and Kegan Paul, 1975.

Fagan, Patrick. *Catholics in a Protestant country: the papist constituency in eighteenth-century Dublin.* Dublin: Four Courts, 1998.

Gillespie, Raymond and Gerard Moran, eds. *'A various country:' essays in Mayo history, 1500–1900.* Westport: Foilseacháin Náisiúnta, 1987.

———. *Longford: essays in county history.* Dublin: Lilliput, 1991.

Graham, Brian, ed. *In search of Ireland: cultural geography.* London: Routledge, 1997.

Graham, B.J. and L.J. Proudfoot. *An historical geography of Ireland.* London: Academic, 1993.

Hewitt, John. 'The northern Athens and after.' In J.C. Beckett et al. *Belfast.* Pp 71–82.

Hill, Jacqueline. *From Patriots to Unionists: Dublin civil politics and Irish Protestant Patriotism, 1660–1840.* Oxford: Clarendon, 1997.

Hughes, T. Jones. 'The origin and growth of towns in Ireland.' *University Review.* 2:7 (1960). Pp 8–15.

———. 'Administrative divisions and the development of settlement in nineteenth-century Ireland.' *University Review.* 3:6 (1964). Pp 8–15.

———. 'Society and settlement in nineteenth-century Ireland.' *Irish Geography.* 5:2 (1965). Pp 79–96.

———. 'Village and town in mid-nineteenth-century Ireland.' *Irish Geography.* 14 (1981). Pp 99–106.

———. 'Historical geography of Ireland from *circa* 1700.' *Irish Geography.* (1984). Pp 149–66.

Jupp, Peter J and Stephen A. Doyle. 'The social geography of Cork City elections, 1801–30.' *Irish Historical Studies.* 29:13 (1994). Pp 13–43.

Kelly, James, and U. Mac Gerailt, eds. *Dublin and Dubliners: essays in the history and literature of Dublin city.* Dublin: Helicon, 1990.

Kennedy, Tom, ed. *Victorian Dublin.* Dublin: Albertine Kennedy with Dublin Arts Festival, 1980.

Litvack, Leon and Glenn Hooper. *Ireland in the nineteenth century: regional identity.* Dublin: Four Courts, 2000.

Moran, Gerard, Raymond Gillespie and William Nolan, eds. *Galway: history and society: interdisciplinary essays on the history of an Irish county.* Dublin: Geography Publications, 1996.

Nolan, William and Kevin Whelan, eds. *Kilkenny: history and society: interdisciplinary essays on the history of an Irish county.* Dublin: Geography, 1990.

O'Brien, John B. *The Catholic middle classes in pre-famine Cork.* NUI: O'Donnell Lectures, 1980.

———. 'Population, politics and society in Cork, 1780–1900.' In O'Flanagan and Buttimer, eds. *Cork.* Pp 699–720.

Ó Dálaigh, Brian, ed. *The stranger's gaze. Travels in County Clare, 1534–1950.* Ennis: Clasp, 1998.

O'Flanagan, Patrick and Cornelius G. Buttimer, eds. *Cork: history and society.* Dublin: Geography Publications, 1993.

O'Shea, James. *Priest, politics and society in post-famine Ireland: a study of Co. Tipperary, 1850–91.* Dublin: Wolfhound, 1983.

Pettit, Seán. *This city of Cork, 1700–1900.* Cork: Studio, 1977.

Power, Patrick C., ed. *A history of south Tipperary.* Dublin: Mercier, 1989.

Power, Thomas P. *Land, politics and society in eighteenth-century Tipperary.* Oxford: Clarendon, 1993.

Preston, Margaret H. 'Lay women and philanthropy in Dublin, 1860–80.' *Éire-Ireland.* 28:4 (1993). Pp 74–85.

Prunty, Jacinta. *Dublin slums 1800–1925: a study in urban geography.* Dublin: Irish Academic Press, 1999.

Smyth, W.J. and Kevin Whelan, eds. *Common ground: essays on the historical geography of Ireland: presented to T. James Hughes.* Cork: Cork University Press, 1988.

Whelan, Kevin, ed. *Wexford: history and society.* Dublin: Georgraphy Publications, 1987.

INSTITUTIONS

Andrew, John H. *A paper landscape: the ordnance survey in nineteenth-century Ireland.* Oxford: Clarendon, 1975.

Barrow, G.L. *The emergence of the Irish banking system, 1820–45.* Dublin: Gill and Macmillan, 1975.

Boyle, J.W. *The Irish labour movement in the nineteenth century.* Washington, DC: Catholic University of America Press, 1988.

Byrne, Kieran R. 'The Royal Dublin Society and the advancement of popular science in Ireland, 1731–1860.' In L. Irwin, ed. *Explorations: centenary essays, Mary Immaculate College Limerick.* Dublin: Colour, 1998.

Cassell, Ronald Drake. *Medical charities, medical politics: the Irish dispensary system and the poor law, 1836–72.* Suffolk: Boydell, 1997.

Hogan, Daire. *The legal profession in Ireland, 1789–1922.* Dublin: Incorporated Law Society of Ireland, 1986.

Kenny, Colum. 'The exclusion of Catholics from the legal profession in Ireland, 1537–1829.' *Irish Historical Studies.* 25:100 (1987). Pp 337–57.

Meenan, James and Desmond Clarke. *R.D.S.: Royal Dublin Society, 1731–1981.* Dublin: Gill and Macmillan, 1981.

Ó Raifertaigh, T., ed. *The Royal Irish Academy: a bicentennial history, 1785–1985.* Dublin: The Academy, 1985.

Saris, A. Jamie. 'Imagining Ireland in the great exhibition of 1853.' In Litvack and Hooper. *Regional identity.* Pp 66–86.

Turpin, John. 'The academy movement in Dublin, 1730–1880.' *New Hibernia Review.* 1:4 (1997). Pp 119–37.

LAND

Bew, Paul. *Land and the national question in Ireland, 1858–82.* Dublin: Gill and Macmillan, 1978.

Bull, Philip. *Land, politics and nationalism: a study of the Irish land question.* Dublin: Gill and Macmillan, 1996.

Clark, Samuel. *The social origins of the Irish land war.* Princeton, Princeton University Press, 1979.

———. 'The importance of agrarian classes: agrarian class structure and collective action in nineteenth-century Ireland.' In Drudy, ed. *Ireland, land, politics and people.* Pp 11–36.

Crossman, Virginia. 'Emergency legislation and agrarian disorder in Ireland, 1821–41.' *Irish Historical Studies.* 27:108 (1991). Pp 309–23.

Cullen, Louis. *The hidden Ireland: reassessment of a concept.* Mullingar: Lilliput, 1988.

Curtis Jr, L.P. 'On class and class conflict in the land war.' *Irish Economic and Social History.* 8 (1981). Pp 86–94.

Dowling, Martin W. *Tenant right and agrarian society in Ulster, 1600–1870.* Dublin: Irish Academic Press, 1999.

Drudy, P.J., ed. *Ireland, land, politics and people.* Cambridge: Cambridge University Press, 1982.

Fitzpatrick, David. 'The disappearance of the Irish agricultural labourer, 1841–1921.' *Irish Economic and Social History.* 7 (1980). Pp 66–92.

———. 'Class, family and rural unrest in nineteenth-century Ireland.' In Drudy, ed. *Ireland, land, politics and people.* Pp 37–75.

———. 'Unrest in rural Ireland.' *Irish Economic and Social History.* 12 (1985). Pp 98–105.

Freeman, T.W. 'Land and people, c. 1841.' In Vaughan, ed. *Union I, 1801–70.* Pp 242–71.

Geary, Laurence M. *The plan of campaign, 1886–91.* Cork: Cork University Press, 1986.

Jones, David Seth. *Graziers, land reform and political conflict in Ireland.* Washington DC: Catholic University of America Press, 1995.

Jordan, Donald E. *Land and popular politics in Ireland: County Mayo from the plantation to the land war.* Cambridge: Cambridge University Press, 1994.

———. 'The famine and its aftermath in County Mayo.' In Morash and Hayes, eds. *'Fearful realities.'* Pp 35–48.

MacCurtain, Margaret. 'Pre-famine peasantry in Ireland: definition and theme.' *Irish University Review*. 4:2 (1974). Pp 188–98.

O'Flanagan, Patrick, Paul Ferguson and Kevin Whelan, eds. *Rural Ireland: modernization and change*. Cork: Cork University Press, 1987.

Solow, Barbara Lewis. *The land question and the Irish economy, 1870–1903*. Cambridge, MA: Harvard University Press, 1971.

Vaughan, W.E. *Landlords and tenants in Ireland, 1848–1904*. Dublin: Economic and Social History Society of Ireland, 1984.

———. *Landlords and tenants in mid-Victorian Ireland*. Oxford: Oxford University Press, 1994.

Warwick-Haller, Sally. *William Smith O'Brien and the Irish land war*. Dublin: Irish Academic Press, 1990.

Whelan, Kevin. 'An underground gentry? Catholic middlemen in eighteenth-century Ireland.' In Donnelly and Miller, eds. *Irish popular culture*. Pp 118–72.

Winstanley, M. *Ireland and the land question, 1800–1922*. London: Methuen, 1984.

LITERATURE: GENERAL

Althoz, Josef L. 'Daniel O'Connell and the *Dublin Review*.' *Catholic Historical Review*. 74:1 (1988) Pp 1–12.

Backus, Margot Gayle. *The Gothic family romance: heterosexuality, child sacrifice and the Anglo-Irish colonial order*. Durham and London: Duke University Press, 1999.

Belanger, Jacqueline. 'The desire of the west: the Aran Islands and Irish identity in *Grania*.' In Litvack and Hooper, eds. *Regional identity*. Pp 95–107.

Boyd, Ernest. *Ireland's literary Renaissance*. London: Grant Richards, 1919.

Bourke, Angela, Siobhán Kilfeather, Maria Luddy, Margaret MacCurtain, Geraldine Meaney, Máirín Ní Dhonnchadha, Mary O'Dowd, and Clair Wills. *The Field Day anothology of Irish writing volumes IV and V: Irish women's writing and traditions*. Cork: Cork University Press, 2002.

Bramsbäck, Birgit and Martin Croghan, eds. *Anglo-Irish and Irish literature: aspects of language and culture*. 3 vols. Uppsala: Almqvist and Wiksell, 1988.

Brisman, Leslie. *Romantic origins*. Ithaca, NY: Cornell University Press, 1978.

Brown, Malcolm. *The politics of Irish literature: from Thomas Davis to W.B. Yeats*. London: George Allen and Unwin, 1972.

Brown, Stephen J. *Ireland in fiction*. 1916. Dublin: Maunsel 1919.

Brown, Terence. *Ireland's literature: selected essays*. Mullingar, Lilliput, 1988.

———. 'Saxon and Celt: the stereotypes.' In Brown, *Ireland's literature*. Pp 3–13.

———. 'Edward Dowden: Irish Victorian.' In Brown, *Ireland's literature*. Pp 29–48.

———. *The life of W.B. Yeats*. Dublin: Gill and Macmillan, 1999.

Brown, Terence and Nicholas Grene, eds. *Tradition and influence in Anglo-Irish poetry*. London: Macmillan, 1989.

Boyd, Ernest. *Ireland's literary Renaissance*. 1916. Dublin: Allen Figgis, 1968.

Cahalan, James M. *Great hatred, little room: the Irish historical novel*. Dublin: Gill and Macmillan, 1983.

———. *The Irish novel: a critical history*. Dublin: Gill and MacMillan, 1988.

———. *Modern Irish literature and culture, a chronology*. New York: G.K. Hall, 1993.

———. 'Forging a tradition: Emily Lawless and the Irish literary canon.' In Kirkpatrick, ed. *Irish women writers*. Pp 38–57.

Cairns, David and Shaun Richards. *Writing Ireland: colonialism, nationalism and culture*. Manchester: Manchester University Press, 1988.

Carpenter, Andrew, ed. *Place, personality and the Irish writer.* Gerrards Cross: Colin Smythe, 1977.

Carpentier, Godeleine. *Charles Joseph Kickham, écrivain*. Paris: Université de Paris III, 1987.

Colman, Ann Ulry. *A dictionary of nineteenth-century Irish women poets*. Galway: Kenny's Bookshop, 1996.

———. 'Far from silent: nineteenth-century Irish women writers.' In Kelleher and Murphy, eds. *Gender perspectives*. Pp 203–11.

Connolly, Claire. 'Nothing more than feelings: rereading national romance.' In Stewart, ed. *Hearts and minds*. Pp 98–110.

Corbett, Mary Jean. *Allegories of union: Irish and English writing, 1790–1870: politics, history and the family from Edgeworth to Arnold*. Cambridge: Cambridge University Press, 2000.

Costello, Peter. *The heart grown brutal: the Irish revolution in literature from Parnell to the death of Yeats, 1891–1939*. Gill and Macmillan, 1977.

———. *James Joyce: the years of growth, 1882–1915*. Dublin: Roberts Reinhard, 1992.

Cronin, John. *The Anglo-Irish novel*. 2 vols. Vol. 1. The nineteenth century. Belfast: Appletree, 1980.

Deane, Seamus. 'Edmund Burke and the ideology of Irish liberalism.' In Richard Kearney, ed. *The Irish mind: exploring intellectual traditions*. Dublin: Wolfhound, 1985. Pp 141–56.

———. *A short history of Irish literature*. London: Hutchinson, 1986.

———. *Celtic revivals: essays in modern Irish literature, 1880–1980*. London: Faber and Faber, 1987.

———. 'Irish national character, 1790–1900.' In Dunne, ed. *Writer as witness*. Pp 90–113.

———. *Strange country: modernity and nationhood in Irish writing since 1790*. Oxford: Clarendon, 1997.

——— ed. *The Field Day anthology of Irish writing*. 3 vols. Derry: Field Day, 1991.

Denman, Peter. 'Ghosts in Anglo-Irish literature.' In Welch, ed. *Irish writers and religion*. Pp 62–74.

Downer, A.S. *The eminent tragedian William Charles Macready*. Oxford: Oxford University Press, 1966.

Dunne, Tom ed. *The writer as witness: literature as historical evidence*. Historical studies 16. Cork: Cork University Press, 1987.

———. 'Haunted by history: Irish romantic writing, 1800–50.' In Roy Porter and M. Teich, eds. *Romanticism in national context*. Cambridge: Cambridge University Press, 1988. Pp 68–91.

Eagleton, Terry. 'Form and ideology in the Anglo-Irish novel.' *Bullán* 1:1. (1994). Pp 17–26.

———. *Heathcliff and the great hunger: studies in Irish culture*. London: Verso, 1995.

———. 'The ideology of Irish studies.' *Bullán* 3:1 (1997). Pp 5–14.

———. *Crazy John and the bishop*. Cork: Cork University Press, 1998.

———. *Scholars and rebels in nineteenth-century Ireland.* Oxford: Blackwell, 1999.

Fackler, Herbert V. 'Aubrey de Vere's *The sons of Usnach* (1844): a heroic narrative poem in six cantos.' *Éire-Ireland.* 9:1 (1974). Pp 80–89.

Fallis, Richard. *The Irish Renaissance.* Dublin: Gill and Macmillan, 1978.

Farren, Robert. *The course of Irish verse in English.* London: Sheed and Ward, 1948.

Fitzsimon, Christopher. *The Irish theatre.* London: Thames and Hudson, 1983.

Flanagan, Thomas. *The Irish novelists, 1800–50.* Westport: Greenwood, 1976.

———. 'Literature in English, 1801–91.' In Vaughan, ed. *Union I, 1801–70.* Pp 482–522.

Foster. J.W. *Fictions of the Irish literary revival: a changeling art.* Dublin: Gill and Macmillan, 1987.

Foster, R.F. 'Anglo-Irish literature, Gaelic nationalism and Irish politics in the 1890s.' In *Ireland after the Union: proceedings of the second joint meeting of the Royal Irish Academy and the British Academy, London 1986.* Oxford: Oxford University Press, 1989. Pp 61–82.

———. 'Protestant magic: W.B. Yeats and the spell of history.' *Proceedings of the British Academy.* 75. Oxford: Oxford University Press, 1989. Pp 243–66.

———. *W.B. Yeats. A life.* Vol. 1. *The appentice mage, 1865–1914.* Oxford: Clarendon, 1997.

Foster, Sally E. 'Irish wrong: Samuel Lover and the stage Irishman.' *Éire-Ireland.* 13:4 (1978). Pp 34–44.

Frayne, John. P., ed. *The uncollected prose of W.B. Yeats.* Vol. 1. *First reviews and articles, 1886–96.* London: Macmillan, 1970.

Gailey, Alan. *Irish folk drama.* Cork: Mercier,1969.

Genet, Jacqueline. *The big house: reality and representation.* Dingle: Brandon, 1991.

——— ed. *Rural Ireland, real Ireland?* Gerrards Cross: Colin Smythe, 1996.

Gibbons, Luke. ' "A shadowy narrator:" history, art and romantic nationalism in Ireland 1750–1850.' In Brady, ed. *Ideology and the historians.* Pp 99–127.

———. *Transformations in Irish culture.* Cork: Cork University Press, 1996.

———. 'The mirror and the vamp: reflections on the Act of Union.' In Stewart, ed. *Hearts and minds.* Pp 21–39.

Graham, Colin. '"Liminal spaces:" post-colonial theory and Irish culture.' *Irish Review.* 16 (1994). Pp 29–43.

———. *Deconstructing Ireland: identity, theory, culture.* Edinburgh: Edinburgh University Press, 2001.

Graham, Colin and Richard Kirkland, eds. *Ireland and cultural theory: the mechanics of authenticity.* London: Macmillan, 1999.

Hall, Wayne C. *Shadowy heroes: Irish literature of the 1890s.* Syracuse, NY: Syracuse Univeristy Press, 1980.

———. *Dialogues in the margin: a study of the* Dublin University Magazine. Gerrards Cross: Colin Smythe, 2000.

Harmon, Maurice. 'Aspects of the peasantry in Anglo-Irish literature from 1800 to 1916.' *Studia Hibernia.* 15 (1975). Pp 105–27.

Hayley, Barbara. ' "The Eerishers are marchin:" British critical receptions of nineteenth-century Anglo-Irish fiction.' In Wolfgang Zach and Heinz Kosok, eds. *Literary interrelations: Ireland, England and the world.* 3 vols. Vol. 1. *Reception and translation.* Tübingen: Gunter Narr Verlag, 1987. Pp 39–50.

———. 'A reading and thinking nation: periodicals as the voice of nineteenth-century Ireland.' In Hayley and McKay, eds. *Irish periodicals*. Pp 29–48.

———. 'Voices and values: some implications of speech in the nineteenth-century Anglo-Irish novel.' In Bramsbäck and Croghan, eds. *Anglo-Irish literature and Irish literature*. Vol. 1. *Aspects of language and culture*. Pp 159–72.

———. 'Religion and society in nineteenth-century fiction.' In Welch, ed. *Irish writers and religion*. Pp 32–42.

Hayley, Barbara and Enda McKay, eds. *Three hundred years of Irish periodicals*. Dublin: Association of Irish Learned Journals, 1987.

Hayley, Barbara and Christopher Murray, eds. *Ireland and France: a bountiful friendship: literature, history and ideas: essays in honour of Patrick Rafroidi*. Gerrards Cross: Colin Smythe, 1992.

Herbison, Ivan. ' "The rest is silence:" some remarks on the disappearance of Ulster-Scots poetry.' In John Erskine and Gordon Lucy, eds. *Cultural traditions in Northern Ireland: varieties of Scottishness*. Belfast: Institute of Irish Studies, 1997. Pp 129–45.

Huber, Werner. 'Irish writers and the English romantics.' In Michael Gassenmeir and Norbert Platz, eds. *Beyond the suburbs of the mind: exploring English romanticism*. Essen: Verlag Die Blaue Eule, 1987. Pp 79–94.

Hutchinson, John. *The dynamics of cultural nationalism. The Gaelic revival and the creation of the Irish nation state*. London: Allen and Unwin, 1987.

Hyland, Paul and Neil Sammells, eds. *Irish writing: exile and subversion*. London: Macmillan, 1991.

Jeffares, A.N. *Anglo-Irish literature*. London: Macmillan, 1991.

———. *Images of invention: essays on Irish writing*. Gerrards Cross: Colin Smythe, 1996.

Keane, Maureen. *Mrs C.S. Hall: a literary biography*. Gerrards Cross: Colin Smythe, 1997.

Kelleher, Margaret. 'Charlotte Riddell's *A struggle for fame:* the field of women's literary production.' *Colby Quarterly*. 34:2 (2000). Pp 116–31.

———. 'Writing Irish women's literary history.' *Irish Studies Review*. 19:1 (2001). Pp 5–14.

———. ' "Factual fictions:" representations of the land agitation in nineteenth-century women's fiction.'

Kelly, John, ed. *The collected letters of W.B. Yeats*. Vol. 1 (1865–95). Oxford: Clarendon, 1986.

Kelly, J.S. 'The fall of Parnell and the rise of Irish literature: an investigation.' *Anglo-Irish Studies*. 2 (1976). Pp 1–23.

Kenneally, Michael, ed. *Irish literature and culture*. Gerrards Cross: Colin Smythe, 1992.

Kiberd, Declan. *Inventing Ireland: the literature of the modern nation*. London: Cape, 1995.

———. *Irish classics*. London: Granta, 2000.

Kilfeather, Siobhán. 'Origins of the Irish female Gothic.' *Bullán* 1:2. (1994) Pp 35–46.

Kinsella, Thomas. *Davis, Mangan, Ferguson? Tradition and the Irish writer.* Dublin: Dolmen, 1970.

Kirkpatrick, Kathryn, ed. *Border crossings: Irish women writers and national identity*. Tuscaloosa: University of Alabama Press, 2000.

Kosok, Heinz, ed. *Studies in Anglo-Irish literature*. Bonn: Bouvier Verlag Herbert Grundmann, 1982.

Kreilkamp, Vera. *The Anglo-Irish novel and the big house*. Syracuse: Syracuse University Press, 1998.

Leerssen, Joep Th. ' "The cracked lookinglass of a servant:" cultural decolonization and national consciousness in Ireland and Africa.' In H. Dyserinck and K.U. Sundram, eds. *Europe und das nationale selbstverständnis. Imagologische problem in literatur, kunst und kultur des 19 und 20 jahrhunderts.* Bonn: Bouvier, 1988. Pp 103–18.

———. 'On the treatment of Irishness in romantic Anglo-Irish fiction.' *Irish University Review* 20:2 (1990). Pp 251–64.

———. *Mere Irish and Fíor-Ghael: studies in the idea of Irish nationality, its development and literary expression prior to the nineteenth century*. 1988. Cork: Cork University Press, 1996.

———. *Remembrance and imagination: patterns in the historical and literary representation of Ireland in the nineteenth century.* Cork: Cork University Press, 1996.

———. 'Irish cultural nationalism and its European context.' In Stewart, ed. *Hearts and minds*. Pp 170–87.

Leerssen, Joep Th., A.H. van der Weel and Bart Westerweel, eds. *Forging in the smithy: national identity and representation in Anglo-Irish literary history*. Amsterdam: Rodopi, 1995.

Lloyd, David. *Anomalous states: Irish writing and the post-colonial moment.* Dublin: Lilliput, 1993.

———. *Ireland after history*. Cork: Cork University Press, 1999.

Lubbers, Klaus. *Geschichte der irishen erzählprosa von den anfägnen bis zum ausgehenden 19 jahrhundert* A history of Irish narrative prose from the beginning to the end of the nineteenth-century. Vol. 1. Munich: Wilhelm Fink, 1985.

McAteer, Michael. *Standish O'Grady, Yeats and AE.* Dublin: Irish Academic Press, 2002.

McCarthy, Ann. *A search for identity in Irish literature.* Alicante: Universidad de Alicante, 1997.

McCaw, Neil. 'Voicing rebellion in Victorian fiction: towards a textual commemoration.' In Geary, ed. *Rebellion and remembrance.* Pp 159–74.

McCormack, W.J. *Ascendancy and tradition in Anglo-Irish literary history from 1789 to 1939.* Oxford: Oxford University Press, 1985.

———. *From Burke to Beckett: Ascendancy, tradition and betrayal in literary history.* Cork: Cork University Press, 1994.

———. ' "Never put your name to an anonymous letter:" Serial reading in the *Dublin University Magazine*, 1861–9.' *Yearbook of English Studies.* 26 (1996). Pp 100–15.

MacDonagh, Oliver. *The nineteenth-century novel and Irish social history: some aspects.* Dublin: O'Donnell lectures, 1970.

McDonagh, Thomas. *Literature in Ireland.* Dublin: Talbot, 1916.

McKenna, Brian. *Irish literature, 1800–75, a guide to information sources.* Detroit, MI: Gale Research, 1978.

Marcus, Phillip. *Standish O'Grady.* Lewisburg PA: Bucknell University Press, 1970.

Mathews, P.J., ed. *New voices in Irish criticism.* Dublin: Four Courts, 2000.

Melville, Joy. *'Mother of Oscar:' the life of Jane Francesca Wilde.* London: John Murray, 1994.

Mercier, Vivien. *The Irish comic tradition.* Oxford: Clarendon, 1965.

———. *Modern Irish literature: sources and founders.* Oxford: Clarendon, 1994.

Morash, Christopher. 'On minor literature: nineteenth-century Ireland.' In Joseph McMinn, ed. *The internationalism of Irish literature and drama.* Gerrards Cross: Colin Smythe, 1992. Pp 209–18.

———. 'The little black rose revisited: Church, empire and national destiny in the writings of Aubrey de Vere.' *Canadian Journal of Irish Studies.* 20:2 (1994). Pp 45–52.

———. ' "The time is out of joint (O cursèd spite!):" towards a definition of supernatural narrative.' In Stewart, ed. *Supernatural and the fantastic.* Vol. 1. Pp 123–42.

Moynahan, Julian. 'The image of the city in nineteenth-century Irish fiction.' In Maurice Harmon, ed. *The Irish writer and the city.* Gerrards Cross: Colin Smythe, 1984. Pp 1–17.

———. *Anglo-Irish: the literary imagination in a hyphenated culture.* Princeton: Princeton University Press, 1995.

Murphy, James H. *Catholic fiction and social reality in Ireland, 1873–1922.* Greenwood, CT: Greenwood, 1997.

———. ' "Things which seem to you unfeminine:" gender and nationalism in the fiction of some upper middle class Catholic women novelists, 1880–1910.' In Kirkpatrick, ed. *Irish women writers.* Pp 58–78.

———. "Between drawing-room and barricade: the autobiographies and nationalist fictions of Justin McCarthy." In Stewart, ed. *Hearts and minds.* Pp 111–20.

——— ed. Rosa Mulholland. *Marcella Grace.* Washington, DC: Maunsel, 2001.

O'Brien, George. 'The fictional Irishman, 1665–1850.' *Studies.* 66 (1977). Pp 319–29.

Ó Cúiv, Brian. 'Irish language and literature, 1845–1921.' In Vaughan, ed. *Union II, 1870–1921.* Pp 385–435.

Ó Hainle, Cathal. 'Towards the revival: some translations of Irish poetry, 1789–1897.' In Peter Connolly, ed. *Literature and the changing Ireland.* Gerrards Cross: Colin Smythe, 1982. Pp 37–57.

Ó hÓgáin, Dáithí. 'The word, the law and the spirit: folk religion and the supernatural in modern Irish literature.' In Welch, ed. *Irish writers and religion.* Pp 43–61.

O'Neill, Michael, ed. *Literature of the romantic period: a bibliographical guide.* Oxford: Clarendon, 1998.

Paulin, Tom. *Minotaur, poetry and the nation state.* London: Faber and Faber, 1992.

Power, P.C. *The story of Anglo-Irish poetry, 1800–1922.* Cork: Mercier, 1967.

Punter, David. *The literature of terror.* London: Longman, 1980.

Quinn, Antoinette, ed. *The figure in the cave and other essays.* Dublin: Lilliput, 1989.

Rafroidi, Patrick. *Irish literature in English: the romantic period (1789–1850).* 2 vols. Gerrards Cross: Colin Smythe, 1980.

Rauchbauer, Otto, ed. *Ancestral voices: the big house in Anglo-Irish literature.* Dublin: Lilliput, 1992.

Read, C.A., and Katharine Tynan Hinkson, eds. *The cabinet of Irish literature.* 3 vols. London: Gresham, 1902.

Ryan, Philip B. *The lost theatres of Dublin.* Westbury: Badger, 1998.

Schirmer, Gregory A. *Out of what began: a history of Irish poetry in English.* Ithaca: Cornell, 1998.

Sheeran, P.F. 'Colonists and colonized: some aspects of Anglo-Irish literature from Swift to Joyce.' *A Yearbook of English Studies.* 13 (1983). Pp 97–115.

Sloan, Barry. 'Mrs Hall's Ireland.' *Éire-Ireland.* 19:3 (1984). Pp 18–30.

———. *The pioneers of Anglo-Irish Fiction, 1800–50.* Gerrards Cross: Colin Smythe, 1986.

Smyth, Gerry. *Decolonization and criticism: the construction of Irish literature.* London: Pluto, 1998.

Snell, Keith, ed. *The regional novel in Britain and Ireland.* Cambridge: Cambridge University Press, 1998.

Spence, Joseph. '"The great angelic sin:" the Faust legend in Irish literature, 1820–1900.' *Bullán* 1:2 (1994). Pp 47–58.

———. 'Isaac Butt, nationality and Irish Toryism, 1833–52.' *Bullán* 2:1 (1995). Pp 45–60.

Stewart, Bruce, ed. *That other world: supernatural and the fantastic in Irish literature and its contexts.* 2 vols. Gerrards Cross: Colin Smythe, 1998.

———. *Hearts and minds: Irish culture and society under the Act of Union.* Gerrards Cross: Colin Smythe, 2002.

Storey, Mark. *Poetry and Ireland since 1800: a source book.* London: Routledge, 1988.

Taylor, Geoffrey. *Irish poets in the nineteenth century.* Westport, CT: Greenwood, 1951.

Tilley, Elizabeth. 'Charting culture in the *Dublin University Magzaine.*' In Litvack and Hooper. *Regional identity*. Pp 58–65.

Tracy, Robert. *The unappeasable host: studies in Irish identities.* Dublin: University College Dublin Press, 1998.

Trumpener, Katie. 'National character, nationalist plots: national tale and historical novels in the age of *Waverley* 1806–30.' *E.L.H.* 60 (1993). Pp 685–731.

———. *Bardic nationalism: the romantic novel and the British empire*. Princeton: Princeton Univeristy Press, 1997.

Vance, Norman. 'Celts, Carthaginians and constitutions: Anglo-Irish literary relations, 1780–1820.' *Irish Historical Studies.* 22:87 (1981). Pp 216–38.

———. *Irish literature: a social history*. 1990. Dublin: Four Courts, 1999.

———. 'Catholic writing and the literary revival.' In Stewart, ed. *Hearts and minds*. Pp 158–69.

Ward, Patrick. *Exile, emigration and Irish writing*. Dublin: Irish Academic Press, 2002.

Waters, Maureen. ' "No divarshin:" Samuel Lover's *Handy Andy.*' *Éire-Ireland.* 14:4 (1979). Pp 53–64.

———. *The comic Irishman*. Albany, NY: State University of New York Press, 1984.

Watson, G.J. *Irish identity and the Irish literary revival: Synge, Yeats, Joyce and O'Casey*. 1979. Washington DC: Catholic University of America Press: 1994.

Welch, Robert. *Irish poetry from Moore to Yeats.* Gerrards Cross: Colin Smythe, 1980.

———. *A history of verse translation from the Irish, 1789–1897*. Gerrards Cross: Colin Smythe, 1988.

——— ed. *Irish writers and religion*. Gerrards Cross: Colin Smythe, 1992.

———. *Changing states: transformations in modern Irish writing*. London: Routledge, 1993.

———. ed. *The Oxford companion to Irish literature*. Oxford: Clarendon, 1996.

Whelan, Kevin. 'Writing Ireland: reading England.' In Litvack and Hooper, eds, *Regional identity*. Pp 185–98.

Zach, Wolfgang, and Heinz Kosok, eds. *Literary interrelations: Ireland, England and the world.* 3 vols. Tübingen: Gunter Narr Verlag, 1987. Vol. 2. *Comparison and impact.*

LITERATURE: AUTHORS

Allingham

Armstrong, Isobel. *The radical in crisis: Clough*. London: Routledge and Kegan Paul, 1993.

Brown, Malcolm. 'Allingham's Ireland.' *Irish University Review.* 13:1 (1983). Pp 7–13.

Hughes, Linda K. 'Politics of empire and resistance: William Allingham's *Laurence Bloomfield in Ireland.*' *Victorian Poetry.* 28:2 (1991) Pp 103–17.

Husni, Samira Aghacy. 'A bibliography of William Allingham.' *Éire-Ireland.* 22:2 (1987). Pp 155–7.

Warner, Alan. *William Allingham.* Lewisburg: Bucknell University Press, 1975.

Banims

Dunne, Tom. 'The insecure voice: a Catholic novelist in support of emancipation.' In *Culture et pratiques politiques en France et en Irlande xvi-xviii siècle.* Paris: Centre de Researches Historiques, 1989. Pp 213–33.

Escarbelt, Bernard. *Les fréres Banim: témoins et peintres de l'Irlande.* Paris: Université de Paris III, 1985.

———. 'An Irishman in France: John Banim.' In Hayley and Murray, eds. *Ireland and France.* Pp 57–66.

Friedman, Barton R. 'Fabricating history, or John Banim refights the Boyne.' *Éire-Ireland.* 17:1 (1982). Pp 39–56.

Hawthorne, Mark D. *John and Michael Banim (the 'O'Hara brothers'): a study in the early development of the Anglo-Irish novel.* Salzburg: Institut für Englische Sprahe und Literatur, 1975.

Murray, P.J. *The life of John Banim.* London: W. Lay, 1857. New York: Garland, 1978.

Boucicault and the theatre

Basta, Samira. 'The French influence on Dion Boucicault's sensation drama.' In Zach and Kosok, eds. *Comparison and impact.* Pp 199–206.

Cave, Richard Allen. 'Staging the Irishman.' In J.S. Bratton et al., eds. *Acts of supremacy: the British empire and the stage, 1790–1930.* Manchester: Manchester University Press, 1991. Pp 62–128.

Clarke, Brenna Katz. *The emergence of the Irish peasant play at the Abbey Theatre.* Ann Arbor, MI: UMI Research Press, 1982.

Fawkes, Richard. *Dion Boucicault: a biography.* London: Quartet, 1979.

Grene, Nicholas. *The politics of Irish drama: plays in context from Boucicault to Friel.* Cambridge: University Press, 1999.

Harrington, John. P. ' "Rude involvement:" Boucicault, dramatic tradition and ontemporary politics.' *Éire-Ireland.* 30:2 (1995). Pp 89–103.

Harvey, Karen J. and Kevin B. Pry. 'John O'Keefe as an Irish playwright within the theatrical, social and economic context of his time.' *Éire-Ireland.* 22:1 (1987). Pp 19–43.

Hogan, Robert. *Dion Boucicault.* New York: Twayne, 1969.

Hurt, James. 'Dion Boucicault's comic myths.' In J.L. Fisher, ed. *When they weren't doing Shakespeare.* Athens: University of Georgia Press, 1989. Pp 253–65.

Kosok, Heinz. 'The image of Ireland in nineteenth-century drama.' In Jacqueline Genet and Richard Allen Cave, eds. *Perspectives of Irish drama and theatre.* Gerrards Cross: Colin Smythe, 1991. Pp 50–67.

Molin, S.E. and R. Goodfellowe. 'Nationalism on the Dublin stage.' *Éire-Ireland.* 21:1 (1986). Pp 135–8.

Morash, Chris. *A history of Irish theatre, 1601–2000.* Cambridge: Cambridge University Press, 2002.

Nelson, J.M. 'From Rory and Paddy to Boucicault's Myles, Shawn and Conn: the Irishman on the London stage, 1830–80.' *Éire-Ireland* 13:3 (1978). Pp 79–105.

Truninger, Annelise. *Paddy and the Paycock: a study of the stage Irishman from Shakespeare to O'Casey*. Berne: Francke, 1976.

Watt, S.M. 'Boucicault and Whitbread: the Dublin stage at the end of the nineteenth century.' *Éire-Ireland* 18:3 (1983). Pp 23–53.

Carleton

Brown, Terence. 'Unspoken volumes: the representation of violence in three Carleton tales.' In Nela Bureu, Pedro Gallardo and Maria O'Neill, eds. *Voices of Ireland. Veus d'Irlanda*. Lleida: Pagès, 1992. Pp 15–25.

Boué, André. *William Carleton: romancier Irlandais (1794–1869)*. Série Sorbonne 6. Paris: Publications de la Sorbonne, 1978.

Chesnutt, Margaret. *Studies in the short stories of William Carleton*. Göteborg: University of Göteborg Press, 1976.

Hayley, Barbara. *Carleton's 'Traits and stories' and the nineteenth-century Anglo-Irish tradition*. Gerrards Cross: Colin Smythe, 1983.

———. *A bibliography of the writings of William Carleton*. Gerrards Cross: Colin Smythe, 1985.

Hurson, Tess, ed. *Inside the margins: a Carleton reader*. Belfast: Lagan, 1992.

King, Sophia Hillan. 'Pictures drawn from memory: William Carleton's experience of famine.' *Irish Review*. 17–18 (1995). Pp 80–89.

Krause, David. 'Carleton, Catholicism and the comic novel.' *Irish University Review*. 24:2 (1994). Pp 217–40.

———. 'William Carleton, demiurge of Irish carnival. *Fardorougha the Miser* 1839.' *Éire-Ireland*. 29:4 (1994). Pp 24–46.

———. *William Carleton, the novelist, his carnival and pastoral world of tragicomedy*. Lanham, MD: University Press of America, 2000.

O'Brien, Margaret. 'William Carleton: the Lough Derg exile.' In Paul Hyland and Neil Sammells, eds. *Irish writing: exile and subversion*. New York: St Martin's, 1991. Pp 82–97.

O Hainle, Cathal. 'The Gaelic background of Carleton's "Traits and stories."' *Éire-Ireland*. 18:1 (1983). Pp 6–19.

Sullivan, Eileen. *William Carleton*. Boston: Twayne, 1983.

Waters, Maureen. 'Comic form and historic nightmare in Carleton's *Emigrants of Ahadarra*.' *Éire-Ireland* 22:1 (1987). Pp 86–101

Wolff, Robert Lee. *William Carleton: Irish peasant novelist: a preface to his fiction*. New York: Garland, 1980.

Edgeworth

Alteiri, Joanne. 'Style and purpose in Maria Edgeworth's fiction.' *Nineteenth-century Fiction*. 23 (1968). Pp 265–78.

Atkinson, Colin B. and Jo Atkinson. 'Maria Edgeworth, *Belinda* and women's rights.' *Éire-Ireland* 19:4 (1984). Pp 94–118.

Butler, Marilyn. *Maria Edgeworth: a literary biography*. Oxford: Oxford University Press, 1972.

———. *Romantics, rebels and reactionaries: English literature and its background, 1760–1830.* Oxford: Oxford University Press, 1981.

———. 'Introduction.' In Maria Edgeworth. *Castle Rackrent* and *Ennui*. London: Penguin, 1992. Pp 1–58.

———. 'Edgeworth's stern father: escaping Thomas Day, 1795–1801.' In Alvaro Ribeiro and James G. Basker, eds. *Tradition in transition: women writers, marginal texts and the eighteenth-century canon.* Oxford: Clarendon, 1996. Pp 75–93.

Cary, Meredith. 'Privileged assimilation: Maria Edgeworth's hope for the Ascendancy.' *Éire-Ireland.* 26:4 (1991). Pp 29–37.

Colgan, Maurice. 'After Rackrent: Ascendancy and nationalism in Maria Edgeworth's later Irish novels.' In Kosok, ed. *Studies in Anglo-Irish literature*. Pp 37–42.

Connolly, Claire. 'Uncanny *Castle Rackrent*.' In Bruce Stewart. *Supernatural and the fantastic.* Vol. 1. Pp 205–20.

———. 'Reading responsibility in *Castle Rackrent*.' In Graham and Kirkland, eds. *Ireland and cultural theory*. Pp 136–61.

Corbett, Mary Jean. ' "Another tale to tell:" postcolonial theory and the case of *Castle Rackrent*.' *Criticism* 36:3 (Summer 1994). Pp 383–400.

———. 'Public affections and familial politics: Burke, Edgeworth and the "common naturalization" of Great Britain.' *English Literary History*. 61 (1994). Pp 877–97.

Croghan, Martin J. 'Maria Edgeworth and the tradition of Irish semiotics.' In Donald E. Morse and Csilla Bertha, eds. *A small nation's contribution to the world: essays on Anglo-Irish literature.* Gerrards Cross: Colin Smythe, 1993. Pp 194–206.

Dunleavy, Janet Egleson. 'Maria Edgeworth and the novel of Manners.' In Bege K. Bowers and Barbara Brothers, eds. *Reading and writing women's lives*. Ann Arbor MI: UMI Research, 1990. Pp 49–65.

Dunne, Tom. *Maria Edgeworth and the colonial mind.* O'Donnell Lectures. Cork: Cork University Press, 1984.

———. ' "A gentleman's estate should be a moral school:" Edgeworthstown in fact and fiction, 1760–1840.' In Raymond Gillespie and Gerard Moran, eds. *Longford: essays in county history.* Dublin: Lilliput, 1991. Pp 95–121.

Ethridge, Kath. 'Beyond the didactic theme: public and private space in Maria Edgeworth's *Vivian*.' *English*. 46:185 (1997). Pp 97–111.

Figes, Eva. *Sex and subterfuge: women novelists to 1850.* Basingstoke: Macmillan, 1982.

Gallagher, Catherine. 'Fictional women and real estate in Maria Edgeworth's *Castle Rackrent*.' *Nineteenth-century Contexts.* 12:1 (1988). Pp 11–18.

———. *Nobody's story: the vanishing acts of women writers in the marketplace, 1670–1820.* Oxford: Clarendon, 1994.

Gilmartin, Sophie. *Ancestry and narrative in nineteenth-century British literature: blood relations from Edgeworth to Hardy.* Cambridge: Cambridge University Press, 1998.

Gonda, Caroline. *Reading daughters' fictions, 1709–1834: novels and society from Manley to Edgeworth.* Cambridge: Cambridge University Press, 1996.

Graham, Colin. 'History, gender and the colonial moment: *Castle Rackrent*.' *Irish Studies Review* 14 (1996). Pp 21–4.

Greenfield, Susan C. ' "Abroad and at home:" sexual ambiguities, miscegenation, and colonial boundaries in Edgeworth's *Belinda*.' *PMLA* 112:2 (1997). Pp 214–29.

Hack, Daniel. 'Internationalism: *Castle Rackrent* and Anglo-Irish fiction.' *Novel: A Forum on Fiction*. 29:2 (1996). Pp 45–64.

Harden, Elizabeth. *Maria Edgeworth*. Boston: Twayne, 1984.

Hollingsworth, Brian. 'Completing the union: Edgeworth's *The absentee* and Scott the novelist.' In J.H. Alexander and David Hewitt, eds. *Scott as carnival*. Aberdeen: University of Aberdeen, 1993. Pp 502–11.

———. *Maria Edgeworth's Irish writings: language, history, politics*. Basingstoke: Macmillan, 1997.

Hurst, Michael. *Maria Edgeworth and the public scene: intellect, fine feeling and landlordism in the age of reform*. London: Macmillan, 1969.

Inglis-Jones, Elisabeth. *The great Maria: a portrait of Maria Edgeworth*. London: Faber and Faber, 1959.

Kelly, Gary. *English Fiction of the romantic period, 1789–1830*. London: Longman, 1989.

———. *Women, writing and revolution, 1790–1827*. Oxford: Clarendon, 1993.

———. 'Nation and empire: money and merit in the writings of the Edgeworths.' *Wordsworth Circle*. 15 (1994). Pp 89–93.

Kirkpatrick, Kathryn. 'Putting down the rebellion: notes and glosses on *Castle Rackrent* (1800).' *Éire-Ireland*. 30:1 (1995). Pp 77–91.

Kowaleski-Wallace, Elizabeth. *Their father's daughters: Hannah More, Maria Edgeworth and patriarchal complicity*. Oxford: Oxford University Press, 1991.

Lightfoot, Marjorie. ' "Morals for those that like them:" the satire of Edgeworth's *Belinda* (1801)' *Éire-Ireland*. 29:4 (1994). Pp 117–31.

McCann, Andrew. 'Conjugal love and the Enlightenment subject: the colonial contest of non-identity in Maria Edgeworth's *Belinda*.' *Novel: A Forum on Fiction*. 30:1 (1997). Pp 56–77.

McCarthy, Bridget G. *The female pen: women writers and novelists 1621–1818*. Cork: Cork University Press, 1994.

McCormack, W.J. 'French revolution ... Anglo-Irish literature ... beginnings? The case of Maria Edgeworth.' In Gough and Dickson, eds. *Ireland and the French Revolution*. Pp 77–98.

———. ' "The tedium of history:" an approach to Maria Edgeworth's *Patronage* (1814).' In Brady, ed. *Ideology and the historians*. Pp 77–98.

———. 'Setting and ideology with reference to the fiction of Maria Edgeworth.' In Otto Rauchbauer, ed. *Ancestral voices: the big house in Anglo-Irish literature*. Dublin: Lilliput, 1992. Pp 33–60.

MacFadyen, H. 'Lady Delacour, Maria Edgeworth, "Belinda" and fashionable reading.' *Nineteenth-century Literature*. 48:4 (1994). Pp 423–39.

Mellor, Anne K. *Romanticism and gender*. New York: Routledge, 1993.

Moore, Lisa. '"Something more tender than friendship:" romantic friendship in early nineteenth-century England.' *Feminist Studies* 18 (1992). Pp 499–520.

Murray, Patrick. *Maria Edgeworth: a study of the novelist*. Cork: Mercier, 1971.

Myers, Mitzi. 'The dilemmas of gender as double-voiced narrative: or Maria Edgeworth mothers the *Bildungsroman*.' In Robert W. Uphaus, ed. *The idea of the novel in the eighteenth century*. East Lansing MI: Colleagues Press, 1988. Pp 67–96.

———. 'Romancing the moral tale: Maria Edgeworth and the problematics of pedagogy.'

In James Holt McGavran, ed. *Romanticism and children's literature in nineteenth-century England.* Athens: University of Georgia Press, 1991. Pp 96–128.
———. 'De-romanticizing the subject: Maria Edgeworth's "The bracelets," mythologies of origin and the daughter's coming to writing.' In Theresa M. Kelley and Paula R. Feldman, eds. *Romantic women writers.* Hanover, NH: University Press of New England. 1995. Pp 88–110.
———. 'Shot from the canons; or, Maria Edgeworth and the cultural production and consumption of the late eighteenth-century woman writer.' In Ann Bermingham and John Brewer, eds. *The consumption of culture, 1600–1800: image, object, text.* London: Routledge, 1995. Pp 193–214.
———. ' "We must grant a romance writer a few impossibilities:" "unnatural incident" and narrative motherhood in Maria Edgeworth's *Emile de Coulanges.*' *Wordsworth Circle* 27 (1996). Pp 151–7.
———. 'War correspondence: Maria Edgeworth and the engendering of revolution, rebellion and union.' *Eighteenth-century Life.* 22:3 (1998). Pp 74–91.
Newby, Percy Howard. *Maria Edgeworth.* Denver: Swallow, 1950.
Newcomer, James. *Maria Edgeworth the novelist.* Fort Worth: Texas Christian University Press, 1967.
———. *Maria Edgeworth.* Lewisburg: Bucknell Univeristy Press, 1973.
Ó Gallchoir, Clíona. 'Maria Edgeworth's revolutionary morality and the limits of realism.' *Colby Quarterly.* 34:2 (2000). Pp 87–97.
Owens, Cóilín, ed. *Family chronicles: Maria Edgeworth's* Castle Rackrent. Dublin: Wolfhound, 1987. Pp 71–8.
Perry, Ruth. 'Colonizing the breast: sexuality and maternity in eighteenth-century England.' *Journal of the History of Sexuality.* 2 (1991). Pp 204–43.
Ragussis, Michael. 'Representation, conversion and literary form: *Harrington* and the novel of Jewish identity.' *Critical Inquiry.* 16:1 (1989). Pp 113–43.
Shaffer, Julie. 'Not subordinate: empowering women in the marriage plot: the novels of Frances Burney, Maria Edgeworth and Jane Austen.' *Criticism: A Quarterly for Literature and the Arts.* 34:1 (1992). Pp 51–73.
Sobba, Katherine. *The courtship novel 1740–1820: a feminized genre.* Lexington, KY: University Press of Kentucky, 1991.
Topliss, Iain. 'Maria Edgeworth: the novelists and the union.' In MacDonagh and Mandle, eds. *Ireland and Irish-Australia.* Pp 270–84.
Tracy, Robert. 'Maria Edgeworth and Lady Morgan: legality versus legitimacy.' *Nineteenth-century Fiction* 40:1 (1985). Pp 1–22.
Weekes, Anne Owens. *Irish women writers: an uncharted tradition.* Lexington, KY: University Press of Kentucky, 1990.
Wohlgemut, Esther. 'Maria Edgeworth and the question of national identity.' *SEL: Studies in English Literature, 1500–1900.* 39:4 (1999). Pp 645–58.

Ferguson

Brown, Malcolm. *Sir Samuel Ferguson.* Lewisburg: Bucknell, University Press, 1973.
Brown, Terence and Barbara Hayley, eds. *Samuel Ferguson – a centenary tribute.* Dublin: RIA, 1987.

Denman, Peter. *Samuel Ferguson: the literary achievement.* Gerrards Cross: Colin Smythe, 1990.

Fackler, Herbert. 'Sir Samuel Ferguson's "The death of the children of Usnach" (1834) and *Deirdre* (1880).' *Éire-Ireland.* 7:1 (1972). Pp 84–95.

Ferguson, Lady. *Sir Samuel Ferguson in the Ireland of his day.* 2 vols. Edinburgh: Blackwood, 1896.

Graham, Colin. *Ideologies of epic: nation, empire and Victorian epic poetry.* Manchester: Manchester University Press, 1998.

Harmon, Maurice, ed. Ferguson Centenary Edition. *Irish University Review.* 16:2 (1986).

———. 'The enigma of Samuel Ferguson.' In O. Komesu and M. Sekine, eds. *Irish writers and politics.* Gerrards Cross: Colin Smythe, 1990. Pp 62–79.

Hodder, William. 'Ferguson's "The fairy thorn:" a critique.' *Irish University Review.* 21:1 (1991). Pp 118–29.

———. 'Translator as ideologue: Samuel Ferguson and the Gaelic folk-song tradition.' *Canadian Journal of Irish Studies.* 20:1 (1994). Pp 1–16.

O'Driscoll, Robert. 'Ferguson and the idea of an Irish national literature.' *Éire-Ireland.* 6:1 (1971). Pp 82–95.

———. *An Ascendancy of the heart: Ferguson and the beginnings of Irish literature in English.* Dublin: Dolmen, 1976.

Ó Tuathaigh, M.A.G. 'Sir Samuel Ferguson—poet and ideology.' In Brown and Hayley, eds. *Samuel Ferguson.* Pp 3–26.

Yeats, W.B. 'The poetry of Sir Samuel Ferguson II.' In Frayne, ed. *Prose of W.B. Yeats.* Vol. 1. Pp 87–104.

Griffin

Cronin, John. *Gerald Griffin 1803–40: a critical biography.* Cambridge: Cambridge University Press, 1978.

Dunne, Tom. 'Murder or metaphor: Gerald Griffin's portrayal of Ireland in the year of Catholic emancipation.' In MacDonagh and Mandle, eds. *Ireland and Irish-Australia.* Pp 64–80.

Griffin, Daniel. *The life of Gerald Griffin by his brother.* 1843. 1857. Dublin: James Duffy, 1874.

Mannin, Ethel. *Two studies in integrity: Gerard Griffin and the Rev. Francis Mahony ('Father Prout').* London: Jarrolds, 1954.

Moynaghan, Julian. 'Gerald Griffin and Charles Dickens.' In Zach and Kosok, eds. *Comparison and impact.* Pp 173–80.

Tissot, Jacques. *Gerald Griffin.* Brest: University of Brest, 1985.

Le Fanu

Achilles. J. 'Fantasy as psychological necessity: Sheridan Le Fanu's fiction.' In A.L. Smith and V. Sage, eds. *Gothick origins and innovations.* Amsterdam: Rodopi, 1994. Pp 15–68.

Begnal, Michael H. *Joseph Sheridan LeFanu.* Lewisburg: Bucknell University Press, 1971.

Coughlan, Patricia. 'Doubles, shadows, sedan-chairs and the past: the 'ghost stories' of J.S. Le Fanu.' In Michael Allen and Angela Wilcox, eds. *Critical approaches to Anglo-Irish literature.* Gerrards Cross: Colin Smythe, 1989. Pp 17–39.

Crawford, Gary William. *J. Sheridan Le Fanu: a bio-bibliography.* Westport CT: Greenwood, 1995.

Gaïd, Girad. *Aspects et construction du fantastique dans les nouvelles de Joseph Sheridan Le Fanu, 1814–73*. Paris: Université de Paris IV, 1993.

Gates, David. ' "A dish of village chat:" narrative technique in Sheridan Le Fanu's *The house by the churchyard*.' *Canadian Journal of Irish Studies*. 10:1 (1984). Pp 63–70.

Gonzalez, Rosa. 'Sheridan Le Fanu's "Uncle Silas" (1864): an Irish story transposed to an English setting.' *Revista canaria de Estudios ingleses*. 22–3 (1991). Pp 101–10.

Heller, Tamar. 'The vampire in the house: hysteria, female sexuality and female knowledge in Le Fanu's "Carmilla." ' In B. Harman and S. Meyer, eds. *The new nineteenth-century: feminist readings of underread Victorian fiction*. New York: Garland, 1996. Pp 77–95.

Howes, Marjorie. 'Misalliance and Anglo-Irish tradition in Le Fanu's *Uncle Silas*.' *Nineteenth-century literature*. 47:2 (1992). Pp 164–86.

McCormack, W.J. *Sheridan Le Fanu and Victorian Ireland*. Oxford: Clarendon, 1980.

———. *Dissolute characters, Irish literary history through Balzac, Sheridan, Le Fanu, Yeats and Bowen*. Manchester: Manchester University Press, 1993.

Mangum, Teresa. 'Sheridan Le Fanu's ungovernable governess.' *Studies in the Novel*. 29:2 (1997). Pp 214–37.

Melada, Ivan. *Sheridan Le Fanu*. Boston: Twayne, 1987.

Milbank, Alison. *Daughters of the house: modes of the Gothic in Victorian fiction*. London: Macmillan, 1992.

Orel, Harold. 'Rigid adherence to the facts: Le Fanu's *In a glass darkly* (1872).' *Éire-Ireland* 20:4 (1985). Pp 65–88.

Rance, N. *Wilkie Collins and other sensation novelists: walking the moral hospital*. London: Associated University Presses, 1991.

Sage, V.R.L. *Horror fiction in the Protestant tradition*. Basingstoke: Macmillan, 1988.

Shaw, Patricia. 'Sheridan Le Fanu: master of the occult, the uncanny and the ominous.' *BELLS: Barcelona English Language and Literature Studies*. 1 (1989). Pp 189–206.

Stoddart, Helen. ' "The precautions of nervous people are infectious:" Sheridan Le Fanu's symptomatic Gothic.' *Modern Language Review*. 86:1 (1991) Pp 19–34.

Sullivan, Kevin. 'Sheridan Le Fanu: the Purcell papers, 1838–40.' *Irish University Review*. 2:1 (1972), Pp 15–19.

Tracy, Robert. 'Loving you all ways: vamps, vampires, necrophiles and necrofilles in nineteenth-century fiction.' In Regina Barreca, ed. *Sex and death in Victorian literature*. Basingstoke: Macmillan, 1990. Pp 23–59.

———. 'Introduction.' In Seridan Le Fanu. *In a glass darkly*. Oxford: Oxford University Press, 1993. Pp vii-xxviii.

Lever

Bareham, Tony, ed. *Charles Lever: new evaluations*. Gerrards Cross: Colin Smythe, 1991.

———. 'The famous Irish Lever.' In Bareham, ed. *Charles Lever*. Pp 1–17.

———. 'Charles Lever and the outsider.' In Bareham, ed. *Charles Lever*. Pp 96–122.

Fitzpatrick, W.J. *Life of Charles Lever*. London: Ward, Lock, 1884.

Haddelsey, Stephen. *Charles Lever: the lost Victorian*. Gerrards Cross: Colin Smythe, 2000.

Morash, Christopher. 'Lever's post-famine landscape.' In Bareham, ed. *Charles Lever*. Pp 86–95.

———. 'Reflecting absent interiors: the big house in the novels of Charles Lever.' In Rauchbauer, ed. *Ancestral voices*. Pp 61–76.

Rix, Walter T. 'Charles James Lever: the Irish dimension of a cosmpolitan.' In Kosok, ed. *Studies in Anglo-Irish literature*. Pp 54–64.

Stevenson, Lionel. *Dr Quicksilver: the life of Charles Lever.* London: Chapman, Hall, 1939.

Mangan

Andrews, Jean. 'James Clarence Mangan and romantic stereotypes: "old and hoary at thirty-nine." ' *Irish University Review* 19:2 (1989). Pp 240–63.

Baldick, Chris. 'Introduction.' In Charles Maturin. *Melmoth the wanderer.* Oxford: Oxford University Press, 1989. Pp vii-xix.

Buttry, Dolores. 'An Irish Faust: James Clarence Mangan, "The man in the cloak." ' *Journal of Irish Literature.* 18:1 (1989). Pp 50–6.

———. 'The negative side of fantasy: James Clarence Mangan's "The thirty flasks." ' *Journal of Irish Literature.* 22:2 (1993). Pp 38–46.

Chuto, Jacques. 'Mangan, Petrie, O'Donovan and a few others: the poet and the scholars.' *Irish University Review* 6:2 (1976). Pp 169–86.

———. 'James Clarence Mangan and the beauty of hate.' *Éire-Ireland.* 30:2 (1995). Pp 173–81.

——— ed. *James Clarence Mangan: a bibliography of his work.* Dublin: Irish Academic Press, 1999.

Coughlan, Patricia A. ' "Fold over fold, inveterately convolv'd:" some aspects of Mangan's intertextuality.' In Hayley and Murray, eds. *Ireland and France.* Pp 191–200.

Donaghy, Henry J. *James Clarence Mangan.* New York: Twayne, 1974.

Kilroy, James. *James Clarence Mangan.* Lewisburg: Bucknell University Press, 1970.

Lloyd, David. *Nationalism and minor literature: James Clarence Mangan and the emergence of Irish cultural nationalism.* London: University of California, Press, 1987.

MacCarthy, Anne. 'James Clarence Mangan's "A treatise on a pair of tongs:" a parody on a parody.' *Canadian Journal of Irish Studies.* 25:1–2 (1999). Pp 388–99.

MacMahon, Peter. 'James Clarence Mangan, the Irish language and the strange case of *The tribes of Ireland*.' *Irish University Review*. 8:2 (1978). Pp 209–22.

O'Donoghue, D.J. *The life and writings of James Clarence Mangan.* Dublin: M.H. Gill, 1897.

Ryder, Sean. 'Male autobiography and Irish cultural nationalism: John Mitchel and James Clarence Mangan.' *Irish Review*. 13 (1992–3). Pp 70–7.

Shannon-Mangan, Eileen. *James Clarence Mangan: a biography.* Dublin: Irish Academic Press, 1996.

Welch, Robert. ' "In wreathèd swell:" James Clarence Mangan: translator from the Irish.' *Éire-Ireland.* 11:2 (1976). Pp 36–55.

Maturin

Baldick, Chris. 'Introduction.' In Charles Maturin. *Melmoth the wanderer*. Oxford: Oxford University Press, 1989. Pp vii-xix.

Coughlan, Patricia. 'The recycling of "Melmoth": "A very German story." ' In Zach and Kosok, eds. *Comparison and impact*. Pp 181–91.

Cox, Jeffrey N. 'Maturin and Coleridge: identity and morality.' *In the shadow of romance: romantic tragic drama in Germany, England and France.* Athens: Ohio University Press, 1987. Pp 119–26.

Dansky, Richard. 'The wanderer and the scribbler: Maturin, Scott and Melmoth the wanderer.' *Studies in Weird Fiction.* 21 (1997). Pp 2–10.

Ellis, K.F. *The contested castle: Gothic novels and the subversion of domestic ideology.* Urbana, IL: University of Illinois Press, 1989.

Fierobe, Claude. *Charles Robert Maturin (1780–1824): l'homme et l'oeuvre.* Paris: Edition Universitaires, 1974.

———. 'A Gothic-historical sermon: Maturin's last novel, *The Albigenses.*' In Hayley and Murray, eds. *Ireland and France.* Pp 47–56.

Fitzgerald, Mary E.F. 'The unveiling of power: nineteenth-century Gothic fiction in Ireland, England and America.' In Zach and Kosok, eds. *Comparison and impact.* Pp 15–25.

Haggerty, G.E. *Gothic fiction/Gothic form.* University Park, PA: Pennyslvania State University Press, 1989.

Haslam, Richard. 'Maturin and the "Calvinist sublime." ' In Allan Lloyd Smith and Victor Sage, eds. *Gothick origins and innovations.* Amsterdam: Rodpi, 1994. Pp 44–56.

Kosok, Heinz. 'Charles Robert Maturin and colonialism.' In Mary Massoud, ed. *Literary inter-relations: Ireland, Egypt and the Far East.* Gerrards Cross: Colin Smythe, 1996. Pp 228–35.

Kramer, Dale. *Charles Robert Maturin.* New York: Twayne, 1973.

Kullman, T. 'Nature and psychology in Maturin's *Melmoth the wanderer* and Emily Brontë's *Wuthering Heights.*' In V. Tinklet-Villani and P. Davidson, eds. *Exhibited by candlelight: sources and developments in the Gothic tradition.* Amsterdam: Rodopi, 1995. Pp 99–106.

Leerssen, Joep Theodoor. 'Fiction, poetics and cultural stereotype: local colour in Scott, Morgan and Maturin.' *Modern Language Review.* 86:2 (1991). Pp 273–84.

Moynahan, Julian. 'The politics of Anglo-Irish Gothic: Maturin, Le Fanu and "The return of the repressed." ' In Kosok, ed. *Studies in Anglo-Irish literature.* Pp 43–53.

Pearson, Jacqueline. 'Masculinizing the novel: women writers and intertextuality in Charles Robert Maturin's *The wild Irish boy.*' *Studies in Romanticism.* 36:4 (1997). Pp 635–50.

Roberts, Marie. *Gothic immortals: the fiction of the brotherhood of the Rosy Cross.* London: Macmillan, 1990.

Scholten, W. *Charles Robert Maturin: the terror novelist.* Amsterdam: 1933.

St John Stott, G. 'The structure of *Melmoth the wanderer.*' *Études Irlandaises.* Université de Lille III. 12:1 (1988). Pp 41–52.

Smith, Amy Elizabeth. 'Experimentation and "horrid curiosity" in Maturin's *Melmoth the wanderer.*' *English Studies.* 74:6 (1993). Pp 524–35.

Watkins, Daniel P. ' "Tenants of a blasted world:" historical imagination in Charles Maturin's *Bertram.*' *Keats-Shelley Review.* 4 (1981). Pp 61–80.

Moore

Basta, Samira. 'The influence of "Mediterranean" orientalism on Thomas Moore's *The Epicurean.*' In G. Serpillo and D. Badin, eds. *The classical world and the Mediterranean.* Cagliari: University of Tema Press, 1996. Pp 164–9.

Campbell, Matthew. 'Thomas Moore's wild song: the 1821 *Irish Melodies.*' *Bullán* 4:2 (1999–2000). Pp 83–103.

Davis, Leith. 'Irish bards and English consumers: Thomas Moore's *Irish Melodies* and the colonized nation.' *Ariel: a Review of International English Literature.* 24:2 (1993). Pp 7–26.

De Ford, Miriam Allan. *Thomas Moore*. New York: Twayne, 1967.

Flannery, James M. *'Dear harp of my country:' Irish melodies of Thomas Moore*. Dublin: Wolfhound, 1998.

Hickey, Bernard. 'Quis separabit? Tom Moore's loyalties: Lord Byron and Lord Edward Fitzgerald.' In Giulio Marra, ed. *Byron e la cultura Veneziana: atti del congresso Mira/Venezia*. Venezia: Dipartamento di Letteratura e Civilta Anglo-Germanichem, 1989. Pp 31–8.

Jones, Howard Mumford. *The harp that once: a chronicle of the life of Thomas Moore*. New York: Henry Hold, 1937.

Jordan, H.H. *Bolt upright: the life of Thomas Moore*. 2 vols. Salzburg: Institut für Englische Sprache und Literatur, 1975.

O'Sullivan, Tadhg. 'The violence of a servile war: three narratives of Irish rural insurgency, post-1798.' In Geary, ed. *Rebellion and remembrance*. Pp 73–92.

Strong, L.A.G. *The minstrel boy*. London: Hodder and Stoughton, 1937.

Tessier, Thérèse. *La poésie lyrique de Thomas Moore: 1779–1852*. Paris: Didier, 1976.

———. *The bard of Erin: a study of Tomas Moore's 'Irish melodies' 1808–34*. Salzburg: Institut für Anglistik und Amerikanistik, 1981.

White, Terence de Vere. *Tom Moore: the Irish poet*. London: Hamish Hamilton, 1977.

Morgan

Andrews, Elmer. 'Aesthetics, politics and identity in Lady Morgan's *The wild Irish girl*.' *Canadian Journal of Irish Studies*. 13:2 (1987). Pp 7–20.

Atkinson, Colin and Jo Atkinson. 'Lady Morgan: Irish patriot and first professional woman writer.' *Éire-Ireland*. 15:2 (1980). Pp 60–90.

Brihault, Jean. *Lady Morgan et l'Irlande*. Haute Bretagne: Université de Rennes 2, 1985.

———. 'Goethe, Rousseau, Rosa: three continental influences on Lady Morgan.' *Études Irlandaises*. 14:1 (1989). Pp 33–45.

———. 'Lady Morgan, mother of the Irish historical novel.' *Études Irlandaises*. 18:1 (1993). Pp 29–37.

Campbell, Mary. *Lady Morgan: the life and times of Sydney Owenson*. London: Pandora, 1988.

Connolly, Claire. ' "I accuse Miss Owenson:" *The wild Irish girl* as media event.' *Colby Quarterly*. 34:2 (2000). Pp 98–115.

Corbett, Mary Jean. 'Allegories of prescription: engendering union in *The wild Irish girl*.' *Eighteenth-century Life*. 22:3 (1998). Pp 92–102.

Dunne, Tom. 'The best history of nations: Lady Morgan's Irish novels.' In Dunne, ed. *Writer as witness*. Pp 133–59.

———. 'Lady Morgan's Irish novels.' In Dunne, ed. *Writer as witness*. Pp 133–59.

Ferris, Ina. 'Narrating cultural encounter: Lady Morgan and the Irish national tale.' *Nineteenth-century Literature*. 51:3 (1996). Pp 287–303.

Fitzpatrick, W.J. *Lady Morgan: her career, literary and personal*. London: Skeet, 1860.

Haslam, Richard. 'Lady Morgan's novels from 1806–33: cultural aesthetics and national identity.' *Éire-Ireland* 22:4 (1987). Pp 11–25.

Lew, Joseph W. 'Sydney Owenson and the fate of empire.' *Keats-Shelley Journal*. 39 (1990). Pp 39–65.

Leerssen, Joep Th. 'How "The wild Irish girl" made Ireland romantic.' In C.C. Barfoot and Theor D'haen, eds. *The clash of Ireland: literary contrasts and connections.* Amsterdam: Rodopi, 1989. Pp 98–117.

———. 'Fiction, poetics and cultural stereotypes: local colour in Scott, Morgan and Maturin.' *Modern Language Review.* 86:2 (1991). Pp 273–84.

Mergenthal, S. 'Impersonating Ireland: Lady Morgan's *The wild Irish girl* and Maria Edgeworth's *The absentee.*' In W. Riehle and H. Keiper, eds. *Proceedings of the Anglistentag, 1994 in Graz.* Graz, Tübingen: Niemeyer, 1994. Pp 97–106.

Moskal, Jeanne. 'Gender, nationality and textual authority in Lady Morgan's travel Books.' In Theresa M. Kelley and Paula R. Feldman, eds. *Romantic women writers.* Hanover NH: University Press of New England, 1995. Pp 171–93.

Newcomer, James. '*Manor Sackville*: Lady Morgan's study of Ireland's perilous case.' *Éire-Ireland.* 10:3 (1975). Pp 11–17.

———. *Lady Morgan, the novelist.* Lewisburg: Bucknell University Press, 1990.

Sha, Richard C. 'Expanding the limits of feminine writing: the prose sketches of Sydney Owenson (Lady Morgan) and Helen Maria Williams.' In P. Fieldman and T. Kelley, eds. *Romantic women writers.* Hanover, NH: University Press of New England, 1995. Pp 194–206.

Spender, Dale. 'Lady Morgan and political fiction.' In Dale Spender, ed. *Mothers of the novel: 100 good women writers before Jane Austen.* London: Pandora, 1986. Pp 301–14.

Stevenson, Lionel. *The wild Irish girl: the life of Sydney Owenson Lady Morgan, 1776–1859.* London: Chapman, Hall, 1936.

Weekes, Ann Owens. *Irish women writers: an uncharted tradition.* Lexington, KY: Unversity Press of Kentucky. 1990.

Whelan, Kevin. 'Foreword.' In Sydney Owenson, Lady Morgan. *The wild Irish girl: A national tale.* Edited and with introduction and notes by Claire Connolly and Stephen Copley. London: Picking and Chatto, 2000. Pp ix-xxiv.

Williams, Julia McElhattan. *Love beyond the pale: Sydney Owenson's* The wild Irish girl, The absentee *and the boundaries of colonial power.* Boston: Northeastern University Press, 1991.

Trollope

Edwards, Owen Dudley. 'Anthony Trollope, the Irish writer.' *Nineteenth-century Fiction.* 38:1 (1983). Pp 1–42.

Hennedy, Hugh L. 'Love and famine, family and country in Trollope's *Castle Richmond*' *Éire-Ireland.* 7:4 (1972). Pp 48–66.

Johnston, Conor. '*The Macdermots of Ballycloran*: Trollope a Conservative-Liberal.' *Éire-Ireland.* 16:2 (1981). Pp 71–92.

———. 'Parsons, priests and politics: Anthony Trollop's Irish clergy.' *Éire-Ireland.* 25:1 (1990). Pp 80–97.

Mullen, Richard with James Munson. *The Penguin companion to Trollope.* London: Penguin, 1996.

Pollard, Arthur. *Anthony Trollope.* London: Routledge and Kegan Paul, 1978.

Skilton, David. *Anthony Trollope and his contemporaries: a study in the theory and conventions of mid-Victorian fiction.* London: Macmillan, 1996.

Tracy, Robert. ' "The unnatural ruin:" Trollope and nineteenth-century Irish fiction.' *Anthony Trollope, 1882–1982. Nineteenth-century Fiction* 37:3 (1982). Pp 358–82.

Wittig, E.W. 'Trollope's Irish fiction.' *Éire-Ireland*. 9:3 (1974). Pp 97–118.

MUSIC

Breathnach, Breandán. *Folk music and dances of Ireland.* Dublin: Talbot, 1971.

Calder, Grace J. *George Petrie and the 'Ancient music of Ireland.'* Dublin: Dolmen, 1968.

Cronin, Maura. 'Popular memory and identity: street ballads in north Munster in the nineteenth century.' In L. Irwin, ed. *Explorations: centenary essays, Mary Immaculate College Limerick.* Dublin 1998.

Faolain, Turlough. *'Blood on the harp:' Irish rebel history in ballad.* Troy, NY: Whitston, 1983.

Fleishchmann, Aloys. 'Music and society, 1850–1921.' In Vaughan, ed. *Union II, 1870–1921.* Pp 500–22.

O'Boyle, Sean. *The Irish song tradition.* Skerries: Gilbert and Dalton, 1976.

Ó Madagáin, Brendán. 'Functions of Irish song in the nineteenth century.' *Béaloideas.* 53 (1985). Pp 130–216.

Pine, Richard. *Music in Ireland 1848–1998.* Cork: Mercier, 1998.

Pine, Richard and Charles Acton, eds. *To talent alone: the Royal Irish Academy of Music, 1848–1998.* Dublin: Gill and Macmillan, 1998.

White, Harry. *The keeper's recital: music and cultural history in Ireland, 1770–1970.* Cork: Cork University Press, 1998.

Wright, R.L. *Irish emigrant ballads and songs.* Bowling Green, OH: Popular, 1975.

Zimmerman, Georges-Denis. *Songs of Irish rebellion: political street ballads and rebel songs, 1780–1900.* Dublin: Allen Figgis, 1967; reprinted, Dublin: Four Courts: 2002.

POLITICAL CULTURE

Alter, Peter. 'Symbols of Irish nationalism.' *Studia Hibernica.* 14 (1974). Pp 104–23.

Bardon, Jonathan. *A history of Ulster.* Belfast: Blackstaff, 1992.

Bartlett, Thomas. 'Militarization and politicization in Ireland, 1780–1820.' In *Culture et pratiques politiques en France et en Irlande, xvi-xviii siècle.* Paris: Centre de Researches Historiques, 1989. Pp 125–36.

———. *The fall and rise of the Irish nation: the Catholic question, 1690–1839.* Dublin: Gill and Macmillan, 1992.

Bartlett, Thomas, Chris Curtin, Riana O'Dwyer and Gearóid Ó Tuathaigh. *Irish Studies, a general introduction.* Dublin: Gill and Macmillan, 1988.

Bew, Paul. *Conflict and conciliation in Ireland, 1890–1910: Parnellites and radical agrarians.* Oxford: Clarendon, 1987.

Bisceglia, Louis R. 'The Fenian funeral of Terence Bellew McManus.' *Éire-Ireland.* 14:3 (1979). Pp 45–64.

Blackstock, Allan. *An Ascendancy army: the Irish yeomanry 1796–1834.* Dublin: Four Courts, 1998.

Boyce, D. George. *Nineteenth-century Ireland: the search for stability.* Dublin: Gill and Macmillan, 1990.

———. *Nationalism in Ireland.* 1982. London: Routledge, 1995.

Boyce, D. George, Robert Eccleshall and Vincent Geoghegan, eds. *Political thought in Ireland since 1700.* London: Routledge, 1993.

Boyce, D. George and Alan O'Day, eds. *The making of modern Irish history: revisionism and the revisionist controversy.* London: Routledge, 1996.

Brady, Ciaran, ed. *Ideology and the historians.* Historical Studies 17. Dublin: Lilliput, 1991

Brynn, Edward. *Crown and Castle: British rule in Ireland, 1800–30.* Dublin: O'Brien, 1978.

Buckland, P.J. *Irish Unionism, one: the Anglo-Irish and the new Ireland, 1885–1922.* Dublin: Gill and Macmillan, 1972.

———. *Irish Unionism, two: Ulster Unionism and the origins of Northern Ireland, 1886–1922.* Dublin: Gill and Macmillan, 1973.

Callan, Patrick. 'Aspects of the transmission of history in Ireland during the latter half of the nineteenth century.' *Irish Educational Studies.* 6:2 (1986–7). Pp 56–75.

Callanan, Frank. *The Parnell split 1890–1.* Cork: Cork University Press, 1992.

———. *T.M. Healy.* Cork: Cork University, Press, 1996.

Comerford, R.V. 'Nation, nationalism and the Irish language.' In T.E. Hachey and L.J. McCaffrey, eds. *Prespectives on Irish nationalism.* Lexington, KY: University of Kentucky Press, 1984.

———. *The Fenians in context: Irish politics and society, 1848–82.* Dublin: Wolfhound, 1985.

———. 'Ireland, 1850–70: post-famine and mid-Victorian.' Pp 372–95. 'Churchmen, tenants and independent opposition.' Pp 396–414. 'Conspiring brotherhoods and contending elites, 1857–63.' Pp 415–30. 'Gladstone's first Irish enterprise, 1864–70.' Pp 431–50. ' In Vaughan, ed. *Union I, 1801–70.*

———. 'Comprehending the Fenians.' *Saothar* 17 (1992). Pp 52–56.

———. 'Isaac Butt and the home rule movement, 1870–7.' Pp 1–25. 'The land war and the politics of distress, 1877–82.' Pp 26–52. 'The Parnell era, 1883–91.' Pp 53–80. In Vaughan, ed. *Union II, 1870–1921.*

Connolly, S.J. 'Aftermath and adjustment.' Pp 1–23. 'The Catholic question, 1801–12.' Pp 24–47. 'Union government, 1812–23.' Pp 48–73. 'Mass politics and sectarian conflict, 1823–30.' Pp 74–107. ' In Vaughan, ed. *Union I, 1801–70.*

——— ed. *Kingdoms united? Ireland and Great Britain from 1500: integration and diversity.* Dublin: Four Courts, 1998.

——— ed. *The Oxford companion to Irish history.* Oxford: Oxford University Press, 1998.

Crossman, Virginia. *Local government in nineteenth-century Ireland.* Belfast: Institute of Irish studies, 1994.

Cullen, L.M. 'The social basis of Irish cultural nationalism.' In Rosalind Mitchison, ed. *The roots of nationalism.* Edinburgh: John Donald, 1980.

———. *The emergence of modern Ireland, 1600–1900.* London: Batesford, 1981.

Curtis, L. Perry. *Coercion and conciliation in Ireland, 1880–92.* Oxford: Univeristy Press, 1963.

———. *Anglo-Saxons and Celts: a study of Anti-Irish prejudice in Victorian England.* Bridgeport, CT: Conference on British studies at the University of Bridgeport, 1968.

———. *Apes and angels: the Irishman in Victorian caricature.* 1971. Washington: Smithsonian Institution Press, 1997.

Dickson, David. ' "Centres of motion:" Irish cities and the origins of popular politics.' In *Culture et pratiques politiques en France et en Irlande, xvi-xviii siècle.* Paris: Centre de Researches Historiques, 1989. Pp 101–22.

Esher, Viscount. *The girlhood of Queen Victoria: a selection of Queen Victoria's diaries, 1832–40.* 2 vols. London: John Murray, 1912.

Farrell, Sean. *Rituals and riots: sectarian violence and political culture in Ulster, 1784–1886.* Lexington KY: University of Kentucky Press, 2000.

Feingold, W.L. *The revolt of the tenantry: the transformation of local government in Ireland, 1872–86.* Boston: Northeastern University Press, 1984.

Foster, R.F. *Modern Ireland, 1600–1972.* London: Allen Lane, 1988.

———. *Paddy and Mr Punch: connections in Irish and English history.* London: Allen Lane, 1993.

Gailey, Andrew. *Ireland and the death of kindness: the experience of constructive Unionism, 1890–1905.* Cork: Cork University Press, 1987.

Garvin, Tom. *The evolution of Irish nationalist politics.* Dublin: Gill and Macmillan, 1981.

———. *Nationalist revolutionaries in Ireland, 1858–1928.* Oxford: Clarendon, 1987.

Geary, Laurence M., ed. *Rebellion and remembrance in modern Ireland.* Dublin: Four Courts, 2001.

Gibbon, Peter. *The origins of Ulster Unionism: the formation of popular Protestant politics and ideology in nineteenth-century Ireland.* Manchester: Manchester University Press, 1975.

Hadfield, Andrew and John McVeagh, eds. *Strangers to that land: British perceptions of Ireland from the Reformation to the famine.* Gerrards Cross: Colin Smythe, 1994.

———. *Irish travel writing: a bibliography.* Dublin: Wolfhound, 1996.

Harrington, John P., ed. *The English traveller in Ireland: accounts of Ireland and the Irish through five centuries.* Dublin: Wolfhound, 1991.

Harvie, C.T. 'Ireland and the intellectuals, 1848–1922.' *New Edinburgh Review.* 38–9 (1977). Pp 35–42.

Hazelkorn, Ellen. 'Reconsidering Marx and Engels on Ireland.' *Saothar.* 9 (1983). Pp 79–87.

Hickey, D.J. and J.E. Doherty. *A dictionary of Irish history, 1800–1980.* Dublin: Gill and Macmillan, 1980.

Hill, J.R. 'The intelligentsia and Irish nationalism in the 1840s.' *Studia Hibernica.* 20 (1980). Pp 73–109.

———.'National festivals, the state and "Protestant Ascendancy" in Ireland, 1537–1829.' *Irish Historical Studies.* 24:93 (May 1984). Pp 30–51.

———. 'The meaning and significance of Protestant Ascendancy, 1787–1840.' In *Ireland after the Union: proceedings of the second joint meeting of the Royal Irish Academy and the British Academy, London 1986.* Oxford: University Press, 1989. Pp 1–22.

Hoppen, K.T. 'Nationalist politics and local realities in mid-nineteenth-century Ireland.' In A. Cosgrove and D. McCartney, eds. *Studies in Irish history presented to R. Dudley Edwards.* Dublin: University College Dublin Press, 1979. Pp 190–227.

———. *Elections, politics and society in Ireland, 1832–85.* Oxford: Oxford University Press, 1984.

———. 'Landlords, society and electoral politics in mid-nineteenth-century Ireland.' In Philpin, ed. *Nationalism and popular protest.* Pp 284–319.

———. *Ireland since 1800: conflict and conformity.* London: Longman, 1989.

Hultin, Neil C. and Warren U Ober. 'An O'Connellite in Whitehall: Thomas Crofton Croker, 1798–1854.' *Éire-Ireland.* 28:3 (1993). Pp 61–86.

Jackson, Alvin. *Ireland, 1798–1998*. Oxford: Blackwell, 1999.

Jenkins, Brian. *Era of emancipation: British government of Ireland, 1812–30*. Kingston Ont: McGill-Queen's University Press, 1988.

Jordan. Thomas E. ' "A great statistical operation:" A century of Irish censuses, 1812–1911.' *New Hibernia Review*. 1:3 (1997). Pp 94–114.

———. 'The quality of life in Victorian Ireland.' *New Hibernia Review*. 4:1 (2000). Pp 103–21.

Jupp, Peter. *British and Irish elections, 1784–1831*. Newton Abbot: David and Charles, 1973.

Kelly, Matthew. 'Dublin Fenians in the 1880s: "The Irish culture of the future"?' *Historical Journal*. 4:3 (2000). Pp 729–50.

Kinzer, Bruce L. *England's disgrace: J.S. Mill and the Irish question*. Toronto: University of Toronto Press, 2001.

Lebow, R.N. *White Britain and Black Ireland: the influence of stereotypes on colonial policy*. Philadelphia: Institute for the Study of Human Issues, 1976.

Legg, Marie-Louise. *Newspapers and nationalism: the Irish provincial press, 1850–92*. Dublin: Four Courts, 1999.

Lyons, F.S.L. *Culture and anarchy in Ireland, 1890–1939*. Oxford: 1979.

Lyons, F.S.L. and R.A.J. Hawkins, *Ireland under the union: varieties of tensions: essays in honour of T.W. Moody*. Oxford: Clarendon, 1980.

McBride, Ian, ed. *History and memory in modern Ireland*. Cambridge: Cambridge University Press, 2001.

Macauley, Ambrose, *The Holy See, British policy and the Plan of Campaign*. Dublin: Four Courts, 2002.

McCaffrey, L.J. *Irish federalism in the 1870s: a study in Conservative nationalism*. American Philosophical Society, Transactions, 53:6. Philadelphia: 1962.

———. *Daniel O'Connell and the repeal year*. Lexington, KY: University of Kentucky Press, 1966.

McCartney, Donal. 'The writing of history in Ireland, 1800–30.' *Irish Historical Studies*. 10:40 (1957). Pp 347–62.

———. 'Lecky's *Leaders of public opinion in Ireland*.' *Irish Historical Studies*. 14:54 (1964). Pp 119–41.

———. *Democracy and its nineteenth-century Irish critics*. Dublin: NUI, 1979.

———. *The dawning of democracy in Ireland, 1800–70*. Dublin: Helicom, 1987.

———. *W.E.H. Lecky, historian and politician, 1838–1903*. Dublin: Lilliput, 1994.

MacDonagh, Oliver. *Ireland: the Union and its aftermath*. London: Allen and Unwin, 1977.

———. *States of mind: a study of Anglo-Irish conflict, 1780–1980*. London: George Allen, Unwin, 1983.

———. 'Introduction: Ireland and the Union, 1801–70.' Pp xlvii-lxv. 'The age of O'Connell, 1830–45.' Pp 158–168. 'Politics, 1830–45.' Pp 169–92. 'Ideas and institutions 1830–45.' Pp 193–217. 'The economy and society, 1830–45.' Pp 218–41. ' In Vaughan, ed. *Union I, 1801–70*.

———. *O'Connell: the life of Daniel O'Connell, 1775–1847*. London: Weidenfeld and Nicolason, 1991.

MacDonagh, Oliver, W.F. Mandle and Pauric Travers, eds. *Irish culture and nationalism, 1750–1950*. London: Macmillan, 1983.

MacDougall, Hugh A. *Racial myth in English history: Trojans, Teutons, and Anglo-Saxons.* University Press of New England: 1982.

Miller, D.W. *Queen's rebels: Ulster loyalism in historical perspective.* Dublin: Gill and Macmillan, 1978.

Moody, T.W. *Davitt and the Irish revolution, 1846–82.* Oxford: Oxford University Press, 1981.

Murphy, James H. *Abject loyalty: nationalism and monarchy in Ireland during the reign of Queen Victoria.* Washington, DC: Catholic University of America Press; Cork: Cork University Press, 2001.

Newsinger, John. 'Fenianism revisited: pastime or revolutionary movement?' *Saothar* 17 (1992). Pp 46–52.

———. *Fenianism in mid-Victorian Britain.* London: Pluto Press, 1994.

O'Callaghan, Margaret. 'Irish history 1780–1980' *Historical Journal.* 29:2 (1986). Pp 481–95.

———. *British high politics and a nationalist Ireland: criminality, land and the law under Forster and Balfour.* Cork: Cork University Press, 1994.

O'Day, Alan. *The English face of Irish nationalism: Parnellite involvement in British politics, 1880–6.* Dublin: Gill and Macmillan, 1977.

O'Day, Alan and D. George Boyce, eds. *Irish nationalism, 1798 to the present.* London: Routledge, 1998.

O'Donoghue, Patrick. 'Causes of the opposition to tithes, 1830–8.' *Studia Hibernica.* 5 (1965). Pp 7–28.

———. 'Opposition to tithe payment in 1830–1.' *Studia Hibernica.* 6 (1966). Pp 69–98.

O'Farrell, Patrick. *Ireland's English question: Anglo-Irish relations, 1534–1970.* London: Batsford, 1971.

———. 'Millennialism, messianism and utopianism in Irish history.' *Anglo-Irish Studies.* 2 (1976). Pp 45–78.

O'Ferrall, Fergus. *Catholic emancipation: Daniel O'Connell and the birth of Irish democracy, 1820–30.* Dublin: Gill and Macmillan, 1985.

O'Gorman, Frank. *Edmund Burke: his political philosophy.* London: George Allen and Unwin, 1973.

Ó Tuathaigh, Gearóid. 'The folk-hero and tradition.' In Donal McCartney, ed. *The world of Daniel O'Connell.* Dublin: Mercier, 1980. Pp 30–42.

Owens, Gary. ' "A moral insurrection:" faction fights, public demonstrations and the O'Connellite campaign, 1828.' *Irish Historical Studies.* 30:120 (1997). Pp 513–40.

———. 'Visualizing the liberator: self-fashioning, dramaturgy and the construction of Daniel O'Connell.' *Éire-Ireland.* 33:3 and 34:1 (1998–9). Pp 103–29.

———. 'Constructing the martyrs: the Manchester executions and nationalist imagination.' In McBride, ed. *Irish nationalist imagination.* Pp 18–36.

Parker, C.S., ed. *Sir Robert Peel from his private papers.* 3 vols. London: John Murray, 1899.

Paseta, Senia. *Before the revolution: nationalism, social change and Ireland's Catholic elite, 1879–1922.* Cork: Cork University Press, 1999.

Peatling, G.K. *British opinion and Irish self-government, 1865–1925: from Unionism to Liberal commonwealth.* Dublin: Irish Academic Press, 2001.

Philpin, C.H.E., ed. *Nationalism and popular protest in Ireland.* Cambridge: Cambridge University Press, 1987.

Pilling, Norman. 'Lecky and Dicey: English and Irish histories.' *Éire-Ireland.* 16:3 (1981). Pp 43–56.

Quinlivan, Patrick, and Paul Rose. *The Fenians in England, 1865–72: a sense of insecurity.* London: Calder, 1982.

Rafferty, Oliver P. *The Church, the state and the Fenian threat, 1861–75.* London: Macmillan, 1999.

Reynolds, J.A. *The Catholic emancipation crisis in Ireland, 1823–9.* New Haven, CT: Yale University Press, 1954.

Roach, John. 'Liberalism and the Victorian intelligentsia.' *Cambridge Historical Journal.* 13 (1957). Pp 71–88.

Senior, Hereward. *Orangeism in Britain and Ireland, 1795–1836.* London: Routledge and Kegan Paul, 1966.

Short, K.R.M. *The dynamite war: Irish-American bombers in Victorian Britain.* Dublin: Gill and Macmillan, 1979.

Steele, E.D. 'J.S. Mill and the Irish question: the principles of political economy, 1848–1970.' *Historical Journal.* 13:2 (1970). Pp 216–36.

———. 'J.S. Mill and the Irish question: reform and the integrity of the empire, 1865–70.' *Historical Journal.* 13:3 (1970). Pp 419–50.

——— . *Irish land and British politics: tenant rights and nationality, 1865–70.* London: Cambridge University Press, 1974.

Takagami, Shin-ichi. 'The Fenian rising in Dublin, March 1867.' *Irish Historical Studies.* 29:115 (1995). Pp 340–62.

Townshend, Charles. *Political violence in Ireland: government and resistance since 1848.* Oxford: Oxford University Presss, 1983.

——— . 'The making of modern Irish public culture.' *Journal of Modern History.* 61:3 (1989). Pp 535–54.

Travers, Pauric. ' "Our Fenian dead:" Glasnevin cemetery and the genesis of the republican funeral.' In James Kelly and U. Mac Gerailt, eds. *Dublin and Dubliners: essays in the history and literature of Dublin City.* Dublin: Helicon, 1990. Pp 52–72.

Vaughan, W.E., ed. *Ireland under the Union I, 1801–70.* F.X. Martin, J.F. Byrne, W.E. Vaughan, Art Cosgrove and J.R. Hill, eds. *A new history of Ireland Vol V.* Oxford: Clarendon, 1989.

———. 'Ireland c. 1870.' In Vaughan, ed. *Union I, 1801–70.* Pp 726–800.

——— ed. *Ireland under the Union II, 1870–1921.* F.X. Martin, J.F. Byrne, W.E. Vaughan, Art Cosgrove and J.R. Hill, eds. *A new history of Ireland Vol VI.* Oxford: Clarendon, 1996.

Vaughan, W.E., and A.J. Fitzpatrick, ed. *Irish historical statistics: population, 1821–1921.* Dublin: Royal Irish Academy, 1978.

Walsh, Oonagh. *Ireland's independence, 1880–1923.* London: Routledge, 2002.

Whelan, Kevin. 'Catholic mobilization, 1750–1850.' In *Culture et pratiques politiques en France et en Irlande, xvi-xviii siècle.* Paris: Centre de Researches Historiques, 1989. Pp 235–58.

———. *The tree of liberty: radicalism, Catholicism and the construction of Irish identity, 1760–1830.* Cork: Cork University Press, 1996.

White, Terence de Vere. *The Anglo-Irish.* London: Victor Gollancz, 1972.

Whyte, J.H. *The Independent Irish Party, 1850–9.* Oxford: Oxford University Press, 1958.
———. *The Tenant League and Irish politics in the eighteen-fifties.* Dundalk, Dundalgan, 1972.
Williams, Leslie. ' "Rint" and "repale:" *Punch* and the image of Daniel O'Connell, 1842–7.' *New Hibernia Review*. 1:3 (1997). Pp 74–93.
Williams, Martin. 'Ancient mythology and revolutionary ideology in Ireland, 1878–1916.' *Historical Journal.* 26:2 (1983). Pp 307–28.
Wyatt, Anne. 'Froude, Lecky, and "the humblest Irishman." ' *Irish Historical Studies.* 19:75 (1975). Pp 261–85.
Zastoupil, Lynn. 'Moral government: J.S. Mill on Ireland.' *Historical Journal.* 26:3 (1983). Pp 707–17.

RELIGION

Akenson, Donald H. *The Church of Ireland: ecclesiastical reform and revolution, 1800–85.* London: Yale University Press, 1971.
Bew, Paul. 'A vision of the dispossessed? Popular piety and revolutionary politics in the Irish land war, 1879–82.' In Devlin and Fanning, eds. *Religion and rebellion.* Pp 137–51.
Bowen, Desmond. *Souperism: myth or reality.* Cork: Mercier, 1970.
———. *The Protestant crusade in Ireland, 1800–70. A study of Protestant-Catholic relations between the Act of Union and disestablishment.* Dublin: Gill and Macmillan, 1978.
———. *History and the shaping of Irish Protestantism.* New York: Peter Lang, 1995.
Brown, Stewart J., 'The new Reformation movement: the Church of Ireland, 1801–29.' In Brown and Miller, eds. *Piety and power.* Pp 180–208.
Brown, Stewart J. and David W. Miller, eds. *Piety and power in Ireland, 1760–1960.* Belfast: Institute of Irish Studies, 2000.
Brooke, Peter. 'Religion and secular thought, 1800–75.' In J.C. Beckett et al. *Belfast: the making of a city, 1800–1914.* Belfast: Appletree, 1983. Pp 111–28.
———. *Ulster Presbyterianism: the historical perspective, 1610–1970.* Dublin: Gill and Macmillan, 1987.
Carroll, Michael P. *Irish pilgrimage: holy wells and popular Catholic devotion.* Baltimore, MD: Johns Hopkins, 1999.
Claydon, Tony and Ian McBride, eds. *Protestantism and national identity: Britain and Ireland, c.1650–c.1850.* Cambridge: Cambridge University Press, 1998.
Clear, Caitriona. *Nuns in nineteenth-century Ireland.* Dublin: Gill and Macmillan, 1987.
Connolly, S.J. *Priests and people in pre-famine Ireland, 1780–1845.* Dublin: Gill and Macmillan, 1982.
———. *Religion and society in nineteenth-century Ireland.* Dundalk: Dun Dealgan, 1985.
———. *Religion, law and power: the making of Protestant Ireland, 1660–1760.* Oxford: Clarendon, 1992.
Corish, Patrick J. *The Irish Catholic experience: a historical survey.* Dublin: Gill and Macmillan, 1985.
Devlin, Judith and Ronan Fanning, eds. *Religion and rebellion.* Historical Studies 20. Dublin: University College Dublin Press, 1997.
Donnelly Jr, James S. 'The Marian shrine of Knock: the first decade.' *Éire-Ireland* 28:2 (1993). Pp 54–99.

———. 'Lough Derg: the making of a modern pilgrimage.' In William Nolan, Liam Ronayne and Mairead Dunlevy, eds. *Donegal, history and society: interdisciplinary essays on the history of an Irish county*. Dublin: Geography Publications, 1995. Pp 491–508.

Elliott, Marianne. *The Catholics of Ulster, a history*. London: Penguin/Allen Lane, 2000.

Ford, Alan, James McGuire and Kenneth Milne, eds. *As by law established: the Church of Ireland since the Reformation*. Dublin: Lilliput, 1995.

Hempton, David. 'The Methodist crusade in Ireland, 1795–1845.' *Irish Historical Studies*. 22:85 (1980). Pp 33–48.

Hempton, David and Myrtle Hill, eds. *Evangelical Protestantism in Ulster society, 1740–1890*. London: Routledge, 1992.

Hinde, Wendy. *Catholic emancipation: a shake to men's minds*. Oxford: Blackwell, 1992.

Holmes, Janice. *Religious revivals in Britain and Ireland, 1859–1905*. Dublin: Irish Academic Press, 2000.

Hynes, Eugene. 'The great hunger and Irish Catholicism.' *Societas*. 8 (1978). Pp 137–56.

———. 'Nineteenth-century Irish Catholicism, farmers' ideology and national religion: explorations in cultural explanation.' In Roger O'Toole, ed. *Sociological studies in Roman Catholicism: historical and contemporary perspectives*. Lewiston: Edwin Mellen Press, 1990. Pp 45–69.

Keenan, Desmond J. *The Catholic Church in nineteenth-century Ireland: a sociological study*. Dublin: Gill and Macmillan, 1983.

Kennedy, Liam. 'The Roman Catholic Church and economic growth in nineteenth-century Ireland.' *Economic and Social Review*. 10 (1978–9). Pp 45–57.

———. *Colonialism, religion and nationalism in Ireland*. Belfast: Institute of Irish Studies: 1996.

Kerr, Donal. *Peel, priests and politics: Sir Robert Peel's administration and the Roman Catholic Church in Ireland, 1841–6*. Oxford: Clarendon, 1982.

———. 'Under the union flag: the Catholic Church in Ireland, 1800–70.' In *Ireland after the Union: proceedings of the second joint meeting of the Royal Irish Academy and the British Academy, London 1986*. Oxford: Oxford University Press, 1989. Pp 23–43.

———. *'A nation of beggars' Priests, people and politics in famine Ireland, 1846–52*. Oxford: Clarendon, 1994.

Knowlton, Steven R. *Popular politics and the Irish Catholic Church: the rise and fall of the Independent Irish Party, 1850–5*. New York: Garland, 1991.

Larkin, Emmet. 'Economic growth and capital investment and the Roman Catholic Church in nineteenth-century Ireland.' *American Historical Review*. 72:3 (1967). Pp 854–84.

———. 'The devotional revolution in Ireland 1850–75.' *American Historical Review*. 77.3 (1972). Pp 625–52.

———. 'Church, state and nation in modern Ireland.' *American Historical Review*. 80:5 (1975). Pp 1244–76.

———. *The Roman Catholic Church and the creation of the modern Irish state, 1878–86*. Dublin: Gill and Macmillan, 1975.

———. *The Roman Catholic Church and the plan of campaign, 1886–8*. Cork: Cork University Press, 1978.

———. *The Roman Catholic Church in Ireland and the fall of Parnell, 1888–91*. Liverpool: Liverpool University Press, 1979.

———. *The making of the Roman Catholic Church in Ireland, 1850–60.* Chapel Hill: University of North Carolina Press, 1980.

———. *The consolidation of the Roman Catholic Church in Ireland, 1860–70.* Dublin: Gill and Macmillan, 1987.

———. *The Roman Catholic Church and the home rule movement in Ireland, 1870–4.* Dublin: Gill and Macmillan, 1990.

———. *The Roman Catholic Church and the emergence of the modern Irish political system, 1874–8.* Dublin: Four Courts, 1996.

———. *The historical dimensions of Irish Catholicism.* Dublin: Four Courts, 1997.

McBride, Ian. ' "The son of an honest man:" William Drennan and the dissenting tradition.' In Dickson, Keogh and Whelan, eds. *The United Irishman.* Pp 49–61.

Macauley, Ambrose, *The Holy See, British policy and the Plan of Campaign.* Dublin: Four Courts, 2002.

McGrath, Thomas. 'The Tridentine evolution of modern Irish Catholicism, 1563–1962: a re-examination of the 'devotional revolution' thesis.' *Recusant history* 20:4 (1991). Pp 512–23.

———. *Politics, interdenominational relations and education in the public ministry of Bishop James Doyle of Kildare and Leighlin, 1786–1834.* Dublin: Four Courts, 1999.

———. *Religion, renewal and reform in the pastoral ministry of Bishop James Doyle of Kildare and Leighlin, 1786–1834.* Dublin: Four Courts, 1999.

Miller, D.W. *Church, state and nation in Ireland, 1898–1921.* Dublin: Gill and Macmillan, 1973.

———. 'Irish Catholicism and the great famine.' *Journal of Social History.* 9 (1975). Pp 81–98.

———. 'Presbyterianism and "modernization" in Ulster.' In Philpin, ed. *Nationalism and popular protest.* Pp 80–109.

———. 'Irish Presbyterians and the great famine.' In Hill and Lennon, eds. *Luxury and austerity.* Pp 165–81.

———. 'Mass attendance in Ireland in 1834.' In Brown and Miller, eds. *Piety and power.* Pp 158–79.

———. 'The 1859 revival and Ulster Presbyterianism.' American Conference for Irish Studies. University of Limerick, 2000.

Murphy, James H. 'The role of Vincentian parish missions and the "Irish Counter Reformation" of the mid-nineteenth century.' *Irish Historical Studies.* 23: 94 (1984). Pp 152–71.

Norman, E.R. *The Catholic Church in Ireland in the age of rebellion, 1859–73.* London: Longmans, 1965.

O'Ferrall, Fergus. 'Daniel O'Connell and Henry Cooke: the conflict of civil and religious liberty in modern Ireland.' *Irish Review.* 1 (1986). Pp 20–7.

Prunty, Jacinta. *Margaret Aylward, 1810–89, lady of charity, sister of faith.* Dublin: Four Courts, 1999.

Rafferty, Oliver P. *Catholicism in Ulster, 1603–1983: an interpretative history.* Dublin: Gill and Macmillan, 1994.

———. 'Carleton's ecclesiastical context: the Ulster Catholic experience.' *Bullán.* 4:1 (1999–2000). Pp 105–24.

Smyth, Jim. 'The making and undoing of a confessional state: Ireland 1660–1829.' *Journal of Ecclesiastical History*. 44 (1993). Pp 506–13.

Steele, E.D. 'Cardinal Cullen and Irish nationality.' *Irish Historical Studies* 19:75 (1975). Pp 239–60.

Sullivan, Mary C. *Catherine McAuley and the tradition of mercy*. Dublin: Four Courts, 1995.

Taylor, Lawrence. *Occasions of faith: an anthropology of Irish Catholics*. Dublin: Lilliput, 1995.

Whelan, Kevin. 'The Catholic parish, the Catholic chapel and village development in Ireland.' *Irish Geography* 16 (1983). Pp 1–15.

———. 'The regional impact of Irish Catholicism, 1700–1850.' In Smyth and Whelan, eds. *Common ground*. Pp 253–77.

SOCIAL LIFE

Ballard, Linda May. *Forgetting frolic: marriage traditions in Ireland*. Belfast: Institute of Irish Studies, 1998.

Beames, Michael. *Peasants and power: the Whiteboy movements and their control in pre-famine Ireland*. Sussex: Harvester, 1983.

———. 'The Ribbon societies: lower-class nationalism in pre-famine Ireland.' In Philpin, ed. *Nationalism and popular protest*. Pp 245–63.

Bew, Paul and Frank Wright. 'The agrarian opposition in Ulster politics.' In Clark and Donnelly, eds. *Irish peasants*. Pp 192–229.

Bonsall, Penny. *The Irish R.M.s: the resident magistrates in the British administration in Ireland*. Dublin: Four Courts, 1997.

Bourke, Angela. 'More in anger than in sorrow: Irish women's lament poetry.' In Joan Newlan Radner, ed. *Feminist messages: coding in women's folk culture*. Urbana and Chicago: University of Illinois Press, 1993. Pp 160–82.

Broeker, Galen. *Rural disorder and police reform in Ireland, 1812–36*. London: Routledge and Kegan Paul, 1970.

Burke, Helen. *The people and the poor law in nineteenth-century Ireland*. Dublin: Women's Educational Bureau, 1987.

Carroll-Burke, Patrick. *Colonial discipline: the making of the Irish convict system*. Dublin: Four Courts, 2000.

Casey, Daniel J. and Robert E. Rhodes, eds. *Views of the Irish peasantry, 1800–1916*. Hamden, CT: Archon, 1977.

Clark, Desmond. 'An outline of the history of science in Ireland.' *Studies*. 62 (1973). Pp 287–302.

Clark, Samuel and James S. Donnelly Jr., eds. *Irish peasants: violence and political unrest, 1780–1914*. Dublin: Gill and Macmillan, 1983.

Connell, K.H. *Irish peasant society*. Oxford: Clarendon, 1968.

Connolly, S.J. ' "The blessed turf:" cholera and popular panic in Ireland, June 1832.' *Irish Historical Studies*. 23:91. (1983). Pp 214–32.

———. 'Popular culture in pre-famine Ireland.' In C.J. Byrne and Margaret Harry, eds. *Talamh an eisc: Canadian and Irish essays*. Halifax, NS: Nimbus, 1986. Pp 12–28.

Cronin, Denis, Jim Gilligan and Karina Holton, eds. *Irish fairs and markets: studies in local history*. Dublin: Four Courts, 2000.

Cronin, Maura. '"Of one mind:" O'Connellite crowds in the 1830s and 1840s.' In Jupp and Magennis, eds. *Crowds in Ireland.* Pp 139–72.

Cronin, Mike. *Sport and nationalism in Ireland: Gaelic games, soccer and Irish identity since 1870.* Dublin: Four Courts, 1999.

Crossman, Virginia. *Politics, law and order in nineteenth-century Ireland.* Dublin: Gill and Macmillan, 1996.

Donnelly Jr, James S. 'Pastorini and Captain Rock: millenarianism and sectarianism in the Rockite movement of 1821–4.' In Clark and Donnelly, eds. *Irish peasants.* Pp 102–39.

———. 'The social composition of agrarian rebellions in early nineteenth-century Ireland: the case of the Carders and Caravats, 1813–16.' In Patrick J. Corish, ed. *Radicals, rebels and establishments.* Historical Studies 15. Belfast, Appletree, 1985. Pp 151–69.

Donnelly Jr, James S. and Kerby A. Miller, eds. *Irish popular culture 1650–1850.* Dublin: Irish Academic Press, 1998.

Dunleavy, Mairead. *Dress in Ireland.* Cork: Collins, 1989.

Ellis, Peter Berresford. *A history of the Irish working class.* London: Victor Gollancz, 1972.

Evans, E. Estyn. *Irish folk ways.* 1957. London: Routledge, 1988.

———. 'Peasant beliefs in nineteenth-century Ireland.' In Casey and Rhodes, eds. *Irish peasantry, 1800–1916.* Pp 37–56.

Finnane, Mark. *Insanity and the insane in post-famine Ireland.* London: Croom Helm, 1981.

Fitzpatrick, David. 'Marriage in post-famine Ireland.' In Art Cosgrove, ed. *Marriage in Ireland.* Dublin: College, 1985. Pp 116–31.

Fleetwood, J.F. *The history of medicine in Ireland.* Dublin: Skellig, 1983.

Foley, Tadhg and Sean Ryder, eds. *Ideology in Ireland in the nineteenth century.* Dublin: Four Courts, 1998.

Garvin, Tom. 'Defenders, Ribbonmen and others: underground political networks in pre-famine Ireland.' *Past and Present.* 96 (1982). Pp 133–53.

Geary, Laurence M. ' "The was in motion:" mendicancy and vagrancy in pre-famine Ireland.' In Hill and Lennon, eds. *Luxury and austerity.* Pp 121–36.

———. 'Prince Hohenlohe, Signor Pastorini and miraculous healing in early nineteenth-century Ireland.' In Malcolm and Jones eds. *Medicine, disease and the state.* Pp 40–58.

Geoghegan, Vincent. 'The emergence and submergence of Irish socialism, 1821–51.' In Boyce, Eccleshall and Geoghegan, eds. *Political thought in Ireland.* Pp 100–23.

Griffin, Brian. *The Bulkies: police and crime in Belfast, 1800–65.* Dublin: Irish Academic Press, 1997.

Herlihy, Jim. *The Royal Irish Constabulary: a short history and genealogical guide with a select list of medal awards and casualties.* Dublin: Four Courts, 1997.

———. *The Dublin Metropolitan Police: a short history and genealogical guide.* Dublin: Four Courts, 2000.

Hill, Jacqueline and Colm Lennon, eds. *Luxury and austerity.* Dublin: University College Dublin Press, 1999.

Inglis, Brian. 'The press.' In McDowell, ed. *Social life.* Pp 92–105.

Jenkins, R.P. 'Witches and fairies: supernatural aggression and deviance among the Irish peasantry.' *Ulster Folklife.* 23 (1977). Pp 48–56.

Jones, David S. 'The cleavage between graziers and peasants in the land struggle, 1890–1910.' In Clark and Donnelly, eds. *Irish peasants.* Pp 374–417.

Jupp, Peter, and Eoin Magennis, eds. *Crowds in Ireland, c.1720–1920.* London: Macmillan, 2000.

Kearney, H.F. 'Fr Mathew: apostle of modernization.' In A. Cosgrove and D. McCartney, eds. *Studies in Irish history presented to R. Dudley Edwards.* Dublin: University College Dublin Press, 1979. Pp 164–75.

Kelly, James. *That damn'd thing called honour: duelling in Ireland 1570–1860.* Cork: Cork University Press, 1995.

Kerrigan, Colm. *Father Mathew and the Irish temperance movement, 1838–49.* Cork: Cork University Press, 1992.

Keogh, Dermot. *The rise of the Irish working class.* Belfast: Appletree, 1982.

Lee, Joseph. 'The Ribbonmen.' In Williams, ed. *Secret societies.* Pp 26–35.

McDowell, R.B., ed. *Social life in Ireland, 1800–45.* Dublin: Three Candles, 1957.

Malcolm, Elizabeth. 'The Catholic Church and the Irish temperance movement, 1838–1901.' *Irish Historical Studies.* 23:89 (1982). Pp 1–16.

———. 'Popular recreation in nineteenth-century Ireland.' In MacDonagh, Mandle and Travers, eds. *Irish culture and nationalism.* Pp 40–55.

———. *Ireland sober, Ireland free: drink and temperance in nineteenth-century Ireland.* Dublin: Gill and Macmillan, 1986.

———. 'The rise of the pub: a study in the disciplining of popular culture.' In Donnelly and Miller, eds. *Irish popular culture.* Pp 50–77.

———. ' "The house of strident shadows:" the asylum, the family and emigration in post-famine rural Ireland.' In Malcolm and Jones, eds. *Medicine, disease and the state.* Pp 177–91.

———. 'Troops of largely diseased women: VD, the Contagious Diseases Act and moral policing in late nineteenth-century Ireland.' *Irish Economic and Social History.* 26 (1999). Pp 1–14.

Malcolm, Elizabeth and Greta Jones, eds. *Medicine, disease and the state in Ireland, 1650–1940.* Cork: Cork University Press, 1999.

Mandle, W.F. *The Gaelic Athletic Association and Irish nationalist politics, 1884–1924.* Dublin: Gill and Macmillan, 1987.

Miller, D.W. 'The Armagh troubles, 1784–95'. In Clark and Donnelly, eds. *Irish peasants.* Pp 155–91.

———. ed. *Peep o' Day Boys and Defenders.* Belfast: Public Records Office of Northern Ireland, 1990.

O'Brien, Gerard. 'The establishment of poor-law unions in Ireland, 1838–43.' *Irish Historical Studies.* 23:90. (1982) Pp 97–120.

O'Connor, Emmet. *A labour history of Ireland, 1824–1960.* Dublin: Gill and Macmillan, 1992.

Ó Crualaoich, Gearóid. 'The "merry wake." ' In Donnelly and Miller, eds. *Irish popular culture.* Pp 173–200.

O'Donnell, P.D. *The Irish faction fighters in the nineteenth century.* Dublin: Anvil, 1975.

Ó Giolláin, Diarmuid. 'The pattern.' In Donnelly and Miller, eds. *Irish popular culture.* Pp 201–21.

———. *Locating Irish folklore: tradition, modernity, identity.* Cork: Cork University Press, 2000.

O'Neill, Timothy P. *Life and tradition in rural Ireland.* London: Dent, 1977.

———. 'The charities and famine in mid-nineteenth-century Ireland.' In Hill and Lennon, eds. *Luxury and austerity*. Pp 137–64.

Ó Suilleabháinn, Seán. *Irish folk custom and belief.* Dublin: 1967.

O'Sullivan, Donal J. *The Irish constabularies, 1822–1922.* Dingle: Brandon, 1999.

Owens, Gary. 'Nationalism without words: symbolism and ritual behaviour in the repeal "monster meetings" of 1843–5.' In Donnelly and Miller, eds. *Irish popular culture*. Pp 242–69.

Patterson, Henry. *Class conflict and sectarianism: the Protestant working class and the Belfast labour movement, 1868–1920.* Belfast: Blackstaff, 1980.

Rafroidi, Patrick. 'The uses of the Irish myth in the nineteenth century.' *Studies.* 62 (1973). Pp 251–61.

Roberts, Paul E.W. 'Caravats and Shanavests: Whiteboyism and faction fighting in east Munster, 1802–11.' In Clark and Donnelly, eds. *Irish peasants*. Pp 64–101.

Robins, Joseph. *Fools and mad: a history of the insane in Ireland.* Dublin: Institute of Public Administration, 1986.

———. *The miasma: epidemic and panic in nineteenth-century Ireland.* Dublin: Institute of Public Administration, 1995.

Scheper-Hughes, Nancy. *Saints, scholars and schizophrenics: mental illness in rural Ireland.* Berkeley: University of Berkeley Press, 1979.

Thuente, Mary Helen. 'Violence in pre-famine Ireland: the testimony of Irish folklore and fiction.' *Irish University Review*. 15:2 (1985). Pp 129–47.

Townend, Paul A. *Fr Mathew, temperance and Irish identity*. Dublin: Irish Academic Press, 2002.

Wall, Maureen. 'The rise of the Catholic middle class in eighteenth-century Ireland'. *Irish Historical Studies* 9:42 (1958), Pp 91–115.

Walker, Brian M. 'The land question and elections in Ulster, 1868–86.' In Clark and Donnelly, eds. *Irish peasants*. Pp 230–68.

Williams, T.D., ed. *Secret societies in Ireland.* Dublin: Gill and Macmillan, 1973.

Witoszek, Nina. 'Ireland: a funerary culture?' *Studies.* 76 (1987). Pp 206–15.

Witoszek, Nina, and Pat Sheeran. *Talking to the dead: a study of Irish funerary traditions.* Amsterdam: Rodopi, 1998.

VISUAL ARTS

Arnold, Bruce. *A concise history of Irish art.* 1968. London: Thames and Hudson, 1977.

Barrett, Cyril and Jeanne Sheehy. 'Visual arts and society, 1830–1900.' In Vaughan, ed. *Union II, 1870–1921*. Pp 436–99.

Bhreathnach-Lynch, Síghle. 'Framing the Irish: Victorian paintings of the Irish peasant.' *Journal of Victorian Culture*. 2:2 (1997). Pp 245–63.

———. 'A national gallery of Ireland: issues of ideological significance.' In Stewart, ed. *Hearts and minds*. Pp 230–48.

Crawford, Margaret. 'The great Irish famine, 1845–9: image versus reality.' In Gillespie and Kennedy, eds. *Ireland: art into history*. Pp 75–88.

Crookshank, Anne. *Irish art from 1600 to the present day.* Dublin: Foreign Affairs, 1979.

———. *Irish sculpture from 1600 to the present day.* Dublin: Foreign Affairs, 1984.

Cullen, Fintan. *Visual politics: the representation of Ireland, 1750–1930.* Cork: Cork University Press, 1997.

Curtis Jr, Perry L. *Images of Erin in the age of Parnell.* Dublin: National Library of Ireland, 2000.

Dalsimer, Adele M., ed. *Visualising Ireland: national identity and pictorial tradition.* London: Faber and Faber, 1993.

De Courcy, Catherine. *The foundation of the National Gallery of Ireland.* Dublin: National Gallery of Ireland, 1985.

Douglas, Roy, Liam Harte, Jim O'Hara. *Drawing conclusions: a cartoon history of Anglo-Irish relations, 1798–1988.* Belfast: Blackstaff, 1998.

Dunne, Tom. ' "One of the tests of national character:" Britishness and Irishness in paintings by Barry and Maclise.' In Stewart, ed. *Hearts and minds.* Pp 260–90.

Fallon, Brian. *Irish art, 1830–1990.* Belfast: Appletree, 1994.

Gibbons, Luke. 'Between Captain Rock and a hard place: art and agrarian insurgency.' In Foley and Ryder, eds. *Ideology and Ireland.* Pp 23–44.

Gillespie, Raymond and Brian P. Kennedy, eds. *Ireland: art into history.* Dublin: Town House, 1994.

Harbison, Peter, Homan Potterton and Jeanne Sheehy. *Irish art and architecture from prehistory to the present.* London: Thames and Hudson, 1978.

Hill, Judith. *Irish public sculpture: a history.* Dublin: Four Courts, 1998.

Hollander, Joel A. 'Beauty and the beast: depictions of Irish female types during the era of Parnell, *c.*1880–91.' In McBride, ed. *Irish nationalist imagination.* Pp 53–72.

Larmour, Paul. *The arts and crafts movement in Ireland.* Belfast: Friars Bush, 1992.

Loftus, Belinda. *Mirrors: William III and mother Ireland.* Dundrum: Picture Press, 1990.

———. *Mirrors: orange and green.* Dundrum: Picture Press, 1994.

McBride, Lawrence W., ed. *Images, icons and Irish nationalist imagination, 1870–1925.* Dublin: Four Courts, 1999.

———. 'Nationalist political illustrations and the Parnell myth.' In McBride, ed. *Irish nationalist imagination.* Pp 73–94.

O'Connor, Ciaran, and John O'Regan, ed. *Public works: the architecture of the Office of Public Works, 1831–1987.* Dublin: Architectural Association of Ireland, 1987.

O'Sullivan, Niamh. 'The iron cage of feminity: visual representation of women in the 1880s land agitation.' In Foley and Ryder, eds. *Ideology in Ireland.* Pp 181–96.

———. *Aloysius O'Kelly. Re-orientations: painting, politics and popular culture.* Dublin: Hugh Lane Municipal Gallery of Modern Art, 1999.

Reilly, Eileen. 'Beyond the gilt shamrock: symbolism and realism in the cover art of Irish historical and political ficiton, 1880–1914.' In McBride, ed. *Irish nationalist imagination.* Pp 95–112.

Richardson, D.S. *Gothic revival architecture in Ireland.* 2 vols. New York: Garland, 1983.

Rowan, Alistair. 'Irish Victorian churches: denominational distinction.' In Gillespie and Kennedy, eds. *Ireland: art into history.* Pp 207–30.

Sheehy, Jeanne. *J.J. McCarthy and the Gothic revival in Ireland.* Belfast: Ulster Architectural Heritage Society, 1977.

Turpin, John. 'Daniel Maclise and his place in Victorian art.' *Anglo-Irish Studies.* 1 (1975). Pp 51–69.

———.'Daniel Maclise, Disraeli and *Fraser's Magazine.*' *Éire-Ireland.* 15:1 (1980). Pp 46–63.

———. 'Exhibitions of art and industries in Victorian Ireland: part 1, the Irish arts and industries exhibition movement, 1834–64.' *Dublin Historical Record.* 35:1 (1981). Pp 2–13.

———. 'Exhibitions of art and industries in Victorian Ireland: part 2, Dublin exhibitions of art and industries, 1865–85.' *Dublin Historical Record.* 35:2 (1982). Pp 42–51.

———. 'The Royal Dublin Society and its school of art, 1849–77.' *Dublin Historical Record.* 36:1 (1982). Pp 2–20.

———. 'The South Kensington system and the Dublin Metropolitan School of Art, 1877–1900.' *Dublin Historical Record.* 36:2 (1983). Pp 42–64.

———. 'The Dublin Society and the beginnings of sculptural education in Ireland, 1750–1850.' *Éire-Ireland.* 24:1 (1989). Pp 40–58.

———. 'Irish history painting.' *Irish Arts Review Yearbook.* (1989–90). Pp 233–47.

Wedgwood, Alexandra. *A.W.N. Pugin and the Pugin family.* London, Victoria and Albert Museum, 1985.

Weston, Nancy. *Daniel Maclise: an Irish artist in Victorian London.* Dublin: Four Courts, 2000.

YOUNG IRELAND

Anton, Brigitte. 'Women and the *Nation.*' *History Ireland.* 1:3 (1993). Pp 34–38.

Buckley, David N. *James Fintan Lalor: radical.* Cork: Cork University Press, 1990.

Davis, Richard. *The Young Ireland movement.* Dublin: Gill and Macmillan, 1987.

———. *Revolutionary imperialist: William Smith O'Brien.* Dublin: Lilliput, 1998.

Flanagan, Thomas. 'Rebellion and style: John Mitchel and the *Jail Journal.*' *Irish University Review* 1:1 (1970). Pp 1–29.

Kenny, Desmond. 'The ballads of the *Nation*: a study in a popular concept.' *Cahiers du Centre d' Études Irlandaises.* 3 (1978). Pp 31–45.

Knowlton, Steven. 'The politics of John Mitchel: a reappraisal.' *Éire-Ireland.* 22:2 (1987). Pp 38–55.

———. 'The enigma of Charles Gavan Duffy: looking for clues in Australia.' *Éire-Ireland.* 31:3 and 4 (1996). Pp 189–208.

Molony, John N. *A soul came into Ireland. Thomas Davis 1814–45.* Dublin: Geography, 1995.

Morash, Chris. 'The rhetoric of rights in Mitchel's *Jail Journal.*' In Leerssen, Weel and Westerweel, eds. *Forging in the smithy.* Pp 207–18.

Owens, Gary. 'Popular mobilization in the rising of 1848: the clubs of the Irish Confederation.' In Geary, ed. *Rebellion and remembrance.* Pp 51–63.

Sloan, Barry. 'The autobiographies of John Mitchel and Charles Gavan Duffy: a study in contrasts.' *Éire-Ireland.* 22:2 (1987). Pp 27–37.

Sloan, Robert. *William Smith O'Brien and the Young Ireland rebellion of 1848.* Dublin: Four Courts, 2000.

Sullivan, Eileen A. *Thomas Davis.* Lewisburg: Bucknell, 1978.

Touhill, B.M. *William Smith O'Brien and his Irish revolutionary companions in penal exile.* Columbia: University of Missouri Press, 1981.

1790s

Bartlett, Thomas. 'An end to moral economy: the Irish militia disturbances of 1793.' In Philpin, ed. *Nationalism and popular protest*. Pp 191–218.

Blackstock, Allan. 'The social and political implications of the raising of the yeomanry in Ulster, 1796–8.' In Dickson, Keogh and Whelan, eds. *The United Irishmen*. Pp 234–43.

Chambers, Liam. *Rebellion in Kildare, 1790–1803*. Dublin: Four Courts, 1998.

Connolly, S.J. 'Eighteeenth-century Ireland: colony or *ancien régime*?' In Boyce and O'Day, eds. *Revisionist controversy*. Pp. 15–33;

———. *Political ideas in eighteenth-century Ireland*. Dublin: Four Courts, 2000.

Cronin, Maura. 'Memory, story and balladry: 1798 and its place in popular memory in pre-famine Ireland.' In Geary, ed. *Rebellion and remembrance*. Pp 112–34.

Curtin, Nancy. *The United Irishmen: popular politics in Ulster and Dublin, 1791–8*. Oxford: Clarendon, 1994.

Dickson, David, ed. *New foundations: Ireland 1660–1800*. Dublin: Irish Academic Press, 2000.

Dickson, David, Dáire Keogh and Kevin Whelan, eds. *The United Irishmen: republicanism, radicalism and rebellion*. Dublin: Lilliput, 1993.

Donnelly Jr, James S. *Irish agrarian rebellion, 1760–1800*. Dublin: Irish Academic Press, 2001.

———. 'Sectarianism in 1798 and in Catholic nationalist memory.' In Geary, ed. *Rebellion and remembrance*. Pp 15–37.

Dunne, Tom. 'Popular ballads, revolutionary rhetoric and politicization.' In Gough and Dickson, eds. *Ireland and the French revolution*. Pp 139–55.

———. 'Subaltern voices? Poetry in Irish, popular insurgency and the 1798 rebellion.' *Eighteenth-century Life*. 22:3 (1998). Pp 31–44.

Elliott, Marianne. *Wolf Tone: prophet of Irish independence*. London: Yale University Press, 1989.

Geoghegan, Patrick M. *The Irish Act of Union: a study in Irish high politics, 1798–1801*. Dublin: Gill and Macmillan, 1999.

Gough, Hugh, and David Dickson, eds. *Ireland and the French Revolution*. Dublin: Irish Academic Press, 1990.

Gray, John. 'Mary Anne McCracken: Belfast revolutionary and pioneer of feminism.' In Keogh and Furlong, eds., *The women of 1798*. Pp 47–63.

Keogh, Dáire. *'The French disease': the Catholic Church and Irish radicalism*. Dublin: Four Courts, 1993.

Keogh, Dáire and Nicholas Furlong, eds. *The mighty wave: the 1798 rebellion in Wexford*. Dublin: Four Courts, 1996.

———. *The women of 1798*. Dublin: Four Courts, 1998.

Keogh, Dáire and Kevin Whelan, eds. *Acts of union: the causes, contexts and consequences of the Act of Union*. Dublin: Four Courts, 2001.

Kinsella, Anna. 'Nineteenth-century perspectives: the women of 1798 in folk memory and ballads.' In Keogh and Furlong, eds. *The women of 1798*. Pp 187–99.

Leighton, C.D.A. *Catholicism in a Protestant kingdom: a study of the Irish ancien régime*. Dublin: Gill and Macmillan, 1994.

McBride, Ian. 'The harp without the crown: nationalism and republicanism in the 1790s.' In Connolly, ed. *Political ideas*. Pp 159–84.

O'Donnell, Ruán. *The rebellion in Wicklow 1798*. Dublin: Irish Academic Press, 1998.

———. *Aftermath: post-rebellion insurgency in Wicklow, 1799–1803*. Dublin: Irish Academic Press, 1999.

———. 'Foreign enemies and internal rebels: the French war and the United Irishmen in New South Wales.' In Geary, ed. *Rebellion and remembrance*. Pp 38–50.

Power, T.P. and Kevin Whelan, eds. *Endurance and emergence: Catholics in Ireland in the eighteenth century*. Dublin: Irish Academic Press, 1990.

———. 'Converts.' In Power and Whelan, eds. *Endurance and emergence*. Pp 101–27.

Reilly, Eileen. 'Who fears to speak of '98? The rebellion in historical novels, 1880–1914.' *Eighteenth-century Life*. 22:3 (1998). Pp 118–27.

Smyth, Jim. *The men of no property: Irish radicals and popular politics in the late eighteenth century*. London: Macmillan, 1992.

——— ed. *Revolution, counter-revolution and union: Ireland in the 1790s*. Cambridge: Cambridge University Press, 2000.

Stewart, A.T.Q. *A deeper silence: the hidden roots of the United Irish movement*. London: Faber & Faber, 1993.

———. *Summer soldiers: the 1798 rebellion in Antrim and Down*. Belfast: Blackstaff, 1995.

Thuente, Mary Helen. *The harp re-strung: the United Irishmen and the rise of literary nationalism*. Syracuse: Syracuse University Press, 1994.

———. 'Liberty, Hibernia and Mary Le More: United Irish images of women.' In Keogh and Furlong. *Women of 1798*. Pp 9–25.

Whelan, Kevin. 'The United Irishmen, the Enlightenment and popular culture.' In Dickson, Keogh and Whelan, eds. *The United Irishmen*. Pp 269–96.

———. 'Reinterpreting the 1798 rebellion in County Wexford.' In Keogh and Furlong, eds. *The mighty wave*. Pp 9–36,

———. *Fellowship of freedom: the United Irishman and the 1798 rebellion*. Cork: Cork University Press, 1998.

Wilkinson, David. ' "How did they pass the union?" Secret service expenditure in Ireland, 1799–1804.' *History*. 82:266 (1997). Pp 223–51.

Wilson, David A. *United Irishmen, United States: immigrant radicals in the early republic*. Dublin: Four Courts, 1998.

Index